URBAN LIFE *and* URBAN LANDSCAPE SERIES

CHANGING PLANS FOR AMERICA'S INNER CITIES

CINCINNATI'S
OVER-THE-RHINE AND
TWENTIETH-CENTURY
URBANISM

Zane L. Miller and
Bruce Tucker

OHIO STATE UNIVERSITY PRESS
Columbus

Library of Congress Cataloging-in-Publication Data

Miller, Zane L.
    Changing plans for America's inner cities : Cincinnati's Over-The-Rhine
and twentieth-century urbanism / Zane L. Miller and Bruce Tucker.
        p.   cm. — (Urban life and urban landscape series)
    Includes bibliographical references and index.
    ISBN 0-8142-0762-6 (cloth : alk. paper). —ISBN 0-8142-0763-4
(pbk. : alk. paper)
        1. Urban renewal—Ohio—Cincinnati—History.   2. Over-the-Rhine
(Cincinnati, Ohio)—History.   I. Tucker, Bruce, 1948–   .   II. Title.
III. Series.
    HT177.C53M55   1997
    307.3'416'0977178—dc21   97-26206
                                                                                          CIP

Text and jacket design by Gary Gore.
Type set in ITC New Baskerville by Wilsted & Taylor Publishing Services.
Printed by Thomson-Shore.

The paper in this publication meets the minimum requirements of American
National Standard for Information Sciences—Permanence of Paper for
Printed Library Materials. ANSI Z39.48-1992.

9 8 7 6 5 4 3 2 1

For Henry

CONTENTS

ILLUSTRATIONS

ACKNOWLEDGMENTS

T HE project that yielded this book began in the early 1980s, and we have since then drawn on the assistance of more people than we can acknowledge here. Most important among them stands Henry D. Shapiro, who contributed seminal ideas for our exploration, prompted our interest in taxonomies of social reality, and helped draft grant proposals that produced the money to keep us going. The grants came from the American Association for State and Local History, the National Endowment for the Humanities (RO-20821-85), the Ohio Board of Regents Urban Universities Research Program and Linkage Grant Program, and the Murray Seasongood Foundation of Cincinnati. We are indebted to Nancy Grey Osterud for helping to prepare the project statement on which we based the grant proposals.

Others at the University of Cincinnati also helped us. The board of trustees provided in-kind matching support by granting Zane Miller two quarters of academic leave for researching and writing. The Department of History and the McMicken College of Arts and Sciences made it possible for us to try out our ideas in the give and take of teaching. At the undergraduate level this took place in the Laboratory in American Civilization (a research seminar), in a McMicken College special topics honors course on the politics of the neighborhood organization revolution, and in a summer continuing education course on recent trends in city and neighborhood planning. We hope that the students learned as much from us as we did from them, particularly Robert Burnham, Penelope Cunningham, Theresa Eisenberg, Jana Morford, and Rose Vitale. This project also insinuated its way into the department's graduate level instruction through its Frontiers of Urban Research seminar, out of which came several useful papers, theses, and dissertations, especially those of Robert Burnham, Charles Casey-Leininger, Bradley Cross, Jon Dowling, Roger Hansen, Andrea Kornbluh, and Rose Vitale. Kevin Grace in the Department of Archives and Rare Books and Karen Kottsy, Sally Moffitt, and Donald Tolzmann of the reference department at the University of Cincinnati Libraries graciously responded to our requests and often guided us to sources we otherwise would have overlooked.

Maureen Sullivan and the staff of the Urban Appalachian Council, especially Brenda Saylor, helped locate material on Appalachians in Cincinnati, and Michael Maloney shared both his knowledge and personal archival collection on the Appalachian ethnic movement in Cincinnati. Loyal Jones, then director of the Appalachian Center at Berea College, and Shannon Wilson, archivist of the Hutchins Library at Berea, provided welcome assistance and encouragement.

The project benefited, too, from researchers who worked long hours at meager wages. These included especially Bruce Tucker, who joined us on NEH support as a research associate. He wrote two of the twenty-three chapters of the initial typescript and several drafts of chapters 4 and 5. Elliot Shapiro and Lisa Thomas conducted careful newspaper research, and Ellen Cangi prepared a long oral history with Harris Forusz.

Several people helped us dig up hard-to-find information. At Cincinnati's city hall we relied heavily on Charles Nuckolls in the clerk of council's office, Ely Ryder in the city solicitor's office, and Charlotte Birdsall (now Thompson), Christopher Cain, Ed Mangold, Steve Schuckman, and Dan Young in the Department of City Planning. Franco Ruffini of the Ohio Historic Preservation Office located, photocopied, and mailed to us important material, and Bruce Goetzman donated his collection of documents and newspaper clippings on the Over-the-Rhine historic designation controversy. W. Joseph Dehner gave us access to the records of the Queen City Housing and Heritage Preservation Development Corporations, and Jon Hughes contributed choice selections from his folio of photos of sites and events in Over-the-Rhine. We also learned a great deal informally from members of the Ohio Historic Sites Preservation Advisory Board and Cincinnati's Historic Conservation board, on both of which Zane Miller served during the 1980s when these two bodies figured prominently in the story we tell.

Others helped us in equally important ways. Hope Earls, the administrative secretary in the history department at the University of Cincinnati, provided us with working materials and technical and managerial assistance, and even found time to type clean copies of parts of the manuscript and other items related to the project. Evelyn Schott efficiently, patiently, and promptly typed the second draft and four revisions of the manuscript that finally became this book. Barbara Hanrahan, director of the Ohio State University Press, supervised the transformation of the manuscript into a book, and Lynne M. Bonenberger applied diligence, judiciousness, and good taste in copyediting our work.

To these acknowledgments we add the name and memory of Nancy K. Shapiro, who not only constructed excellent oral history interviews but also provided us a model of intelligence, curiosity, commitment, good humor, and wit, even in the face of an illness that ended her life just as the book began to take shape. She and the others acknowledged here share in whatever merits readers might find in this book. The authors are responsible for its shortcomings.

ZANE L. MILLER

INTRODUCTION

Why Cincinnati, Why Over-the-Rhine?

THIS book started as an examination of a cultural conflict over who should live in a particular neighborhood, who should design its physical fabric, and who should decide. The contest stemmed from an effort by the city, state, and federal authorities to use recently developed historic preservation techniques to revitalize a poor, predominantly black, inner-city tract called Over-the-Rhine,[1] 110 blocks (362 acres) of mostly nineteenth-century architecture on the northern edge of Cincinnati's central business district. The nature of the neighborhood, the national popularity of historic preservation as a neighborhood conservation treatment, and the length of the battle (1979–85) over the appropriate social and physical environment for this old and richly historic area seemed of sufficient significance and general interest to warrant a study of how anti-preservationists beat city hall and what pro-preservationists might learn from it.

But we soon discovered two things that extended the scope and duration of our work. First, the proposal of historic preservation as an appropriate treatment for rejuvenating Over-the-Rhine stood as merely one in a long string of cultural transformation programs devised for the area since the 1920s, when the city government first embraced the manipulation of the social and physical environment for broadly cultural purposes

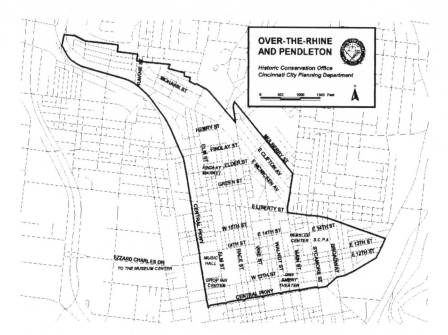

Over-the-Rhine, 1997. Map by Dan Young, Cincinnati Department of City Planning.

and when the Queen City emerged as a nationally recognized and applauded leader in this new field. Second, a double shift in the history of these treatments for Over-the-Rhine and other old neighborhoods around downtown took place at mid-century. Between 1920 and 1950 the city government called such neighborhoods "slums" and tried to eliminate them by two methods. After 1950, however, officials redefined them as "inner-city" neighborhoods and sought to conserve them with a plethora of programs.

These discoveries raised two kinds of questions. At one level of analysis we wondered how the city government justified some very expensive attempts to solve the slum problem by clearing out dwellings that housed thousands of people. What did the city propose to do with those uprooted people, and how did it hope to accomplish it? Why and how did some neighborhoods, such as Over-the-Rhine, survive the slum clearance campaign? Why did the inner-city conservation campaign after

Cincinnati's neighborhoods, 1982. Map by Mark Abell, Hamilton County Regional Planning Commission.

1950 leave Over-the-Rhine near the top of municipal priorities in the 1970s? Why did the attempt to apply historic preservation as a revitalization technique provoke such a long (and nasty) fight in the late 1970s and 1980s? How might we account for the outcome of that argument? And was that outcome inevitable?

At another level, we wondered how to account for the shift at mid-century from slum clearance to inner-city conservation and why that shift yielded a proliferation of treatments for the inner city. We suspected that the answers to these questions would be crucial to working out explanations for the "lower-level" questions that would not trivialize, patronize, or demonize any of the actors in our story. To resolve the two higher questions, we used simple techniques. We looked at how our Cincinnati actors defined problems. We looked for patterns in what they said and did not say and in what they did and did not do as they attempted to solve their problems. And we placed these patterns of talk, action, and inaction in the context of contemporary general discussions of American civilization that might have informed their thinking and activities.

We concluded that the mid-century shift from slum clearance to inner-city conservation stemmed from a revulsion against totalitarianism in Europe and conformity at home that changed the way Americans thought about their society, culture, and cities. The rationale for slum clearance took as its chief concern the welfare of the whole city. It defined the social mission of the city as the fostering of cosmopolitanism (the sharing of ideas and behavioral traits among groups of people without destroying each group's sense of its given and distinctive cultural identity), and viewed slums as cancerous entities that posed the most serious threat to the cosmopolitan project.

This slum clearance regimen seemed both sensible and responsibly democratic in its day. But in the 1950s it looked like a variety of cultural engineering resembling that associated with the outrages committed by the Nazi and Soviet governments on their own people during the late 1930s and 1940s. This juxtaposition produced a new mode of thinking that took the autonomy of individuals as its chief concern, defined the social mission of the city as the fostering of cultural individualism (the pursuit by individuals of their self-constructed cultures/life styles), and regarded inner-city neighborhoods as scruffy but redeemable entities essential for the full flowering of cultural individualism, which required by definition the creation of widely diverse types of residential places to accommodate the tastes of widely diverse types of self-constructed life styles.

Over-the-Rhine provides an ideal vehicle for the exploration of the broad range of treatments generated by these two modes of thought for old neighborhoods around downtown because our actors seriously considered or tried all of them. Before mid-century the two slum clearance techniques consisted of zoning inner-city neighborhoods for non-residential land uses or demolishing them to make way for community building public housing projects. After 1950, conservation treatments for inner-city tracts included remodeling them as chic downtown residential neighborhoods; rehabilitating them as low-income housing districts; using them as models for improving the participation of poor people in neighborhood planning and plan implementation; loading them with public and private social service agencies responsive to the problems of the poor as defined by the poor; reserving them as homes for members of minority groups (African Americans and "urban" Appalachians in our case) who felt deprived of their right to practice cultural individualism; and using historic preservation techniques to conserve them as places of residence for low-income minorities, homeless people, alcoholics, and more prosperous people regardless of their race or life style.

This book, then, uses the treatment of Over-the-Rhine by Cincinnati's city government to illustrate some of the consequences of the two modes of thought about American cities and their neighborhoods. We especially hope to point out some neglected explanations for the decline that afflicted Over-the-Rhine and other old neighborhoods in American cities during the twentieth century, particularly after 1960. Over-the-Rhine's population peaked at about 44,475 in 1900 and fell gradually to about 30,000 by 1960. A decade later that number had shrunk by half, and included 5,380 African Americans, a newly significant minority in the neighborhood. In 1990, census takers counted just 9,752 people in Over-the-Rhine, 6,875 of them (71 percent) African Americans. By then, too, more than a quarter of the neighborhood's apartments stood vacant and the area's median household income was just $5,000, well below the figure for the city, $21,006.[2]

These impoverished people lived in the city's most crime-ridden turf, a territory haunted by pimps, drug pushers, prostitutes, thieves, and muggers. Over-the-Rhine also accounted for more than its share of the city's domestic violence cases, street fights, and murders. For the most part, the criminals picked on their neighbors. But occasionally they hit an unlucky outsider, as in the 1996 robbery-killing of a popular young, white rock musician who worked in a nightspot along the short strip of restaurants, bars, nightclubs, and coffeehouses that catered to young adults and middle-aged people, mostly whites, some from Cincinnati's outer neighborhoods or suburbs and some businesspersons or tourists from other cities.

The persistence of such conditions and events in one of the city's most visible and historic neighborhoods generated continuing concerns about its future.[3] Many of these concerns now focused on the prevalence of drugs and prostitution in the neighborhood, the blatancy of which prompted the Over-the-Rhine Chamber of Commerce, a recently established improvement association, to run an ad in a metropolitan daily newspaper listing the names and addresses of twenty-five persons arrested in the neighborhood for soliciting or for drug-related offenses during a four-month period in 1996. "Your illegal activities," read the ad, "have brought degradation and suffering to the citizens who live and work here, especially our children . . . we ask that you stay out . . . unless you plan to help us build a healthier, more liveable community."[4]

These pleas touched city council member Phil Heimlich, Cincinnati's premier law and order legislator in the mid-1990s. He responded by securing the passage of yet another treatment for Over-the-Rhine: its designation as a "crime exclusion zone" (an idea borrowed from Portland, Oregon). The provisions of his ordinance included banning from the neighborhood for ninety days non-residents arrested there on drug or prostitution charges and extending the exile to one year for those convicted of those crimes.[5]

Others who worried about Over-the-Rhine in the mid-1990s took a larger view that depicted the neighborhood as part of a problem that threatened the welfare of the whole city and its mission as a facilitator of cultural individualism. They contended that thirty years of wrong-headed policies had converted Over-the-Rhine into part of Cincinnati's "second" black ghetto. And residential apartheid, these critics contended, mocked the idea of cultural individualism by denying blacks the right to a full and free choice of better homes in neighborhoods of their preference or design. The situation especially embittered middle-class blacks, for it not only discriminated against these successful adults but also reminded them and their children that even those who secured good educations and decent jobs, built families, and conducted socially and civically responsible lives stood little chance of escaping the confines of their involuntary residential enclaves, including the gilded ones in outlying and suburban neighborhoods.

In this view, then, the persistence and growth of the ghetto, America's most visible stamp of disdain for African Americans since the time of slavery, constitutes Cincinnati's major problem at the approach of the twenty-first century. It encourages social and civic alienation among African American adults and undermines the confidence of middle-class blacks in their ability to compete on everything from standardized tests to on-the-job performance. It tempts their children to drop out and into the underclass. It fosters a climate of fear, misunderstanding, and mistrust among the races that erodes faith on both sides of the color line in the city's political system and economic prospects. It threatens the viability of the city as an agency for the nurturing of cultural pluralism, whether of the trait-sharing or multi-cultural variety. And as in the 1960s, the persisting ghetto in the 1990s frustrates attempts to solve other problems because attacks on such issues as sexism, education, affordable housing, poverty, and the enrichment of the wealthy at the expense of the middle class and poor get caught up in the interracial crossfire and are deflected or buried.[6]

The concerns of this book focus on Over-the-Rhine and Cincinnati. But people familiar with the experience of other American cities will find our story characteristic of processes occurring elsewhere in the nation. We concede the uniqueness of the *details* of what happened in Cincinnati. But they are *particularities* rather than peculiarities, for the plot of the drama, its divisions into acts or periods, its dramatis personae, and the issues, concerns, and problems they confronted and the solutions they devised mirror the drama played out in other places.[7]

PROLOGUE
1850s–1910s

OUR neighborhood of concern lay in the mid-nineteenth century on the northern edge of a basin on the north bank of the Ohio River in which rested the city of Cincinnati. Hills about 400 feet high surrounded the basin, and the Miami and Erie Canal (Cincinnati's "Rhine") ran across it about halfway between the hills and the river, then turned sharply to the north, forming the southern and western sides of the triangular piece of land that became known as Over-the-Rhine. The area, like peripheral areas of other mid-nineteenth-century cities, attracted a diversity of people who lived in extraordinarily high densities amidst a mix of land uses. And Over-the-Rhine, like other peripheral neighborhoods in this period, attracted a large number of immigrants (almost half of the city's population in 1850 came from abroad), including so many from the German states that they made up 60 percent of the neighborhood's population in 1850, and 50 percent a decade later. But these men and women formed no coherent community, for they came from a variety of independent states, spoke a variety of dialects, adhered to a variety of religions and ideologies, belonged to a variety of political parties, pursued diverse occupations, ranged in wealth from rich to poor, and moved frequently, both within and beyond this large area and generally up the social ladder.[1]

1

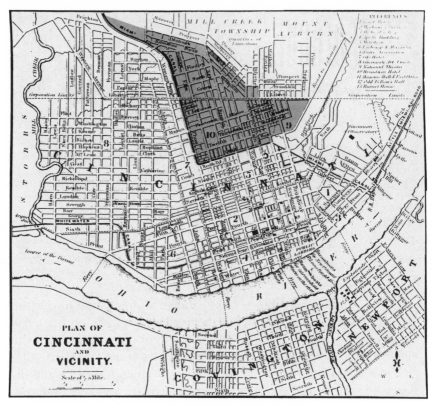

Street map of Cincinnati, 1846. Over-the-Rhine is shown as the shaded area tucked into the angle of the Miami and Erie Canal. Courtesy of the University of Cincinnati, Over-the-Rhine Design Studies Project, 1988.

By the turn of the century Over-the-Rhine still contained most of the city's German institutions, though a lower percentage of German and other immigrants, and Germans still led the city's immigrant groups in social and residential mobility. Most Cincinnatians regarded Over-the-Rhine as the city's premier entertainment district, for it offered a gaudy array of saloons, restaurants, shooting galleries, arcades, gambling dens, dance halls, burlesque halls, and theaters. Upper Vine Street especially attracted throngs of out-of-town visitors, traveling salesmen, politicians, show people, and "sports" who gave the neighborhood an evil reputation among some respectable people. Over-the-Rhine, lamented one,

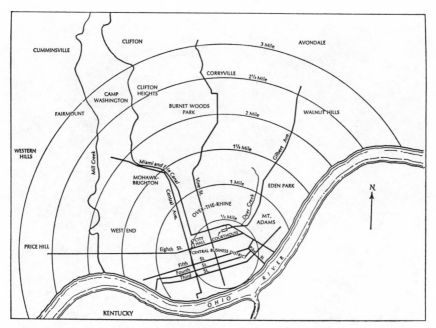

Cincinnati in 1875. The concentric circles illustrate the growth of the city and its suburbs. Reprinted, with permission of the author, from Zane L. Miller, *Boss Cox's Cincinnati* (New York: Oxford University Press, 1968).

combines "all the tarnished tinsel of a Bohemianism with the trimmings of a gutter and the morals of a sewer."[2]

Over-the-Rhine also worried city planners at the turn of the century, but their mode of thinking restricted their remedial options. They took groups as the basic units of society and attributed to them not only an inherited physiological character but also a biologically transmitted and indivisible essence that included intelligence, morality, and culture (that is, total way of life). These planners also divided the groups into categories of superior and inferior and regarded a culturally homogeneous nation-state as the sturdiest foundation for social and civic coherence. But their sense of biology as destiny rendered city planning useless in eradicating group distinctions, including those that separated in their minds the superior and "naturally" more modern, more prosperous, and more powerful "American stock" Anglo-Saxon group from the culturally different and "naturally" inferior groups, such as Polish Americans, Italian

Cincinnati's "Rhine," ca. 1900. Photograph shows a segment of the east-west axis of the Miami and Erie Canal, with Mt. Adams in the background and downtown to the right. Courtesy of the Cincinnati Historical Society.

Americans, and African Americans, who occupied and accepted lower niches in a hierarchical American society. In addition, turn-of-the-century biological determinism and homogenetic nationalism focused attention on the United States rather than on cities as the territorial unit of concern and led frustrated cultural homogenizers to worry more about dominant-group birth rates, the perils and possibilities of amalgamation, and the survival of inferior groups in a rapidly modernizing country than about urban problems.[3]

As a consequence city planners of that era tended to be architects, landscape designers, engineers, and sanitarians who offered advice on particular municipal problems by now and then devising a city plan as part of their larger practice. They normally worked independently of government as part of a general effort to keep important matters out of the hands of the presumably corrupt politicians who allegedly catered to special interests and who so often controlled city hall. They focused, moreover, on defective elements of the infrastructure of cities, such as the transportation system, park system, or sewerage system, in an effort to mitigate problems of poverty, vice, crime, disease, and high mortality rates while encouraging the construction of imposing civic centers and other beautiful and monumental public buildings to inculcate a sense of municipal and civic patriotism among the diverse and, in their view, unequal and culturally incompatible groups that lived uneasily together in crowded cities. Some of these part-time planners put their infrastructure and public buildings programs together in one elaborate and artfully designed document so that the plan itself might serve as a monumental symbol to inspire civic patriotism. "Make no little plans," advised Daniel Burnham, the author of such a plan for Chicago. "They have no magic to stir men's blood. Make big plans; aim high in hope and work. . . . Let your watchword be order and your beacon beauty."[4]

This way of thinking yielded in Cincinnati the boss system in politics and government to manage conflict among diverse groups and "reform" activities to manage the social problems inherent in the presumption of unequal diversity. Divisions of local government planned separately for the development of park, transit, and sewerage systems to facilitate the movement of slum dwellers into healthier and morally more wholesome social and physical environments, and the Park Board proposed the creation of a centrally located and monumental civic center along a parkway to inspire a general sense of city patriotism transcending the persisting differences and competition among various groups. In this context charitable and social work agencies addressed the problems of dependent and/or deviant groups by attempting to accommodate them to the dominant American stock's alien culture.[5]

In 1915, then, when our story begins, the physical fabric of Over-the-Rhine and its unsavory reputation remained intact. But the proliferation of suburbs after 1850 had created a less densely heterogeneous rim of new neighborhoods in the hills around the basin, which now ranked as the oldest section of town and seemed destined for occupation entirely by the expanding central business district. Over-the-Rhine sat on downtown's northern edge, its foreign population now thinned because

Cincinnati, unlike the more rapidly growing cities along the Great Lakes corridor, attracted a relatively small stream of new immigrants from eastern and southern Europe. Nonetheless, many of them, like American migrants, started their lives in the Queen City in Over-the-Rhine, the population of which remained as diverse as ever in all respects but one: almost all the prosperous people had left.

Given this history, Over-the-Rhine in the early twentieth century may be seen as a characteristically American slum, an old and declining area of mixed land uses and mixed peoples that formed part of a band of similar neighborhoods surrounding the central business district. Like such neighborhoods elsewhere, it retained that mix of land uses and peoples through the 1920s and 1930s, and after 1940 attracted large numbers of both Appalachians and African Americans. Unlike many such neighborhoods, however, Over-the-Rhine survived into the 1950s despite the adoption by city government after 1920 of new and drastic efforts to revitalize Cincinnati, including such dramatic slum clearance treatments as demolition and redevelopment.

PART **ONE**

ZONING, RAZING, OR REHABILITATION

INTRODUCTION

From Cultural Engineering
to Cultural Individualism

THE idea of slum clearance as an appropriate treatment for old neighborhoods such as Over-the-Rhine took shape in the 1920s and 1930s and flourished until the mid-1950s. It found some of its staunchest supporters among city planners who sought to encourage cosmopolitanism as a characteristic of residents in the metropolis. These planners defined cosmopolitanism as the sharing of behavioral traits among diverse groups of people without the destruction of each group's sense of its given and distinctive cultural identity, and they sought to promote cosmopolitanism by making it a new and key element of good citizenship. The planners meant, of course, that good citizens should possess the will and ability to earn their living, lead responsible social lives, and obey the law. But the planners also thought that good citizens bore a responsibility to understand and tolerate the various cultural groups in the city, and that all groups should be willing to subordinate from time to time their special interests for the sake of the public interest. By this planners now meant not only steps to advance the safety, comfort, and mental and physical health of all city residents, but also steps to promote the city's cosmopolitan social mission.[1]

The linking of good citizenship to cosmopolitanism did not itself justify slum clearance. But the cosmopolitan project took shape from a

9

social deterministic viewpoint that suggested both the focus on the city as a whole and the drastic treatment of slums. This viewpoint defined cities in culturally pluralistic terms that took groups as the basic units of society and assumed that each possessed or should possess a coherent and durable culture, defined as a total way of life. Groups acquired their culture, according to this line of thought, from their history and experience in varying social and physical environments, an explanation that made each group's identity and behavior the product of inexorable processes beyond the control of its members. This perspective also made all groups seem equal or potentially equal as components of urban life by positing a tangled complex of urban interdependence in which the dysfunctioning or disintegration of one group or part of the system not only impeded the functioning of the whole but also affected the operation of each of the other groups and parts.

This understanding of the city made slums seem extremely dangerous, for comprehensive city planners not only defined them as areas of mixed land uses and peoples who lived under congested conditions in old, obsolescent, and dilapidated dwellings. They also contended that slums eroded the coherence of cultural groups and left a residue of freestanding, impoverished, anomic, and alienated individuals, hapless people bereft of social and civic will who provided fodder for demagogues and political opportunists and were likely recruits into lives of crime, vice, violence, and disease. Worse still, city planners saw slums as cancerous, for they seemed to spread both contiguously and in leap-frog fashion, creating blight in adjacent and more remote territories, a condition that weakened the social and civic will of even more residents and diminished the possibility of establishing in those areas good citizenship based on intergroup tolerance and understanding and a willingness to sacrifice for the public welfare.

But comprehensive planners did not worry exclusively about slums and blight, for social determinism prompted profound concerns about the disruption of democracy through intense competition and conflict among groups outside of slums. This prospect seemed likely if not inevitable in a city composed of groups with given and distinctive ways of life, a situation that made intergroup understanding, tolerance, and cooperation virtually impossible and sacrifice for cosmopolitanism unlikely. So planners, city officials, and civic leaders touted good citizenship ideals not only in the slums but throughout the varied neighborhoods of the city. Short-term tactics featured civic education campaigns that stressed the social rather than the biological determinism of group cultures, emphasized the legitimacy and equality of all cultural groups, praised the virtues of compromise, denounced extremism and political opportunism, preached the gospel of intergroup respect, understanding, and tolerance, and exhorted all groups to make sacrifices for the promotion of the welfare of the whole.[2]

The long-term strategy for promoting good citizenship and cosmopolitanism extended well beyond the realm of civic education. It consisted of a cultural engineering program involving the use of city planning as a key element in forging a cosmopolitan population. Social determinism, that is, contended that the culture of groups might be altered and alienation forestalled by manipulating the social and physical environment, a bracing notion for persons concerned with cancerous slums, inevitable conflicts among groups outside the slums, and the maintenance of the culture and civic morale of groups everywhere in the city. From this perspective the comprehensive planners insisted on two items. They contended that experts in urban life and culture should work under governmental auspices and through governmental agencies to produce for all parts and groups in the city a single master plan, a document containing detailed, long-term recommendations for changes in the social and physical environment designed to implement the cosmopolitan project. And they argued that the chief guardian of the master plan should be a strong planning commission that would negotiate disputes over the implementation of particular public and private development proposals by working out settlements that did not endanger the cosmopolitan project.[3]

Ironically, the cosmopolitanizing comprehensive planners sought to inaugurate a new era of intergroup understanding, cooperation, and conflict-free urban life by more thoroughly segregating the city geographically by class and race. Comprehensive plans, that is, focused on the construction of carefully crafted, regulated, and homogeneous neighborhoods, including sometimes the creation of new ones on tracts cleared of slums in the inner city. The planners promoted territorial segregation by race and class to advance the cosmopolitan agenda in two ways. They wanted to separate the cultural groups to keep the peace among them and to assign them to physical and social environments designed to promote intragroup coherence. Under these conditions, the planners felt, other governmental and civic agencies could foster trait-sharing by orchestrating discretely managed intergroup contacts in the city's social, recreational, and political life.

Attempts to realize this vision in Cincinnati earned it a reputation as one of the nation's best governed cities[4] and produced several programs that classified Over-the-Rhine as a slum and proposed to eliminate it. These consisted of a comprehensive zoning scheme adopted in 1924 that targeted Over-the-Rhine for commercial and industrial but not residential land uses, a master plan in 1925 intended to assure that outcome, a design in the 1930s to clear part of Over-the-Rhine for a community development public housing project, and another comprehensive plan in 1948 that called for the clearance of all the city's slums, including Over-the-Rhine, and the construction in Over-the-Rhine of three community building public housing projects. This plan also sought in two ways to protect the new Over-the-Rhine housing projects from succumbing to blight and the spread of slums. It proposed to subject nearby slum neighborhoods to clearance and redevelopment with either public or privately financed and managed community development housing and to apply to nearby blighted neighborhoods conservation and rehabilitation treatments to forestall the inevitable day when they too would become slums and qualify for clearance and redevelopment. The failure of this program led to a rethinking of the nature of the metropolis problem that pushed the city in a new direction in dealing with these (and other) neighborhoods during the 1950s.

1

Social Groups, Slums, and Comprehensive Planning, 1915–1944

THE drive to wipe out slums through comprehensive planning began in the 1920s and made sense in the context of the work of the so-called Chicago school of sociology, some members of which proposed a theory of society and the city that rested on the idea that cultural groups derived their identity and behavioral characteristics from their history and experience in a particular place. These sociologists defined the city as a pluralistic organism with its own evolving way of life and portrayed its groups, parts, and systems as so interdependent that a change in one affected all the rest.[1] The Chicago school also stressed the tendency of city growth to dissolve old forms of social organization but contended that this did not mean that the emergence of the modern city would eliminate a vital local life. According to the Chicago school, local unity and cohesion developed in areas dominated by first-, second-, and third-generation ethnic groups that forged and sustained formal institutions of local community in response to the outside threat of discrimination. This suggested that a similar sense of local community could develop in areas of the city in which city planning or natural processes of urban growth had separated residential from other land uses, segregated population elements by economic and ethnic categories, and concentrated community organizing activities on homogeneous territorial units. Such an arrangement, the Chicago school argued, created "competent" communities, localities that stimulated residents to cooperate on such critical issues as assuring individuals a home, work, new experiences, leisure activities, status, and affection—the necessary prerequisites for the inculcation and development of civic patriotism.[2]

One member of the Chicago school, Louis Wirth, also thought that the contact and interaction of groups in the modern city tended toward cosmopolitanism, the creation of integrated societies comprised of a pluralistic blend of all the cultures that had and would participate in a given social system. Wirth conceived of this as stemming from the human capacity for empathy, that is, the ability to understand others' perspectives, motives, goals, and systems of thought even while disagreeing on particular questions. This suggested that contact and interaction among groups led to a process of interpenetration so that some groups came to share traits and outlooks while remaining cognizant of, proud of, and loyal to the heritage of their own group. (From this angle, of course, "natural" or trained cosmopolites seemed ideally suited as "experts" in discerning the public interest.)[3]

The Chicago school analysts of the city drew optimistic political implications from their view of the disorganizing, reorganizing, and integrating processes of urbanization. The city's disorganizing characteristics, if unchecked, might produce an anomic and alienated citizenry, perpetual social group conflict, and an undemocratic political system intolerant of subcultures offensive to the dominant group. But the city's reorganizing tendencies, if channeled by the use of segregative city planning and social welfare techniques, might fulfill the promise of the modern city for a new era of tolerance among subcultures, an era of urbanity, cosmopolitanism, and metropolitan civic patriotism.[4]

Yet the specter of disorganized and therefore incompetent local communities in the disorganizing and reorganizing dynamics of the modern city haunted this potentially optimistic view of modern American society. The threat lurked in every neighborhood but loomed largest in the slums, where losers in the competition of urban life found cheap habitations in places devoid of unity and cohesion. As Robert E. Park, the dean of the Chicago school, noted, all "the slum areas that invariably grow up just on the edge of the business areas of great cities, areas of deteriorated houses, of poverty, vice, and crime, are areas of social junk" that tended to spread outward into adjacent old neighborhoods and contiguously from there toward newer places on the periphery of the city.[5]

Views such as these about the perils and promises of urbanization made sense of and fueled Cincinnati's effort in the 1920s to simultaneously wipe out its slums and cosmopolitanize its population, a campaign that opened a new era of reform that targeted every group and neighborhood in the city. Social workers, for example, moved beyond their exclusive concern for dependent and/or defective groups to the promotion of social welfare, by which they meant the welfare of all groups and neighborhoods in the metropolis and the facilitating of cosmopolitanism. For these purposes they created the Council of Social Agencies as an executive federation to supervise the activities of every helping organization in the metropolitan area, and they established the Community Chest to raise funds for distribution by the Council. Cosmopolitan social workers also created new social agencies to assure the separate but equal treatment and participation in Council deliberations of all groups, including those, like blacks, who in the past had failed to establish their own comprehensive social welfare program to care for them as a group. Cosmopolitan social workers also helped establish in 1926 the city's Recreation Commission, which promptly developed an ambitious policy of encouraging the cultural consciousness of groups and promoting intergroup relations through such programs as "The Bowl of Promise," a pageant that celebrated both the civic history of the city and the contributions of various groups to its emerging cosmopolitanism.[6]

The cosmopolitan revolution reached well beyond the invention of social welfare. By the mid-1920s Cincinnati's cosmopolitan civic activists had also ousted the Republican machine and its hierarchically organized boss system and replaced it with a horizontally organized system of politics and government. The new city charter set up a city manager to coordinate on a separate but equal basis the activities of the various departments, boards, and commissions, including the new and powerful Cincinnati Planning Commission, and to arrange for the cooperation of civic organizations and other pressure groups with city government. In addition, the new charter established a merit system of civil service to eliminate group favoritism from the regulation of personnel matters and created a nine-member council to make policy, a body that chose from among its members a "weak" mayor as presiding officer. The charter also prescribed the election of city council through an at-large nonpartisan ballot and a system of proportional representation (PR). At-large elections sought to encourage city council to focus on the welfare of the city as a whole, PR acknowledged the legitimacy of cultural group pluralism, and nonpartisanship made it easier for minority representatives to secure a place on the ballot.[7]

But comprehensive city planning ranked as the key element in the cosmopolitanizing campaign against slums, and its advocates based their programs on ideas similar to those of the Chicago school sociologists, including their views of competent communities and of the poorest slum dwellers as social junk so demoralized they could never become good citizens. In their view that justified slum clearance programs, and they persuaded city council to adopt two master plans, one in 1925 and another in 1948, each of which took different approaches to the slum clearing task. Each, however, stemmed from the same understanding of the city, one that justified comprehensive city planning as the centerpiece of the drive to promote trait-sharing among the city's cultural groups and to eliminate slums.

The campaign for the creation of a planning commission and the adoption of a comprehensive plan for Cincinnati began in 1915 under the tutelage of Alfred Bettman, a forty-eight-year-old lawyer and former city solicitor who in the 1920s became a nationally recognized expert in planning and zoning. Bettman assembled a United City Planning Committee composed of representatives of seventeen civic organizations, including the Council of Social Agencies, the Chamber of Commerce, the Federated (Neighborhood) Improvement Association, the City Club, the Woman's City Club, the Central Labor Council, the Better Housing League, and the Smoke Abatement League. Through this committee Bettman orchestrated a persistent and intense effort to persuade the public to support comprehensive planning under government auspices by trumpeting the social, economic, aesthetic, civic, and health benefits of such planning. By 1920 the coalition had persuaded the state legislature to authorize city planning and zoning by municipalities, and had amended Cincinnati's charter to provide city government with a planning commission.[8]

The Cincinnati Planning Commission in 1921 took its first step to-

ward the creation of an official comprehensive city plan by engaging, for
a fee of $14,000, the Technical Advisory Corporation of New York (TAC)
to conduct a survey of the city. Ladislas Segoe, a Hungarian immigrant
and engineer who became by the 1930s one of the nation's premier planning consultants, prepared the survey under the supervision of George
Ford and E. C. Goodrich, the founders of TAC.[9]

Cincinnati, Segoe reported, badly needed a comprehensive plan because one-third of the city's population lived in the basin (the old city),
which contained just one-nineteenth of the city's area and broad
stretches of depressed property values. The report pointed to crowded
housing conditions in the basin and the absence of open space as breed-
ers of disease and delinquency, especially in the Negro lower West End,
where population densities ran as high as 1,500 persons per acre. It also
observed that the city's comparatively small foreign-born contingent,
mostly Germans, occupied the western and northern portions of the basin but under the pressure of business expansion had started migrating
to a hilltop district between Eden Park and Avondale, a location far removed from jobs. The movement, the report said, had a "harmful effect
on the surrounding [middle-class] residential districts."[10]

The survey suggested only tentative solutions to these problems, but
it especially emphasized the virtues of zoning. This device, Segoe explained, created land use, height, setback, court, and occupancy restric-
tions in different parts of the city to "direct the growth of each function
and each part of the city along logical lines."[11] Zoning also could help alleviate several problems identified in the report. It could, for example, de-
flect the migrating foreign-born to homes within walking distance of
their work and to districts more appropriate to their working-class and
ethnic status. It could encourage the development of well-organized residential neighborhoods in outlying districts with community centers containing commercial, recreation, civic, and business facilities, amenities
that would reduce the attractiveness of the basin as the "center of city
life." And it could lower mortgage costs in outlying subdivisions by stabi-
lizing land values and protecting property from harmful neighbors.

Indeed, Segoe contended, comprehensive zoning as an integral part
of a plan would eventually solve the problem of Cincinnati's uneven and
illogical distribution of population and property values. A plan combined with a zoning code would reserve the basin for business and industry in the future and disperse its residential population to the hilltops,

into better organized communities segregated by ethnicity, race, and class. These large movements would not happen suddenly, Segoe acknowledged, but in the meantime a good plan would provide more open space and playgrounds for basin residents. And as basin housing wore out, collapsed, burned, or gave way to the invasion of commercial or industrial facilities, its occupants would be dispersed to outlying neighborhoods and suburbs equipped with community institutions appropriate for healthy urban life.[12]

Three years later, TAC's preliminary solutions to Cincinnati's problems became law in the form of the master plan of 1925, a document that focused on creating and improving the functionally differentiated units of the metropolis and on shoring up real estate values as a means to protect the city's tax revenues and ensure a healthy rate of population and economic growth. Beyond the basin, the plan would foster in existing residential sections the development of competent neighborhood communities, each with a business and commercial recreation center and an adjacent civic center surrounded by residences. The plan identified several such nascent communities of wage-earners close to the basin, and others inhabited by more prosperous persons living nearby in detached houses on larger lots. The plan also declared it "obvious" on historical grounds that the nearby older neighborhoods "will gradually give place to more intensive development and the best type of housing will move farther out."[13]

This picture of the growth of the city indicated that the bulk of poor newcomers—most of them rural and southern in origin, the plan predicted—would occupy temporary quarters in the basin.[14] As a consequence, the plan did not provide an enduring role for the basin as a portal of entry for newcomers or as a major residential district of any sort, even though the area contained 80 percent of the city's tenements. Indeed, the plan reserved all of the basin for commercial, industrial, and civic uses, each in its own segregated zoning district. And the plan noted with satisfaction that natural forces, "the spread of business and industry," were decreasing the basin's population of 120,000 at the rate of 2 percent per year, a calculation suggesting that the basin's new zoning maps would merely accelerate the inevitable.[15]

The plan of 1925 also made other recommendations to hasten the transformation of the basin, several of which involved changes in or near

Over-the-Rhine. In so doing it consolidated and reformulated into a single bold design four previous plans—one of them as old as 1907[16]—for civic facilities on or near the southern edge of Over-the-Rhine. The plan suggested the construction by 1950 of a cluster of new developments in the elbow of Central Parkway between City Hall on the south and Music Hall, which sat across the street from Washington Park. The park itself occupied the equivalent of four city blocks and contained a bandstand, benches, curvilinear paths, and statues. In addition, the plan urged the location around Washington Park of new cultural facilities, such as a natural history museum, a historical museum, and a technical museum, and the extension of Central Parkway straight west to a proposed union railroad passenger terminal in Mill Creek Valley at the west end of Lincoln Park. The erection of a colonnaded memorial tower between the proposed post office and Board of Education building at the beginning of the westward extension of Central Parkway also was suggested. The plan proposed to extend the civic center to the other end of Central Parkway, where the Ohio Mechanic's Institute (with its acoustically marvelous Emery Auditorium) and the county courthouse stood. Near the courthouse, at the confluence of Eggleston Avenue and Reading Road, the plan called for an underground rapid transit terminal covered by a transfer plaza containing planted terraces from which passengers could make connections to trolley and bus lines.[17]

This list of projects did not exhaust the plan's schemes for the basin, which with its civic center and other embellishments would serve as "a visible focus, an expression of civic pride, a tangible medium for the awakening of civic consciousness."[18] In pushing for this goal the plan promoted cosmopolitanism, sometimes by reproducing pictures of old civic designs in European and American cities as worthy of emulation.[19] But it also claimed for Cincinnati "all the picturesqueness of Boston, New Orleans, Quebec [and] the hill towns of Italy," a characteristic derived not only from the Queen City's hills and vistas but also from its eighty-eight public parks and the charming streetscapes of its "innumerable corners," some of them in the "picturesque" slums "that delight the artist." The plan proposed several ways of enhancing the city's "real and vivid personality," including the designation of twenty-three historic sites, most of them in the basin but none above Central Parkway, and recommended their identification "by tablets, monuments, or small parks, or by the

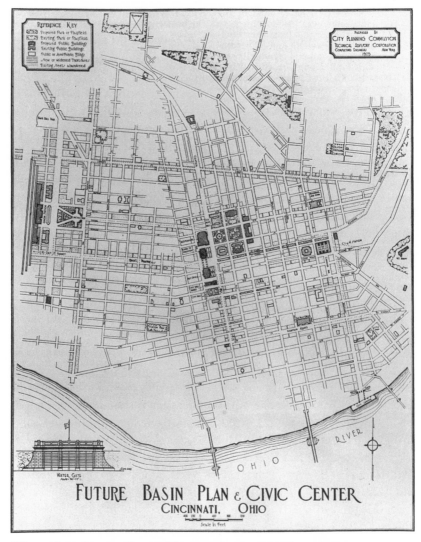

The projected twenty-five- to fifty-year plan for the basin and civic center, 1925. Reprinted from City Planning Commission, *The Official City Plan of Cincinnati, Ohio*, 1925.

erection of dignified public or semi-public buildings appropriately named or marked." The plan also urged the preservation of the city's abundant "natural and inherited charm" by the establishment of an "art jury" to approve "the location, character and design of all public structures, and ... to influence the design of semi-public and private structures."[20]

Zoning and other features of the plan of 1925 ultimately would create a new basin. In the meantime the plan recommended other alterations and policies to make Over-the-Rhine and the rest of the basin palatable for those residents who could not or would not soon move. These included the opening of courtyards in large, poorly ventilated, and dimly lighted tenements, the creation of new neighborhood parks and play-fields and additional playgrounds next to schools, and the merger and elimination of several school districts and buildings. The plan noted, too, that stall rentals in the city's five public markets, all of them in the basin, produced little revenue for municipal coffers but remained useful because they helped "to lower somewhat the cost of living for poorer residents." Nonetheless, the plan recommended the closing of two of the markets because their clientele "is moving away with the incursion of business." The other three, including Findlay Market, the only one in Over-the-Rhine, could remain without serious damage to traffic or the extension of business, though the plan concluded that "their usefulness does not warrant any large expenditures for enlargement or even renewal."[21]

The plan also recommended the melioration of the housing problem with special reference to the basin, where conditions had become so acute that social agencies found it "impossible ... to provide anything like a satisfactory solution to the family problems which they are attempting to adjust." The problem stood out most starkly in the lower West End, where "the majority of the colored people" lived with six to twelve people per room crowded into the oldest and most unsanitary dwellings. Here, as in other black enclaves outside the basin, rents had more than doubled and families spent at least one-quarter of their average annual income for rent. But the plan emphasized that the housing shortage also bore heavily on the white low-wage earners of the basin. Since these two groups could not afford newly constructed accommodations, they would have to be provided for by the decentralization of the population into the competent communities the plan sought to create in older districts beyond the basin.[22]

Such decentralization "should be encouraged by every means," the plan insisted, including transit, viaduct, boulevard, and cross-town thoroughfare projects designed to open the western hills for more intensive settlement and to fill the gaps between the bands of settlement along existing traffic corridors that stretched out of the basin to the north and east like the fingers of a hand. The planners, moreover, thought that decentralization could be hastened without involuntary displacement, because questionnaires and the history of city growth indicated that low-wage earners wanted better dwellings in better (and therefore farther out) neighborhoods. The plan predicted that silk-stocking neighborhoods such as Clifton, Hyde Park, and Avondale would eventually fall to a lower status, replaced as the city's choicest and most exclusive residential sites by four even more remote areas, including three outside Cincinnati, where "the best type of housing should be encouraged."[23]

In its decentralization scheme, then, the plan of 1925 pictured a metropolis with residents constantly in motion through several classes of homogeneous and stable competent communities. It depicted this mobility as the solution to the housing problem: low-wage earners forced to live in unzoned neighborhoods that lacked community centers, often close to or in the midst of the "social junk" of the slums and therefore exposed to influences likely to render them incompetent citizens. Population decentralization would solve the housing problem, the plan said, for "as fast as the families in better circumstances move out of the older tenements and houses, they will become available for housing the lower wage earners."[24] This policy also held out the hope that the basin might continue, albeit temporarily, to serve as a staging ground for mobility, but it provided no place or remedy for those slum dwellers described by Robert Park as "social junk," and the comprehensive plan remained silent on the question of what to do with or for them.

After 1929 the persistence of the low-cost housing shortage and its aggravation by the Great Depression changed the minds of the Planning Commission members and other supporters of comprehensive planning about the elimination of residences from the entire basin. In the early 1930s the Planning Commission staff began work on a proposal for slum clearance and the creation of newly constructed competent communities in the West End and Over-the-Rhine (which they called the north basin).[25] City officials in 1932 and 1933 supported several efforts by limited dividend corporations to secure loans from the federal Reconstruction Finance Corporation for slum clearance and competent community housing development projects, all of which failed for lack of adequate local financing. Prospects for such projects brightened in 1933, however, when the New Deal's Public Works Administration authorized its housing division to make loans and grants covering 30 percent of project costs to states, municipalities, or other public bodies engaged in low-cost or slum housing redevelopment. That same year Cincinnati planning advocates and housing reformers helped persuade the state legislature to establish the Cincinnati Metropolitan Housing Authority (CMHA) for a territory covering both Cincinnati and three outlying townships. The CMHA hoped to accommodate those displaced from slums in low-density projects in the basin and on vacant land sites in outlying areas, including the suburbs.

But the CMHA wanted to start with slum clearance in the basin, and the Planning Commission unveiled in 1933 an ambitious basin redevelopment plan prepared by the Commission's secretary, Myron Downs. This plan treated the north and west basin problems as identical and proposed to correct them by razing 145 blocks of slums and replacing them with sixteen superblocks in two community development housing projects. One of the projects straddled Lincoln Park Drive (now Ezzard Charles Drive) between the newly constructed Union Terminal and Music Hall on the west side of the northern axis of Central Parkway. The other lay parallel to the West End project on the east side of Central Parkway and included Washington Park in Over-the-Rhine and additional land up to Findlay Street. The selection of these sites ignored the worst slums of the lower West End, whose residents the planners regarded as socially and civically irredeemable. But surveys of the target areas by the Planning Commission and other agencies persuaded the planners that high levels of sickness, crime, juvenile delinquency, and unemployment qualified the two target areas for slum clearance and redevelopment, even though some residents objected to the designation of their neighborhoods as slums.

In defense of the scheme the planners contended that the North and West Central Basin District Plan would relieve congestion, provide more

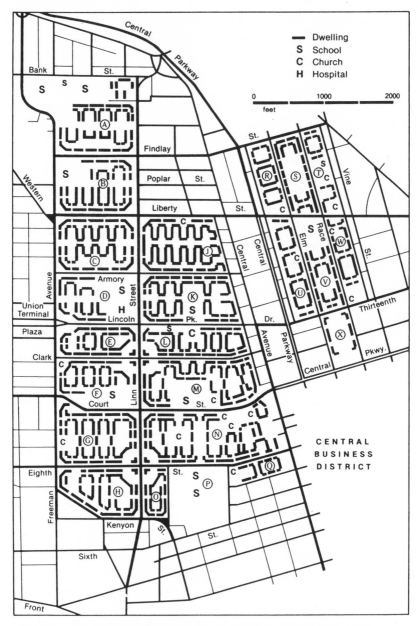

Planning Commission's proposed basin redevelopment plan, 1933. The plan proposed razing slums and replacing them with superblocks of housing. Cincinnati Historical Society, Rowe Papers. Reprinted in Robert B. Fairbanks, *Making Better Citizens* (Urbana: University of Illinois Press, 1988).

The dense West End in 1930, before the construction of Laurel Homes. Courtesy of the Cincinnati Historical Society.

light and air, and give residents the experience of competent community living. The plan called for neighborhood schools scattered throughout the area, and each superblock offered abundant space within rectangular residential developments for recreation facilities, churches, businesses, and meeting places. Each possessed distinct boundaries formed by thoroughfares to enhance the sense of a self-contained community.

The plan for the north and west central basin never came to fruition, but the CMHA did complete two smaller public community housing projects, Laurel Homes for whites and Lincoln Court for blacks, both located one block west of Music Hall on either side of Lincoln Park Drive, the approach to Union Terminal. By subjecting prospective tenants to credit, employment, and crime-record checks, CMHA weeded out those it deemed hopelessly corrupted by slum living, and by setting income maximums for tenants it designated the projects as way stations, temporary but competent communities that prepared their residents to acquire the resources, community spirit, and cosmopolitanism necessary for successful urban life in other communities farther out. To assure this outcome, Laurel Homes contained not only 1,309 housing units in low-rise apartment buildings in a park-like setting, but also a shopping center, playgrounds, and a supervised community building where tenants could meet, establish social organizations, hold dances, read the project's newspaper, and develop community and civic spirit. Lincoln Court, a project for black defense workers completed in the early 1940s, operated on the same principles, separate but equal.

The creation of Laurel Homes and Lincoln Court under the New Deal public housing program left Over-the-Rhine untouched, as did other major New Deal housing initiatives—the provision through the Home Owners Loan Corporation and the Federal Housing Administration of guaranteed mortgages for housing improvements and new residential construction. Indeed, these measures benefited outlying city and suburban districts at the expense of the basin because the federal agencies endorsed the homogeneous community ideal, which regarded areas of mixed land uses and/or mixed peoples as slums or proto-slums and therefore at high risk for housing investments. The policies also helped preserve Over-the-Rhine into the 1950s as a predominantly white enclave, for they encouraged the confining of blacks to black areas or mixed areas near black enclaves, a practice endorsed by the Cincinnati Board of Realtors, which supported the homogeneous neighborhood policy by refusing to assist the movement of blacks into white neighborhoods as a matter of high ethical principal.[26]

During World War II, however, a sense of crisis led to the writing of a new metropolitan master plan that revived the issue of redeveloping Over-the-Rhine. In 1940, the Urban Land Institute, an agency of the National Board of Realtors, commissioned Walter S. Schmidt, a leading Cincinnati Realtor, to undertake an analysis of the city's problems and what might be done about them. Called *Proposals for Downtown Cincinnati*, the study in fact sought to rejuvenate the entire metropolitan area. It identified two new problems, the difference in the rate of population growth between Cincinnati and its suburbs, which seemed to threaten the status of Cincinnati as the core of the metropolis, and the slowing of activity in the central business district, which had suffered a 20 percent drop in retail business since 1920.

The study did not call for the rebuilding of the central business district. Instead, it made a host of recommendations, including several to address the principal causes of the stagnation of the central business district, which it identified as the obsolescent housing around the district and the desire of residents of older sections for new homes in outlying neighborhoods. As correctives the study proposed the development of a new metropolitan master plan that would include proposals for the rehabilitation of the old stock of housing around the central business district and improved transportation facilities to make downtown more accessible to people from city and suburban neighborhoods.[27]

That same year the *Real Property Survey* of Cincinnati and urbanized Hamilton County, a study carried out by the Cincinnati Planning Commission and the Hamilton County Regional Planning Commission (established in 1929), intensified the sense that the city faced grim problems. The survey reported some familiar news—66,100 substandard or overcrowded living units in the basin, for example—but also endorsed Schmidt's conclusion that Cincinnati was growing much less rapidly than its suburbs. The real property survey, however, eschewed the rehabilitation of old neighborhoods in favor of the clearance and "physical redevelopment of . . . blighted neighborhoods" as the proper check for the "outward flow," the perpetuation of which would create a fiscal crisis for Cincinnati.[28]

In this context of conflicting strategies for dealing with the suburban exodus and the basin's obsolescence, Alfred Bettman, the chair of the Planning Commission, pushed for a revision of the plan of 1925.[29] Instead of reviving the United City Planning Committee, he put together a support group consisting of the chief executive officers of the area's biggest businesses. It organized in December 1943 as the Cincinnati Citizens Development Committee (CDC) to back not only comprehensive planning but also "every movement of a broad nature for the improvement of business and living conditions in the Cincinnati area." In that capacity it lobbied city council and the state legislature on planning issues, put out a newsletter urging public support for planning and public works projects, and raised $100,000 to underwrite a successful bond issue campaign to raise $41 million for capital expenditures by the city and county and Cincinnati public schools.[30]

City council also responded favorably to the pleas of the CDC and others for a new master plan. In February 1944 it appropriated $100,000 to the Planning Commission to create a Division of City and Metropolitan Planning and to hire a separate staff headed by experts in regional planning. After a careful nationwide search, the city hired Sherwood L. Reeder, a former director of the regional federal Public Housing Authority in Detroit, as director of the division. As consultants, Reeder selected Ladislas Segoe, who had served in the 1930s as research director for the Urbanism Committee of the New Deal's National Resources Planning Board, and Tracy Augur, a planner for the Tennessee Valley Authority, another New Deal venture.[31]

They faced a daunting task. After two decades of comprehensive metropolitan planning the slum problem remained unsolved. Planners in the 1920s had sought to resolve it by encouraging the use of zoning to eliminate all housing in the basin, and by the 1940s two alternative proposals had appeared: slum clearance and redevelopment for competent community living in public housing, or housing rehabilitation. Questions remained about the last option, including the issue of which neighborhoods would be rehabilitated, but it did not necessarily run counter to the competent community ideal. That ideal had focused on the rehabilitation of salvageable slum dwellers by creating for them a new and cosmopolitanizing social and physical environment to foster metropolitan civic patriotism, a project conceivable in a physical environment created in the past but rehabilitated physically and socially to serve the present and the future.

2

Neighborhoods and a Community, 1948–1960

T HE Cincinnati Metropolitan Master Plan of 1948 eschewed the idea of rehabilitation as the best treatment for slums. Instead, the plan proposed to tear down slums and redevelop the land for other uses, a proposition that rested on the conventional planning wisdom of the past, including the ideas of social determinism, trait-sharing cosmopolitanism, and the creation of competent communities along the lines developed for public housing projects in the 1930s. The plan of 1948 called for just such a redevelopment project for Over-the-Rhine as part of its larger program to offset the more rapid rate of suburban as opposed to city growth and to avert the economic and residential decline of Cincinnati as the dynamic core of the metropolitan area. As the principal solution to these problems the plan called for the demolition of *all* slums to make way for industrial and low-density residential redevelopment projects in the inner city and an expressway system,[1] each of which would displace thousands of people, especially blacks, as well as many institutions and businesses.

The planners of 1948 intended to handle the relocation issue as part of their larger effort to promote citywide social stability and civic pride.[2] This broad scheme covered outer- as well as inner-city areas and rested on the conviction that unregulated urban growth eventually "reaches a

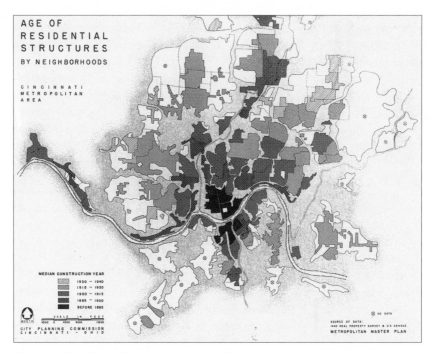

The age of residential structures by neighborhood, 1940. Reprinted from City Planning Commission, *Residential Areas: An Analysis of Land Requirements for Residential Development, 1945 to 1970,* December 1946.

point of diminishing returns in terms of the advantages which a city, as a social community, should provide for its inhabitants." The plan proposed to solve this problem by organizing all of the Queen City's residential districts into communities of 20,000 to 40,000 people, not self-governed but "self-contained in respect to the everyday life of their inhabitants except for such facilities and services . . . located in or supplied by Cincinnati as the central city, and by institutions serving the Metropolitan Area."[3]

This conception of the metropolitan residential area as a cluster of medium-sized communities stemmed from an optimistic interpretation of the history of the metropolis that made the grandiose scheme seem plausible. The planners depicted Cincinnati as a product of the growth of a plethora of neighborhoods around the original settlement, the

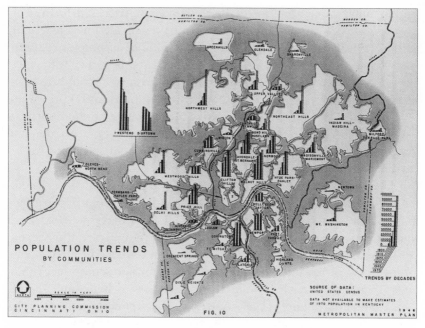

Projected population trends by community, 1900–1970. Reprinted from City Planning Commission, *Residential Areas*, December 1946.

annexation of a number of them to Cincinnati, and the grouping of some of them into self-contained communities by hills and valleys. This seemed most "fortunate" because it tended "to preserve as the city grew, some of the better qualities of small town life, such as the spirit of neigh- borliness and the sense of attachment to locality." Specifically, the plan- ners asserted, small-town people "participate to a greater extent in community activities; a larger percentage goes to the polls; a higher pro- portion contribute to the Community Chest; more are interested in pub- lic affairs." And "here in the Cincinnati Area, to a greater degree than in most large cities, residents enjoy the economic and cultural advantages of a metropolis while living in residential localities small enough to satisfy the urge for intimacy in home surroundings and a social life in scale with the average family."[4]

Unfortunately, history had not adequately completed the task of community building, and the plan proposed "to strengthen the present rudimentary . . . composition of the Metropolitan Area . . . to form an organized 'cluster' of communities, each further divided into neighborhoods." The boundaries of each community should encompass 20,000 to 40,000 people on 1,000 to 2,000 acres of land and be drawn with reference to separators such as topographic features, industrial belts, railroads, large parks, greenbelts, cemeteries, institutions, and expressways. Each community would be connected to others by intercommunity thoroughfares and in turn to expressways leading to the larger metropolitan community of work, entertainment, education, and social and recreational activities.[5]

The plan cited several features as critical to the viability of each community. Ideally, each should be served by a high school, one or two junior high schools, and several neighborhood elementary schools. Each should also possess "a community business district" and near it a civic center composed of a branch library, a recreation center, a health center, a branch post office, and, in some cases, appropriate semi-public buildings. In addition, each community should possess both single-family homes and apartments of various sizes to accommodate "young couples . . . growing families and . . . elderly persons," thereby eliminating the necessity for a family "to move away from friends, neighbors, churches and other associations as it arrives at various stages of the life cycle."[6]

The community scheme of the plan of 1948 presented each community as separate but equal, and proposed to stabilize for a generation the population of each community and to moderate the rate of incursion by newcomers from other communities. Yet it also provided for racial, ethnic, and class heterogeneity within communities while endorsing residential segregation by race, ethnicity, and class. The mechanism for doing this was the idea of neighborhood, for in forming each community the planners tried to group "traditional" and therefore segregated neighborhoods, an arrangement that frequently put diverse neighborhoods in one community. In such cases each segregated neighborhood functioned as a social unit while the diverse residents of the various neighborhoods intermingled in the community's civic, recreational, and commercial facilities that served all the neighborhoods, an arrangement that made the community the crucible for encouraging individuals to pursue self-fulfillment through trait-sharing cosmopolitanism and civic patriotism.

According to the plan of 1948, a neighborhood should contain 4,000

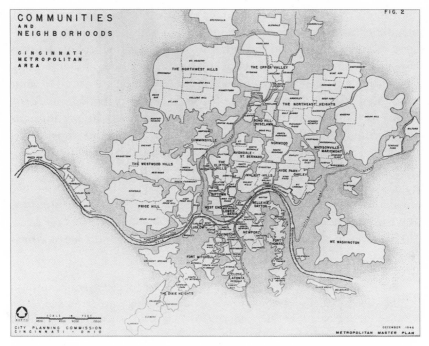

Cincinnati's communities and neighborhoods, 1946. Reprinted from City Planning Commission, *Residential Areas*, December 1946.

to 8,000 people on 400 to 800 acres of land. Each neighborhood should be connected to its community and the metropolis by the thoroughfare and expressway systems and bounded, but not entered, by interneighborhood streets. Moreover, each neighborhood should have all the attributes of a community except a civic center, that is, an elementary school with a playground as well as additional playgrounds where necessary, one or several neighborhood shopping centers, and perhaps additional local shopping areas consisting of a few stores. And each neighborhood should have some mix of single-family homes and apartments, with the proportion of single-family homes increasing with distance from the central business district.[7]

The planners of 1948 recognized that they had to apply their neighborhood and community conception to a real city, not an abstraction. To define that reality, they used a historical analysis that pictured the metropolis roughly as a series of concentric circles of older and newer neighborhoods, with the older neighborhoods at the core, the middle-aged in the next ring, and the new ones on the periphery. This analysis also attributed a common life cycle to all neighborhoods and depicted a city decaying from a process by which old residential areas fell to non-residential uses and neighborhoods deteriorated as blacks and poor whites spread from the oldest and worst neighborhoods into contiguous and declining middle-aged neighborhoods. Each neighborhood, said the plan, experienced an initial period of growth, then stability, then decline, with changes "in the type of population coming into the neighborhood, . . . shift from owner to tenant occupancy, . . . the conversion into smaller apartments of larger homes," heavier traffic, more institutions, and the incursion of industry or commercial facilities.[8]

Finally comes the nadir, exemplified in Cincinnati by the basin, which the plan identified as a deteriorated area.

> In the oldest, and hence most centrally located neighborhoods, not only will the deterioration and obsolescence of the housing have proceeded to a marked degree, . . . but the pattern of the land use may also have changed radically from its original character into what is familiarly known as slum or blighted areas, or in this report, "deteriorated areas." The best examples in Cincinnati of . . . neighborhoods that have reached, or are approaching the end of their life-cycle . . . are found, of course, in the Basin area. Here neighborhoods that were in their time among the finest in the city, have become through force of circumstance ripe for the most complete redevelopment.[9]

The plan of 1948 then classified Cincinnati's neighborhoods by age groups and by the housing conditions in each age group, a classification that yielded five categories of neighborhoods and recommendations for handling each. Deteriorated areas received the most drastic treatment: "complete clearance and a fresh start through redevelopment for either private or public use, in accordance with the master plan." The planners scheduled declining but not yet deteriorated areas for "rehabilitation," a temporary expedient to delay complete clearance and redevelopment that involved the demolition of the worst structures, reduction of heterogeneity in land use and of residential overcrowding, repair and modernization of dwelling units, and the introduction of playgrounds and schools. Middle-aged neighborhoods fell under the "conservation" rubric, a program to prevent deterioration carried out by Planning Commission staff, who would induce property owners to modernize buildings, adhere to the master plan, and help arrange financing for such efforts. Newer neighborhoods required only "protection" through adequate zoning and careful planning. The last category, "preparation for new growth," applied to neighborhoods "just beginning to develop" and involved an assessment of the future character of the neighborhood and community structure to shape the size and nature of these youngest of urban places.[10]

Through these programs the residential strategy of the plan of 1948 aimed to encourage suburbanization while preventing the potentially devastating civic and fiscal effects of Cincinnati's eventual transformation into one great slum. The plan sought also to preserve the area's segregated social and racial geography and to regulate the neighborhood filter-down process that facilitated residential segregation. It encouraged rapid population growth "in the major peripheral communities" of the metropolitan area and modest increases or decreases "in the built-up portions of the urban area lying between the Basin and the peripheral communities." For the basin itself, the plan projected a 50 percent population decrease by 1970, "assuming adequate redevelopment," and a 27 percent decrease without it. The plan also foresaw a destination for that excess basin population by observing that certain "middle-aged sections" (Avondale, Clifton, Cumminsville, Norwood, and Walnut Hills) would experience a change "in the composition and character of the population and in types of residential structures."[11] In short, the plan anticipated that some poor white and black inhabitants of the basin displaced by low-density redevelopment would move out to the next band of neighborhoods on the north and the east, where programs of conservation and rehabilitation would slow the inevitable descent of these neighborhoods into slums requiring clearance and reconstruction.

This vision of outward growth made the redevelopment of Cincinnati's basin slums a key element in the plan's scheme to reverse the decay of the Queen City as the dynamic center of the metropolis. The redevelopment package contained industrial, commercial, and private residential components, but it also proposed to endow the basin with two additional public housing communities, each composed of three neighborhoods. One, called Linconia, encompassed the black neighborhoods west of Music Hall and north of the Laurel Homes and Lincoln Court public housing projects. The other, dubbed Uptown by the planners, occupied the territory north of the central business district still known popularly as Over-the-Rhine.[12]

The planners included but a brief list of redevelopment proposals for Uptown, and they provided no explanation for the meaning of the name (the rationale for Linconia seems self-evident) and suggested no special scheme to recall the area's German past. But the plan laid out drastic changes for Uptown, especially its community thoroughfare scheme. It designated Vine Street as the area's north to south "axis thorofare" and called for the construction of a viaduct running from the convergence of Vine Street and Clifton Avenue to Race Street at Findlay Street, the widening of west Findlay Street to Central Parkway to encourage traffic to bypass the community on the west, and the widening and extension of Liberty Street into a thoroughfare connecting proposed expressways on the east and west flanks of Uptown. The plan also proposed an east bypass around Uptown by widening Clifton Avenue and extending it to Liberty and Sycamore Streets.[13]

Other proposals for the new community proved more modest. The plan recommended the erection of a new building for Peaslee Elementary School in the Over-the-Rhine neighborhood, designated Rothenberg Elementary School to serve the Liberty neighborhood, and suggested the construction of a new elementary school for the Washington Park neighborhood in the north part of the park itself. The plan noted, too, that the Board of Education intended to convert Woodward High School into a junior high school and to build a new high school near Lincoln Park Drive and Central Avenue between the communities of Linconia and Uptown (the plan did not discuss racial integration or segregation in the public schools). The plan suggested the laying out of play areas around all the schools in Uptown and the expansion of the Findlay Street playground to encompass an entire block. It recommended the concentration of commercial facilities on one street (either Walnut, Race, or Elm Street) and suggested the construction of the community civic center for Uptown in the vicinity of Liberty and Vine Streets.[14]

Finally, the plan of 1948 proposed the retention of some industrial land uses in Uptown. It noted disapprovingly that printing, laundry, brewery, and "miscellaneous" industries intruded among residences throughout Uptown, while denser concentrations of diverse industries occurred on the east side of the community along Reading Road and on the northwest along McMicken Street and Central Avenue. In the new community, the plan cautioned, industry should be restricted to the periphery of the area, though the plan contained no industrial redevelopment project for Uptown.[15]

These alterations and the clearance and redevelopment of Uptown would have destroyed both the physical and social fabric of the area, of course. But Over-the-Rhine survived because the Planning Commission, the city administration, and city council took as their top priorities slum clearance and redevelopment and expressway construction in the West End and pushed hard for their implementation. Indeed, Alfred Bettman, who chaired the Planning Commission from 1930 to 1945, played a leading part during the early 1940s in drafting both the Ohio and the federal redevelopment laws of 1949 that together furnished the legal basis and federal financial support for tearing down and rebuilding inner-city neighborhoods.[16]

Both these laws obligated the city government to assure the availability of relocation housing for persons displaced by urban redevelopment, a problem that seemed manageable until its complication by the question of race. This issue appeared early in the clearance and redevelopment process because the Planning Commission proposed to start the program in African American tracts in the West End, after which it intended to send bulldozers to Over-the-Rhine, the predominantly white territory. Council responded favorably to this proposition and authorized two urban redevelopment bond issues for voter approval in November 1951 to cover the city's share of the cost of the federally subsidized project.

But city council also banned racial discrimination in redevelopment residential programs, a policy that Charles Stamm, the city official in charge of redevelopment, initially welcomed with enthusiasm. It would, he thought, help solve several problems, including the notion that "certain groups must be kept in certain places." It would also, he contended, help raise housing standards generally and contribute to the solution of social problems "rising from the slums."[17]

Yet Stamm worried that the anti-discrimination measure combined with the involuntary removal of African Americans might undermine support for the bond issues in both white and black neighborhoods. To avert this, he called on the Mayor's Friendly Relations Committee for assistance. He wanted to counter rumors in the black West End that equated slum clearance with "Negro clearance" by assuring residents of the availability of relocation housing within the city of Cincinnati. He also wanted the Committee to help prepare for the movement of black families into white neighborhoods by persuading residents of such places that the arrival of blacks would not lower property values.[18]

The Committee voted to help out, and both bond issues carried the precincts on the redevelopment sites. But they failed to pass muster with voters citywide (one lost by a margin of 61 percent and the other by 58 percent), a defeat ascribed by the Better Housing League of Greater Cincinnati to fears among most voters that relocation might introduce blacks into white neighborhoods or convert racially mixed areas into black enclaves. Stamm thought such fears might yet be overcome, however, and he turned next for assistance to the Cincinnati Metropolitan Housing Authority. CMHA had also adopted an anti-discrimination policy in response to civil rights advocates who claimed that its once popular large-scale community development projects isolated tenants, stigmatized them as poor, and destroyed their sense of themselves as individuals capable of making choices about their futures. Under the new strategy CMHA retained the old projects but agreed to reserve for relocation housing new ones that would be smaller and lack their own commercial, civic, and social facilities. Relocation units also would be scattered around the city so that tenants would have a choice of neighborhoods in which to live and could use the same local facilities as other residents.[19]

Implementing this integrationist policy in the 1950s proved impossible, even though the CMHA secured federal allocations sufficient to build as many as four or five projects. Most people did not want in their neighborhood a relocation public housing project for slum dwellers displaced from the basin's West End for fear that such projects would lower property values, increase juvenile delinquency and crime, and provide vehicles for the introduction of poor blacks into white or racially mixed but unstable middle-class areas. Between 1952 and 1954 the CMHA abandoned four relocation public housing projects in the face of stiff and racially charged neighborhood opposition.[20]

Meanwhile, Stamm had moved away from racial residential integration in his efforts to alleviate the relocation housing problem and get redevelopment back on track. First, he helped set up a homogeneous community development project for whites (Forest Park) on 3,400 acres of undeveloped land in Cincinnati's northern suburbs. The land had been part of a federal government greenbelt town project that in the 1930s yielded a white community development project called Greenhills.[21] Then Stamm linked basin redevelopment projects with rehabilitation and conservation treatments in the band of hilltop neighborhoods around the basin. The impetus for this move came from the passage of the federal Housing Act of 1954, which provided subsidies for rehabilitation and conservation as well as slum clearance and redevelopment under the new rubric of "urban renewal." Under this program the city launched a redevelopment project in the lower West End in the Kenyon Barr area, the construction of which began in 1955 and displaced additional African Americans. As a relocation site the city government selected for its first rehabilitation and conservation effort the partially integrated Avondale-Corryville neighborhoods to the north and northeast of the basin, places in which it hoped to accommodate poor blacks displaced from the West End but without creating another slum.[22]

Planning for the Kenyon Barr and Avondale-Corryville projects delayed for two years action on the 1948 plan's proposal for a community development public housing project in Over-the-Rhine. But Charles Stamm in 1956 persuaded city council to make it the next item on the slum clearance agenda and filed with the federal government a proposal to survey the area and write a detailed plan for the project.[23] Yet the project did not go forward. Instead, the city manager withdrew the application in 1957 and the Planning Commission incorporated the neighborhood into a new approach to renewal planning in the basin: the designation of Over-the-Rhine, the central riverfront, and the central business district as a single renewal area within which to carry out redevelopment projects one at a time.[24]

This new approach to urban renewal in the heart of the city made it possible to mitigate the housing relocation problem by including large chunks of non-residential territory in the renewal area and by concentrating clearance and redevelopment in that lightly populated territory. But the Planning Commission went further than that. It inaugurated the new policy not only by placing the Over-the-Rhine slum clearance proposal on its inactive list but also by indicating that it would consider using that turf as a residential neighborhood oriented to downtown rather than as a site for a community development public housing project.[25] Meanwhile, the city focused its clearance and redevelopment activities on commercial properties within the central business district well south of Over-the-Rhine and pushed ahead with the Avondale-Corryville conservation and rehabilitation project.

This new approach to treating the basin left the physical and social environment of Over-the-Rhine intact but also suggested in vague terms a future for the neighborhood as a residential appendage to the central business district rather than as the object of slum clearance and community development housing. That proposition might or might not involve clearing the site, for city officials had already acquiesced in the rehabilitation of old structures in one such neighborhood (Mt. Adams) and had sanctioned in another the construction of a new and racially integrated residential complex (Park Town) as part of downtown's "new" West End.[26] Both of these potential precedents, moreover, targeted middle- and/or upper-income people as ideal residents, an indication that Over-the-Rhine as a downtown neighborhood would not provide much if any room for the city's "social junk" and would not need the attributes of a competent community.

The new approach to downtown and Over-the-Rhine rested upon a new conception of the city with profound consequences. It rendered obsolete the idea of cosmopolitan cultural engineering and the various projects flowing from that program, including metropolitan master planning. It also ushered in an era in which the phrase "inner city" replaced "slum" as the designation for the area around downtown and in which that terrain became contested turf for people defining their own cultures by designing a neighborhood of their choice.

PART **TWO**

NEW VISIONS AND VISIONARIES

INTRODUCTION

Community Action and Neighborhood Planning

THE failure of slum clearance and community development residential projects as the final solution to Cincinnati's basin problem led to a rethinking of the issue that, as we have seen, initially suggested two new treatments: conservation and rehabilitation to prevent the spread of blight, and the possibility of rehabilitating some inner-city tracts as residential neighborhoods somehow related to the central business district. This rethinking also produced a new understanding of the city that assigned to it a new social mission, changed the relationship of the municipality to all neighborhoods, and generated additional and often incompatible treatments for troubled neighborhoods, especially Over-the-Rhine. Most important, the new understanding changed the relationship of the city government to neighborhoods because it posited for the municipality a new social mission centered on facilitating the pursuit by individuals of their self-defined cultures and life styles, a notion that suggested the utility of encouraging residents to control their neighborhoods for the purpose of designing their physical and social fabrics.

The new understanding of the city and the idea of neighborhood autonomy derived ultimately not from local circumstances but from a general revolt against the notion of the social (and biological) determination of culture. This now seemed a dangerous mode of thinking because of its association in Europe with fascism, Nazism, and communism. These ideologies differed in detail, of course, but they struck many influential Americans in the 1940s and 1950s as totalitarian social engineering movements that resembled democratic cosmopolitanism because they projected cultural blueprints of the future and preached sacrifice for the welfare of the whole as necessary for realizing them. In addition, such ideas in the context of the Cold War seemed deplorable because they might create a "soft" totalitarianism,[1] a democratic but conformist mass society incapable of appreciating, let alone achieving, cosmopolitanism or any form of cultural pluralism.

The revolt against determinism, in short, suggested the utility of exalting "the ultimate integrity of the individual" by encouraging people to define their own life styles and cultures, a culturally individualistic imperative that inaugurated an era of identity politics.[2] This kind of cultural individualism deplored conformity, took individuals rather than groups as the basic units of concern, attributed to these individuals a need for self-fulfillment through the definition of their own life styles (cultures), and suggested the appropriateness of realizing those life styles through affiliation with self-constructed groups. This apotheosis of the autonomous/liberated individual and of self-actualization through participation in self-constructed groups deflected attention from the idea of the public interest defined as the welfare of the whole, rendered suspect both "experts" and governments as potential repressors of the right of individual self-determination, and regarded intergroup conflict (in the past and present) as a normal method by which individuals might establish for themselves a satisfying way of life and spaces in which to live it.[3]

Cultural individualism also transformed the discourse about downtown.[4] The new emphasis on personal needs and their variety implied not only a tolerance for segregated neighborhoods but also a new interest in the mixing of classes, races, and/or ethnic groups. It drew a particularly sharp distinction between the city and its suburbs, characterizing suburbia as homogeneous and serene and the city as the site of heterogeneity, concentration, mixed land uses, and excitement. In this view the central business district seemed not only the chief center for entertainment and business facilities but also a logical location for chic new residential developments to help make downtown as busy by night as by day and to boost Cincinnati in its competition with its suburbs and with other cities around the country.

The new understanding of the city also cast a transforming light on slums around the central business district that made them appear worthy of conservation for a variety of residential uses, including downtown ones. Their mixed land uses seemed a convenient and delightful contrast to the homogeneity and lower density of outlying neighborhoods, while their variegated stock of old buildings on relatively inexpensive real estate looked intriguingly flexible. These characteristics opened a broad range of potential uses for and users of old neighborhoods, especially when they possessed a rich and complex past that could be interpreted to support the claims for neighborhood control by one or another group of users or potential users. That combination of characteristics fit Over-the-Rhine and made it attractive both to people who wanted to adapt it as a staging ground for mobility and to those who preferred to adapt it for a more stable population because it matched or could be made to match the self-defined needs of current residents, new residents, or some combination of both.

Above all, the new understanding of the city contended that individuals should be consulted about the design of their physical and social environments so that the look and feel of the neighborhoods matched their self-constructed life styles. This provided the basis for the adoption by city government of techniques for involving as directly as possible the residents of neighborhoods in policy making on questions affecting their neighborhood, a process interpreted by some as a formula for community control by residents, the source of a neighborhood organization revolution[5] against the decisive intrusion by outsiders, including those in city hall, in decision-making processes. This is what happened in Over-the-Rhine, and it sparked a long struggle over who should live in the neighborhood, whether and how it should be redesigned, and who should decide.

In the course of this struggle the word "slum" virtually disappeared as people began to apply the term "inner city" to the band of neighborhoods around the central business district and to assume that such places were, were becoming, or ought to become the special home of blacks who might want to live there. Those few who challenged that assumption set off a long conflict to preserve and control Over-the-Rhine, a once scorned physical environment that now seemed indispensable for the playing out of their various scenarios for its future. The conflict began as a consequence of the development of a central business district plan that called for revitalization of Over-the-Rhine and some other parts of the inner city as chic neighborhoods on the downtown fringe for middle- and upper-income persons regardless of ethnicity or race. This proposal prompted tenacious opposition from social workers, black racial separatists, urban Appalachian advocates, and white community organizers of the poor and homeless, all of whom complained that the implementation of the proposal would drive up rents and involuntarily displace low-income people.

All this took place within a political system in which all parties embraced citizen participation governing processes but that otherwise changed significantly in only one way. The Republican Party in 1957 pushed through a charter amendment that retained the non-partisan ballot but replaced proportional representation (PR) for minority political groups with an electoral system that awarded seats on council to the nine candidates with the most votes. The GOP hoped that this individualization of the representational method would kill the Charter Party, the group that engineered the adoption of PR in the 1920s. Instead, Charterites ran their own slates and, like the Democrats, invariably won a seat or two on council until 1971. That year they joined the Democratic Party in a coalition that terminated fourteen years of Republican hegemony and dominated council until 1985, when the Democrats withdrew from the alliance. All but once thereafter the Democrats won majorities on council, but they never shut out either the Republicans or the Charterites.

3
Participatory Planning and the Downtown Renaissance, 1954–1964

CINCINNATI's municipal government adopted cultural individualism as the city's new social mission while planning a neighborhood conservation program to forestall the spread of slums[1] and developing a scheme to revivify the central business district. Both of these projects involved attempts to promote neighborhood autonomy through the maximum feasible participation of citizens in making decisions about their turf. Both rested on a new view of inner-city neighborhoods as physical fabrics with social histories that might be drawn upon to create a residential ambiance desirable to people who might choose to live there in the course of defining and pursuing their cultures and life styles. And both contributed to the reidentification of Over-the-Rhine as a cityscape worth preserving and converting into a chic downtown neighborhood, the first step in a long struggle for control of the area as an autonomous entity with the right of determining for itself its identity and design.

Developing the vision of Over-the-Rhine as a chic neighborhood began with a conservation and rehabilitation project to stop the growth of the city's second African American ghetto and to prevent its deterioration into another inner-city neighborhood occupied solely by poor blacks. By the mid-1950s the displacement of black families from the

47

West End and the continued migration of blacks to the city had created a second ghetto that took shape around an old black enclave in east Walnut Hills, spread west into Avondale and Corryville, and threatened to engulf the nearby white and middle- to upper-class neighborhoods of Clifton and North Avondale. South Avondale and Corryville, moreover, contained several of the city's most valuable assets, including the University of Cincinnati, five hospitals, a large and heavily wooded park (Burnet Woods), and the Cincinnati Zoo. The combination of these factors suggested the possibility of containing the second ghetto at the borders of North Avondale and Clifton while preventing the blighting of Avondale and Corryville by developing for them a neighborhood conservation and rehabilitation program.[2]

The professional planners in city hall approached the Avondale-Corryville project by consulting both the plan of 1948 and the Housing Act of 1954. The plan of 1948 laid out rehabilitation and conservation treatments like those written into the federal urban renewal legislation of 1954 and urged the provision of "guidance" to residents within project areas so that they would participate in the implementation (not the planning) of the program.[3] According to the Housing Act of 1954, moreover, cities receiving urban renewal assistance had to demonstrate that the city would consult with other public agencies in developing urban renewal plans, and that the city had made some provision, unspecified in the act, for citizen participation in the project.[4]

Cincinnati's application for federal support of the Avondale-Corryville project went well beyond the minimum federal requirements for citizen involvement. The first section responded to federal guidelines by establishing a citywide Citizens Conservation Council to advise the city administration on all such projects, and by pledging to consult at the local level with neighborhood associations and individual property owners. The second section vowed to involve citizens not only in implementing but also in planning the projects, a commitment that exceeded both the federal requirements and the guidelines set down in the plan of 1948.[5]

Specifically, the Avondale-Corryville program called on the community relations staff of the Department of Urban Renewal to visit businesspeople, civic leaders, and residents in the target areas to stimulate interest in conservation and rehabilitation and to establish neighborhood councils and improvement associations to secure the voluntary

cooperation of property owners and renters in planning and plan implementation. The program also mandated the holding of public hearings
in the target areas where businesspeople and residents could examine
planning proposals and make suggestions for changes, both at the hearings and later in city hall before the Planning Commission. After these
negotiations the plan would be revised and a new zoning plan prepared,
and the whole would be presented once more to the Planning Commission and then to city council, which would hold public hearings and
either approve the plan or send it back to the Department of Urban Renewal for further study.[6]

City officials estimated that the use of this method in developing a
plan for Avondale and Corryville would take twelve months, but the process took four years, about the length of time it took to finish the metropolitan plans of 1925 and 1948. The delay stemmed from several factors.
The Department of Urban Renewal and the Planning Commission had
to prod residents of the neighborhoods to establish block organizations
and community councils as vehicles for their participation and to push
the University of Cincinnati and several hospitals in the area to engage
in long-range rather than piecemeal planning for the addition of new
facilities. Also, neighborhood residents objected strenuously to the initial plan drawn up by the consultant on the project and insisted on several
changes in the scheme.[7]

A key element of the completed plan was a kind of historical analysis
new to professional planners, one that abandoned the old interpretation
of metropolitan history as driven by social and economic forces that
produced a cycle of neighborhood growth, maturity, decline, and decay.
The new approach focused on neighborhoods rather than the metropolis and aimed to stimulate in residents a sense of neighborhood pride,
loyalty, and patriotism rather than metropolitan pride, loyalty, and patriotism. The dynamic factor in the new history became the struggle of
individuals in the past to make choices about their way of life and to arrange a physical and social environment suitable to that way of life, a
process that gave each neighborhood its own physical fabric and social
legacy. In this context the neighborhood's physical fabric seemed worthy of saving and its social legacy worthy of recording as inspiration
for a new cadre of residents struggling to make choices about their way
of life.

From this new understanding of neighborhood history the Avondale-Corryville plan handled the renewal area as not one but two entities requiring distinctive rehabilitation treatments. The new history of Corryville described it as a century-old residential place, one established as a suburb by people of "Germanic stock, neither wealthy nor poor," who built on small lots solid and sturdy homes that "retain much of their original charm." In the late nineteenth century, after annexation to the city of Cincinnati, Corryville prospered, maintained "its strong Germanic tradition," and persisted as "a neighborhood of craftsmen and artisans, who were frugal and painstaking in their work." When the twentieth century caught up with Corryville its residents lost a measure of control over their physical and social environment and their lives. Custom production gave way to industrialization, "the Germanic tradition faded," original settlers moved out, some newcomers converted houses to apartments, more newcomers arrived, and the area became one of "heavy turnover in rental units." Lending institutions became wary of making loans in the area, and the University of Cincinnati began its piecemeal and unpredictable expansion, making property owners reluctant to improve their buildings, "another factor in the downward trend creeping into the area."[8]

The plan's history of Avondale also documented a change in population. But it noted that Avondale developed later than Corryville and as a suburb for "very wealthy businessmen" who built big, single-family homes and mansions on large lots. By the 1920s some owners converted homes to apartments as "successive waves of migration" brought various "components of the Jewish population" into the area and as entrepreneurs built large apartments along the major arteries leading into and through Avondale. Nonetheless, "a high level of livability" persisted as owners remodeled homes and apartments for families with children, and in the 1940s Avondale was still "one of the higher rental areas in the city." Then came another shift in population and "negro families began moving in" as part of an "orderly expansion of an old negro settlement on the eastern edge of Avondale," a reflection of "the economic well-being of the negro community." By the late 1950s, said the plan, 75 percent of the dwellings in Avondale housed black families "that have moved into the area . . . by choice, not because they have no other place to go," and who "know that this is an area of above average housing" that can become for them "a good neighborhood in which to rear their families, . . . an area of which they can be proud."[9]

Yet these residents, too, said the plan, found their choice of a way of life frustrated by factors beyond their control, for decline characterized the latest stage in the history of Avondale. Old property owners, the plan reported, recognized the eagerness of additional and less prosperous blacks to move to this promising neighborhood and therefore neglected to make improvements as they waited to sell their homes. The newcomers found it difficult to meet mortgage payments, or took out land contracts, in either case meeting the payments by renting rooms or by making illegal conversions. The overcrowding that resulted was "the first step toward a slum"; the lack of maintenance was the second. The plan described these problems as "potentially serious" though not "prevalent."[10]

The new neighborhood histories provided the basis for the principal objective of the Avondale-Corryville plan, the "restoration of value to a valuable area" through the preservation of the historic characteristics that distinguished the two areas from each other and from other neighborhoods. These features included the elegant scale of development in Avondale and the more modest charm of Corryville, and the importance of the presence of the university and the hospitals to the reputation of the two neighborhoods. The plan stressed especially the history of the neighborhoods as physical and social environments, the historic role of the neighborhoods in their local communities, and the historic role of these communities in the complex of communities that made up the city. Those roles and the values attached by people to a particular neighborhood deserved preservation because they sustained civic pride and translated into the potential economic value of residential property.[11]

The Avondale-Corryville plan next laid out a program of private and public action for the various parties concerned with the future of each of the neighborhoods. Most important, it laid out a "mutual assistance program" to enlist and train citizens for participation in the formation and perpetuation of a physical and social environment compatible with their chosen identities and life styles. This program sought to eliminate top-down implementation by assuring "two-way communication" between city hall and citizens. It required the staff of the Department of Urban Renewal to offer, on a house-to-house basis, advice on building improvement contracts, assistance in securing mortgages, and suggestions for architectural design, sometimes by arranging design clinics and exhibitions. It also assigned the department the task of aiding the Avondale Community Council and the Corryville Civic Association in the organization of residents on a block-by-block basis to ensure their representation and credibility in the ongoing implementation processes. In addition, the department proposed to work with the two neighborhood organizations in the "diagnosis of individual, group, and neighborhood social problems, and [their] referral to proper public or semi-public agencies for treatment." Finally, the mutual assistance program called for the department to offer additional "informational and educational services" to "encourage and stimulate rehabilitation by citizen participation" and to ensure an adequate flow of mortgage money into the neighborhoods from lending institutions, both for remodeling and for new investment.[12]

The Avondale-Corryville urban renewal plan of 1960 marked a watershed in the treatment of Cincinnati's neighborhoods. Experts in comprehensive metropolitan planning since the 1920s had believed that socially determined cultural group pluralism drove metropolitan growth in predictable and manageable patterns of change in commercial, industrial, and residential land use districts, patterns by which old districts gave way to new ones unless regulated by such planning devices as zoning or slum clearance and redevelopment. Both the master plan of 1925 and that of 1948, moreover, defined the public interest as the welfare of the whole and emphasized the promotion of intergroup tolerance, cooperation, and metropolitan loyalty by engineering trait-sharing.

The Avondale-Corryville plan abandoned all of these principles and practices. To these planners, individuals and neighborhoods, not socially determined cultural groups and the metropolis, seemed the fundamental elements of concern, and the future of neighborhoods rested in the heads and hands of each of their institutional and human occupants, not in the patterns of metropolitan growth diagnosed and prescribed for by expert metropolitan master planners. This new view of the city and approach to city planning called for a partnership among site occupants, city hall, other governmental bodies, social agencies, lending institutions, and developers to secure the attachment of diverse individuals (human and institutional) to neighborhoods as a means of forestalling the flight to the suburbs and of assuring the viability of Cincinnati as a municipality.

The treatment of Avondale and Corryville as distinctive neighborhoods also indicated that the Planning Commission thought that Cincinnati ought to consist of a vast variety of neighborhoods to provide residents with a wide range of choices.[13] This view led the director of city planning, Herbert Stevens, to establish in 1963 a neighborhood planning service for all the city's "older close-in residential areas,"[14] including Over-the-Rhine, which he now saw as a chic residential component of the central business district slated for rehabilitation and conservation, not slum clearance and redevelopment. This switch occurred in the process of developing a comprehensive central business plan that rested on a new definition of downtown as a distinctive neighborhood encompassing the entire basin and Mt. Adams, and one that required a participatory plan to ward off a new threat, the loss of its economic and entertainment functions to the suburbs.

The Planning Commission began to build the new vision of the slums as an integral part of the central business district in 1956 in a study prepared with the assistance of an advisory committee composed of individuals with an interest in downtown real estate and other downtown businesses.[15] The study divided downtown into three parts, the "Core," the "Frame," and the "Fringe." The Fringe consisted of the central riverfront, the West End adjacent to the Frame, the land immediately east of the Frame, including Mt. Adams, and the land immediately to the north of the Frame (Over-the-Rhine).[16] This was a first step in the reconception of downtown, one that marked a new era in the treatment of downtown and the slums. Never before had the Planning Commission included within downtown such a large and diverse part of the cityscape, defined it as a discrete unit requiring its own plan, and divided it into subareas for the purpose of determining appropriate land uses for them.[17]

As the next step in the reconceptualization of the slums and downtown the planners issued a second study (also prepared with the participation of a group of advisers especially concerned with the central

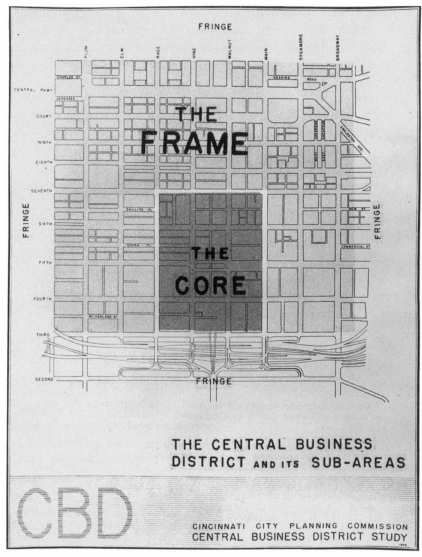

Map of the central business district (the Core) and its surrounding areas. Reprinted from City Planning Commission, *The Cincinnati Central Business District Space Use Study: A Summary,* revised June 1957.

business district) that laid out a framework for determining land uses within all three parts of the central business district.[18] This study proposed urban redevelopment (demolition and reconstruction) as an instrument for improving the Core, the traditional home for large office buildings, financial institutions, and department stores. It also contained suggestions for the Frame and Fringe satisfactory to contemporary proponents of the two-shift downtown, one as lively by night as by day.[19] The boundaries of the Frame and the Fringe encompassed both the Music Hall–Washington Park and the Taft Museum–Lytle Park neighborhoods, thereby acknowledging the importance of high-culture institutions and parks in these subareas of the central business district. The study also recommended the designation of both Lytle Park and Garfield Park as sites for residential and club as well as office development. In addition, the study proposed an exposition/convention hall on the west edge of the Frame and a cluster of new office and commercial buildings between new construction residential redevelopment projects in Kenyon Barr (west edge of downtown) and the Core.[20]

This study for the first time advocated a promiscuous mixing of land uses downtown but said little about the character of Over-the-Rhine as a Fringe residential neighborhood. Yet Over-the-Rhine received special consideration before the adoption of the central business district plan that linked it not only to neighborhood conservation but also to the use of historic preservation as a particular conservation technique. This occurred in the context of a fight over the proposed demolition of several nineteenth-century residential structures and clubs in the Taft Museum–Lytle Park neighborhood to make way for an expressway tunnel. The clubs and their residential allies protested vigorously the proposed demolitions in arguments stressing the historical significance of the buildings and contending that both the historic character of the neighborhood and its contribution to housing in the central business district should be preserved.[21]

This outburst of enthusiasm for historic preservation prompted city council to ask the Planning Commission to prepare a citywide inventory of historic sites that might require more gentle treatment in the future.[22] This document appeared in 1960 and identified just eleven historic areas in all of Cincinnati and Hamilton County, including Upper Broadway in Over-the-Rhine. But the catalogue of individual buildings and sites of historic significance in Over-the-Rhine contained twenty-two citations, more than any other neighborhood in the city. The Over-the-Rhine list, moreover, underscored the growing interest in mixed land uses, for it included Findlay Market, St. John's Roman Catholic Church, Grammer's restaurant, Wielert's beer garden, Turner Hall, Cosmopolitan Hall, Music Hall, the College of Music, the Hamilton County Memorial Building, St. John's Unitarian Church, Washington Park, Heuck's Opera House, the People's Theater, St. Mary's Roman Catholic Church, the Ohio Mechanic's Institute, and St. Paul's Roman Catholic Church.[23]

The new passion for historic preservation and the density of historic sites in Over-the-Rhine helped persuade city planners to handle the area with care as they completed the plan for the downtown renaissance. The Planning Commission and city council adopted in 1963 a new zoning code and maps that reserved space for residential housing in the Fringe, including Over-the-Rhine, and a year later city council approved a design plan for the renewal of the Core[24] that laid out a preservationist philosophy on which rested the entire scheme for downtown, including its Fringe.

From antiquity into the nineteenth century, claimed the design plan, downtowns had been extraordinarily diverse places, a characteristic that suggested three major attributes of a vital modern central business district. It should offer goods and services in such variety, quality, and quantity that no one would be "excluded from the opportunity to participate in the life of downtown." It should be accessible and compact, and should intermingle land uses to provide the "excitement" generated by the concentration of diversity. And it should be pedestrian in scale and aesthetically pleasing, not only as an attraction to Cincinnatians but also as "an intimate place for the traveler moving on foot, as in ancient days," through the heart of the city in "surroundings of special beauty."[25]

The report insisted that this historically based and sensitive approach to the downtown renaissance would serve well the key goal of the plan, the making of Cincinnati into "*the* management center of the Ohio Valley," a proposal in which the Fringe figured prominently. To achieve this goal required the capturing of corporate headquarters and high-technology industries, not only by providing tangible advantages such as superior transportation facilities, but also by fostering intangible attractions such as a two-shift central business district, a strategy requiring an "intermingling of uses including housing." For this purpose the plan stressed the importance of residential development not only in Garfield Park and Lytle Park but also in a broad band extending from Mt. Adams on the east through the Lytle Park area to proposed high-rise apartments on the central riverfront.[26] For Over-the-Rhine, the plan suggested the preservation of its mix of land uses in a program that placed "particular emphasis on conservation and rehabilitation, minimizing clearance except where required by . . . structural conditions" or by opportunities for new uses "compatible with Downtown's functions," such as a branch of a university to serve middle-class downtown workers and residents of its new "residential concentrations,"[27] including retired middle- and/or upper-class persons.

The downtown urban design plan of 1964 and its preservationist philosophy sailed through city council as a scheme drawn up without reference to its relationship to other neighborhoods and as one endorsing the most recent views of the design and function of a modern downtown. It discarded the vision of the plan of 1948 for downtown, which reserved it for business and amusements only and deplored mixed land uses there as well as elsewhere.[28] Instead, the plan of 1964 promised to create a downtown of enormous diversity, mixing historic charm with modern architecture, mass with respect for the human scale, big business with smaller entrepreneurs, money making with pleasure, recreational and cultural facilities with business enterprises, and pedestrians with vehicles. These features, combined with the commitment to the creation of new and the conservation of old residential housing in the Frame and the Fringe, underscored the commitment of the planners to a downtown that combined vitality by day with liveliness by night.

In these ways the plan of 1964 represented the final step away from the plan of 1948 and the intellectual apparatus on which rested its approach to downtown and the slums around it. Yet the urban design plan of 1964 did not raise the question of the compatibility of the predominantly poor people who occupied Over-the-Rhine with the residential functions envisioned for the two-shift central business district. And the planners had neither confronted nor even acknowledged the question of what to do if leaders of the low-income or desperately poor residents of

Over-the-Rhine rejected rehabilitation and conservation on the grounds that their supporters preferred not to move into public housing, into Corryville or Avondale, or into some other neighborhood where they might prove unwelcome to residents seeking to conserve their vision of their neighborhood as a haven for people with more affluent cultures and life styles.

4 Redefining the Problem, 1950–1966

CITY officials put off the conversion of Over-the-Rhine into a chic neighborhood in favor of starting the downtown renaissance with redevelopment projects in the central business district, a delay that permitted neighborhood activists to envision a double-barreled alternative treatment for Over-the-Rhine, designated by some as "community action." Advocates of this new approach to social work proposed the creation of new social agencies in the neighborhood and the overhaul of established ones to make them more sensitive to the way their clients defined and wanted to solve their problems. At the same time, African American neighborhood organizers in the West End persuaded city officials to include poor people in comprehensive planning processes to promote ethnic pride and coherence as a means of revitalizing particular inner-city neighborhoods and their poor residents. The first application of these ideas in the West End suggested the utility of historic preservation techniques for revitalizing neighborhoods through community action programs for the inner city. The second produced an urban redevelopment plan that linked the future of the West End with an "Appalachian" Over-the-Rhine.

The invention of community action flowed from a transformation in social theory. In the 1950s, social workers, like city planners, rejected the idea of socially determined cultural groups that had dominated their past practices[1] in favor of the idea that individuals should define their own cultures and life styles, a notion that proposed a new respect for the choices of clients about how and where to live. This idea also suggested that a slum need not be an environment that entrapped and demoralized its inhabitants, but could be a place that could serve either as a staging ground for mobility or as a residential location chosen by people because it fit their self-defined needs, including cheap housing, social welfare and recreational services, and appropriate jobs. Indeed, this conceptualization of the possibilities of human choice implied that slums, previously regarded as the inevitable result of community reorganization in the metropolis, could be eliminated.[2]

This approach to social work in the inner city came to Over-the-Rhine in 1959 when the Community Health and Welfare Council, the administrative arm of the Community Chest, undertook an assessment of the impact of urban renewal and expressway programs on the delivery of recreational services to individuals in the basin. In this study the social workers, like contemporaneous city planners, abandoned their old idea of the basin as a separate entity and redefined the area as a series of distinct neighborhoods with different needs. The problem now was not what to do about the basin, but how to develop programs to meet the self-identified[3] needs of the residents of distinctive neighborhoods within it.

While figuring this out the social workers prepared a report on the use of leisure time by basin residents that defined a new role for community centers. Such facilities, the report stated, should function not only as providers of recreational and other social services but also as critical links between residents and city agencies engaged in developing plans for neighborhood revitalization and stabilization. The report also suggested the creation of a citywide agency to coordinate the process of working with people at the neighborhood level and described its chief function as developing "a pool of . . . leadership skilled in group social work and community organization" for the purpose of helping residents define the kind of neighborhood they wanted.[4]

But in which neighborhoods should this work start? To answer the question the Community Health and Welfare Council constructed in 1962 what it called a "Problem Index," a table that ranked Over-the-Rhine third highest among all thirty-three neighborhoods in the city on the basis of its poverty, criminal, and infant mortality statistics.[5] The Council described Over-the-Rhine as "one of the highest delinquency and crime areas of the city" and also indicated that it lacked community centers and organizers to help residents play a vital role in planning for the rehabilitation of themselves and their neighborhoods.[6]

Two years before the passage of the federal Economic Opportunity Act, then, Cincinnati's social work administrators had established the principles of community organizing for neighborhood autonomy as the linchpin of their social welfare programs and had identified Over-the-Rhine as one of the city's neediest neighborhoods, one of several pockets of poverty. Not surprisingly, such an identification attracted community organizers to Over-the-Rhine, particularly those who saw it as a neighborhood chosen as a place to live by a large number of migrant southern mountaineers who seemed somehow different from other poor people. In their thinking about Appalachians in Over-the-Rhine as a peculiar people, social workers rejected the conventional explanation of the relationship of migrant groups to American society and constructed a new definition of ethnicity.

Between 1915 and 1950 students of the problem of diversity in American culture defined ethnicity as a socially determined group identification based on place of origin.[7] In the 1950s, however, leading participants in the revolt against determinism began to label culture as an identification defined and freely chosen by autonomous individuals. A classic form of the argument appeared in Oscar Handlin's *The Uprooted* (1952), which examined immigration and its consequences for migrants. The decision to migrate, Handlin suggested, itself signified a self-conscious choice to break with old ways, and the process of moving disrupted the peasant society of face-to-face relationships embodied in church, village, and family and left traditional institutions, ideas, and behavior in disarray. As migrants settled in the United States, according to Handlin, they decided to reorganize themselves into groups according to their national origins, to establish voluntary associations, and to cluster together in inner-city neighborhoods.[8] None of these associations or neighborhoods lasted long, however, because the fluidity of American society offered choices to immigrants through which they continually reconstituted their identities and institutions in new forms as they learned to negotiate their way in American society. Through this process of immigration, Handlin wrote, particular migrants learned "what it was to be an individual, a man apart from place or station," and in the process they came to know "what was essential in the situation of Americans."[9]

Handlin's designation of self-definition as the critical ingredient of ethnic identity played a role both in the more general revolt against social determinism and in that aspect of it that took shape in the 1940s and 1950s as Cincinnatians discovered mountain people in their midst and defined them as social problems. This began as early as 1941, when a report from the Public Library of Cincinnati and Hamilton County suggested that the migration of southern whites into some of Cincinnati's neighborhoods had resulted in decreased use of library services in those neighborhoods and in excessive book loss. Alarmed by the Detroit race riot of 1943, moreover, the Community Chest's Division of Negro Welfare investigated intergroup relations in the Queen City and suggested that whites from the "hill sections of Kentucky [and] Tennessee" brought with them "southern racial prejudices" that contributed to racial tensions in Cincinnati. In 1944 six pastors from the West End issued a joint statement calling on parishioners to practice a "Christ-like neighborliness toward both . . . mountaineer and Negro neighbors," a statement that also defined Appalachians as outsiders whose behavior and attitudes might create serious social problems.[10]

During the next several years, the Appalachian migration to Cincinnati and concern over the presence of mountaineers in the city intensified, prompting social workers, clergy, teachers, and other public officials to hold in 1954 a conference to consider how to work effectively with them. In the opening address, sociologist Roscoe Giffin of Berea College in Kentucky described Cincinnati's mountaineers as temporary victims of an archaic culture who would eventually become successful city dwellers.[11] This point of view rested on an understanding of the migration from the mountains as simply a domestic variant of the Handlinesque process that had brought millions of European immigrants to America's cities as part of their self-conscious rejection of traditional peasant culture and their movement to urban modernity.[12]

Giffin, like Handlin, argued that mountain migrants brought with them some customs and habits that would slow but not obstruct their progress toward becoming independent and choice-making urbanites with a knack for forging their own identities and life styles. He contended, for example, that mountain living had isolated mountaineers from modern economic and social developments. Whereas modern Americans relied on the school system to transmit "important knowledge and behavior patterns," he said, mountain people carried a tradition that "considers a little 'readin' and writin'' the goal of formal education." In addition, Giffin claimed that mountaineers reacted with indifference or suspicion to modern medical practices and eschewed thriftiness and financial planning. Giffin also described mountaineers as "familist" or kin-centered, implying that they lacked the drive and the means to create institutional networks for the purpose of urban survival. And Giffin stressed their religious fundamentalism, a trait, he argued, that encouraged the acceptance of poverty as "evidence of virtue and assurance of eternal salvation," discounted the importance of achievement in the present, and discouraged initiatives for overcoming poverty, ignorance, or disease.[13]

Yet Giffin remained optimistic. Citing Handlin, he argued that the decision of modern mountaineers to leave an agricultural and rurally based society augured well for their future adoption of urban ways.[14] The local press echoed this view, suggesting that family disruption, sporadic school attendance, excessive credit buying, and violence resembled and ran no deeper than the problems of any migrant group. The implication was that mountaineers, like Cincinnati's Germans before them, would eventually devise an appropriately urban life style, with or without an ethnic component.[15]

Giffin's address to the 1954 workshop, along with a summary of the proceedings, appeared in pamphlet form and circulated among social workers, clergy, city planners, and other public officials, who by the early 1960s advocated the adoption of policies that would help mountaineers make the expected transition from peasant migrant to modern American urban dweller by empowering them to define their own life styles. Giffin, for example, advised social workers to "implant the motivations and behavior which go with formal education, dependable work habits, maintenance and improvement of housing conditions, more realistic use of cash income, and sharing in community responsibilities which accompany urban living."[16] Others added that enlightened social workers—

understanding the culture of mountain folk and avoiding judgmental-
ism—would secure their cooperation in broadening their scope of life-
style choices.[17]

The belief that the transition from peasant migrant to urban citizen
would ultimately occur among Cincinnati's mountaineers comforted social theorists. But the recognition that some Appalachians faced difficulties in adjusting resulted in efforts during the late 1950s and early 1960s
in Over-the-Rhine to ease their transition to urban living.[18] In 1957, for
example, the Appalachian Fund, a local philanthropic organization,
hired a social worker to serve as a "curbside counselor" to Appalachians
in Over-the-Rhine, an arrangement institutionalized in 1962 at Emmanuel Community Center on Race Street.[19] In addition, the Mayor's
Friendly Relations Committee established in 1963 the Council on Appalachian Migration, a group of social workers and volunteers who sought
to educate Cincinnatians about newcomers from the mountains by distributing educational materials, organizing a speakers bureau, and participating in radio and television interviews.[20]

The Roman Catholic Church joined this effort to help migrants adjust by reversing its policy, adopted in the 1940s, of gradually abandon-
ing Over-the-Rhine and instead began to expand its presence as the
provider of yet another life-style choice. In 1962, for example, the arch-
bishop designated St. Mary's parish, an immigrant church established
in the 1840s in the heart of Over-the-Rhine, as a special place where
newcomers, including Germans, Hungarians, and Cubans, could hear
masses offered in their native tongues. Two years later students from
Mount St. Mary's seminary started Catholic community organizing activities in Over-the-Rhine by opening a social and recreation center for
Appalachian children and adults called the Main Street Bible Center.
The seminarians soon engaged an Appalachian social worker, Ernie Mynatt, to supervise a block-by-block home visitation team that asked mountain migrants about their problems and helped them find assistance in
mitigating them. The staff members also organized a summer camp for
Appalachians and worked with migrant juvenile offenders in a rehabilitation program.[21]

At this juncture developments in the West End turned up an ally for
the Appalachian advocates in their efforts to serve Over-the-Rhine's mi-

grant population. African American community organizers during the 1960s worked out a technique to help the poor by bolstering ethnic pride on the basis of racial residential segregation, and they indicated their willingness to assist the Appalachian advocates next door in implementing an ethnic program for their constituents. As William Mallory, president of the West End Community Council, put it in September 1966, his group would join forces with the Over-the-Rhine Community Council because "the real problems of the poor," such as substandard housing and "economic exploitation . . . by store operators, finance companies, and landords[,] . . . transcend racial consideration."[22]

The West Enders' ethnic technique for helping the poor consisted of the use of a historic black neighborhood as a center around which to build ethnic pride and as a special place of residence for people who had moved out, involuntarily or otherwise, as well as those who remained on the site. The development of this technique began inauspiciously in January 1964 with a routine review by the Planning Commission of a proposed sale of city property for the construction of a gasoline service station in the West End just as a few blocks from Over-the-Rhine. After hearing the objections of Maurice McCrackin, the minister of the West Cincinnati-St. Barnabas Church, the Commission tabled the matter and directed its staff to reconsider the sale and study the possibility of rezoning the area.[23]

The staff response to this directive extended the scope of the discussion significantly by raising historic preservation as a potential tool in neighborhood revitalization. The report cited several assets of the neighborhood, including schools, churches, and a burgeoning network of community organizations under the auspices of the West End Community Council. And it rated a two-block stretch of Dayton Street between Linn Street and Freeman Avenue as the neighborhood's "most outstanding physical asset" because it contained some forty mid-nineteenth-century three-story structures, including stone-front townhouses with iron fences that once housed the families of Cincinnati's millionaire meat-packers and beer brewers.[24]

The staff asserted that these assets could be preserved and strengthened and the neighborhood revitalized as a residential area if the city dropped its emphasis on industrial redevelopment in the area. The new approach would require a moratorium on slum clearance and the application of conservation and rehabilitation techniques, including the adoption of a "realistic" zoning program to acknowledge existing industrial uses while designating the bulk of the area for residential uses. In addition, the staff thought that efforts to limit traffic and to concentrate such municipal services as rodent control, trash collection, and street sweeping would stimulate private investment in the area. Private improvements in the future could be accelerated by investing public funds in spot clearance and in an advisory service for landlords and developers similar to the one devised for the Avondale-Corryville urban renewal program.[25]

This report offered a new lease on life for the Dayton-Findlay neighborhood and gave both neighborhood residents and outsiders a chance to enter the debate about neighborhood revitalization. The outsiders consisted of historic preservationists, who now pressed hard for assistance from city council in preserving Dayton Street from the wrecker's ball. Representatives of the predominantly black neighborhood expressed distrust for the preservationists, but city council nonetheless requested the Planning Commission to prepare a report on maintaining Dayton Street as a historical and architectural asset under provisions of the city's historic preservation enabling legislation,[26] which included measures for the designation of protected areas and established an Architectural Board of Review to administer design regulations established by separate legislation for each protected area.[27]

The Dayton Street protection area study followed the new tendency to see the basin as a composite of distinctive neighborhoods. Like the Avondale and Corryville plans in the late 1950s, this study sought to establish the neighborhood's character by presenting a brief "historic background" that linked Dayton Street with the "grand era of the late nineteenth century," a period in which pork-packing and brewing magnates constituted the business elite of the Queen City.[28] On that basis the report proposed the adoption of a protection area ordinance for Dayton Street, a step taken by the Planning Commission after it amended the law to increase the membership of the Architectural Board from six to seven persons. The amendment had been requested by the Dayton Street Community Club so that a representative of a particular protected area

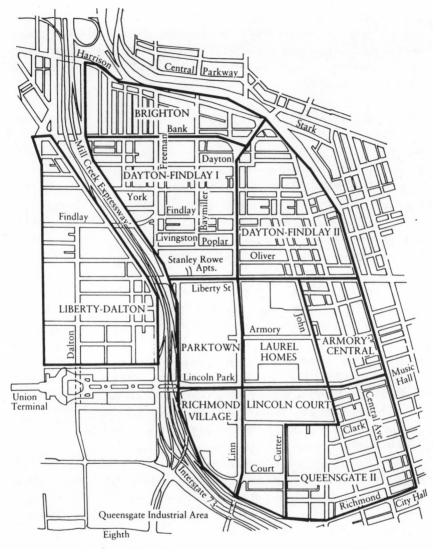

West End neighborhoods, 1975. Reprinted, with permission of the publisher, from John Emmeus Davis, *Contested Ground: Collective Action and the Urban Neighborhood* (Ithaca: Cornell University Press, 1991).

could vote on matters pertaining to that area. The Dayton Street ordinance also sought to take into account the status of the Dayton-Findlay area as a poverty neighborhood by permitting "normal" maintenance if the property owner could not within one year secure financial assistance to carry out more expensive alterations recommended by the Architectural Board.[29]

The new approach to Dayton Street saved one chunk of African American turf in the West End. The next step in the process launched the drive to include Dayton Street in a larger revitalized black neighborhood that could serve as a center around which to build ethnic consciousness and pride. The effort began when West End community organizers expressed fears that the city might construct in the Dayton Street neighborhood additional off-street parking for Crosley Field,[30] then the home of the Cincinnati Reds professional baseball team. As part of the protest the community organizers established another neighborhood association, the Queensgate Community Club, in a section of the West End south of Dayton Street. This organizing campaign gathered momentum and attracted attention outside the neighborhood in 1966 when the city applied to the federal government for a survey and planning grant for an urban renewal project to assist in the construction of a new baseball stadium just outside of the territory represented by the Queensgate Community Club. The West End Community Council vigorously opposed the idea, and to placate the group the city manager appointed a broad-based West End Task Force to survey conditions in the West End and to prepare a plan for a residential urban renewal project in the area.[31]

West End residents and their advocates dominated the Task Force,[32] which began its work by rejecting the stadium idea and insisting on the writing of a comprehensive plan for the Queensgate II area, a 117-acre tract that bordered Over-the-Rhine on its northeastern side and the central business district to the south of Over-the-Rhine. To handle the planning process, the city government used federal funds to hire as a consultant the University of Cincinnati, which established a team of social scientists and planners to submit alternatives to the West End Task Force. The Task Force then molded the suggestions into one scheme for submission to the Planning Commission and city council.

Although contentious, the process yielded a policy plan adopted by city council in September 1970. The plan asserted that the West End and Queensgate II had been since the late nineteenth century a "lively" African American ghetto, the home of people with a variety of occupational, religious, class, and institutional affiliations and therefore well equipped to make their own life-style choices, including either the pursuit of socioeconomic and geographic mobility or the forging of ties in the ghetto. That same analysis contended that slum clearance and public housing in the 1930s and 1940s and expressway construction and urban renewal in the 1950s and 1960s had displaced many blacks and their institutions, reduced cultural, economic, social, and educational opportunities in Queensgate II, and cut the area off from the larger neighborhood and converted it into an isolated enclave of poor individuals who lacked the opportunity but still possessed the will to choose what they might become.[33]

To remedy this situation, the Queensgate II plan called for the razing of Queensgate II and the development of 2,000 low- to moderate- and medium-income housing units for 6,000 people, with the first choice of dwellings to be reserved for current and former residents of the area.[34] The plan also featured a town center next to Over-the-Rhine containing housing, shops, businesses, social service agencies, a plaza, commercial recreation facilities, restaurants, and an African American and possibly an Appalachian cultural center; a parking garage for 5,000 vehicles next to the town center; a pedestrian bridge running from the town center across Central Parkway into Music Hall; an expanded gymnasium and athletic field at Taft High School; a baseball diamond; new industry north of the neighborhood to provide employment for residents of Queensgate II and the rest of the West End; partially subsidized housing in Garfield Park; and a plaza directly east of the city hall building for civic events and festivities.

As some of these features of the Queensgate II plan suggest, it aimed not merely to create an ethnic enclave as a source of ethnic identity and strength but also to link Queensgate II and its residents more effectively to the rest of the West End, to Over-the-Rhine, to the central business district, and to the metropolitan area. The town center was expected to attract and serve people from all over the metropolitan area who might want to browse through its ethnic businesses and shops and the African American and Appalachian heritage centers. Other facilities aimed at the same goal. The pedestrian bridge, for example, was seen as a way of stimulating a two-way flow of people between the town center and Music Hall, Washington Park, and the rest of the Over-the-Rhine neighborhood.[35]

The mayor and both metropolitan daily newspapers applauded the Queensgate II plan, and for a time it seemed that it might become reality.[36] The federal Department of Housing and Urban Development (HUD) had reserved funds for its implementation, and the city's Department of Urban Renewal in August 1970 drafted implementation proposals indicating the level of city expenditures and the phasing in of federal support through HUD's Neighborhood Development Program. The plan was never wholly implemented, however, largely because the Nixon administration substantially reduced its financial commitments to such projects and adopted a racially desegregationist residential policy for the dispersal of low-income housing.[37]

Nonetheless, black community organizers had demonstrated a technique for fighting poverty by building ethnic pride through a program to reestablish and gild a once lively ghetto as the keystone of a larger ethnic separatist movement, a remarkable achievement for a previously powerless enclave of poor people. Some West End black activists attributed their influence to their discovery that influential whites feared confrontational blacks and could be intimidated by aggressive tactics.[38] But blacks also monopolized the West End turf, ran the only community organization in Queensgate II, and possessed allies in the Dayton-Findlay neighborhood, in other black neighborhoods outside the West End, and among sympathetic whites. They also could draw on a long history of black urban experience in Cincinnati, a history that stretched back into the early nineteenth century and that stressed and dramatized not only the persistence of blacks' oppression but also their endurance and their success in building a lively early-twentieth-century ghetto. That same history produced black heroes to be used as role models and a stock of "sacred" ethnic places for inspiration. Indeed, the history portrayed the inner-city ghetto as the historic source of black ethnic strength and coherence.[39] It also suggested that blacks were by historic right the inheritors of a piece of the latter-twentieth-century inner city, which could be seen as a strategic location deserving revitalization because it bordered the central business district, still regarded as the heart of the metropolitan area by the white "power structure."

Finally, events in the West End during the mid- and late 1960s suggested a distinctive and critical role for community councils as the defenders of the general welfare of the territory over which they claimed jurisdiction. During the period of the development of the Queensgate II plan, the West End Community Council identified and defined problems in the West End and assigned priorities for their resolution, in this case placing the redevelopment of Queensgate II at the top of the community's agenda. Thus the Council ordained and supported the activities of various groups, organized and otherwise, within the West End, successfully managing the tendency toward neighborhood parochialism.

By the late 1960s, then, a definition of Over-the-Rhine as a neighborhood inhabited by Appalachian migrants had taken hold and West End activists had pointed the Appalachian advocates to ethnic pride as a way to combat poverty. Indeed, some Over-the-Rhine activists had already taken steps to establish the area as an enclave for Appalachians only. It remained to be seen whether they could match their black counterparts in organizational skill and ideological finesse as they strove to prevent Over-the-Rhine from becoming either a chic downtown neighborhood or another part of the city's growing black ghetto.

5 Collapse of the Appalachian Option, 1964–1974

PROSPECTS of Over-the-Rhine becoming an Appalachian ethnic enclave brightened in the late 1960s because of a surge of interest by a variety of outside parties. The passage of the federal Equal Opportunity Act in 1964 inaugurated a "war on poverty" in Cincinnati that prompted city officials to look favorably on proposals to do something about the inner-city poor, including those in Over-the-Rhine. It also gave Appalachian advocates a chance to conduct studies and develop programs to convince the city government that Over-the-Rhine should be officially designated as Appalachian turf, both to fight poverty and to promote an urban Appalachian identity among all classes of Appalachians, first in the metropolitan area and then nationally. This ambitious campaign failed in part because of competition from anti-poverty warriors who put class above ethnic consciousness, but more importantly because the Appalachianists, unlike African American community organizers in the West End, could not devise a compelling case for their cause.

The war on poverty in Over-the-Rhine focused initially on alleviating conditions without reference to ethnic issues. One emphasis fell on programs to offset the shortage of decent low-income dwelling units and especially to secure better accommodations for blacks who could not find or afford housing elsewhere. The first of these consisted of a concentrated building code enforcement program that sent inspectors into 8,000 of the 8,800 dwelling units in the area, brought 4,200 units up to code, and yielded the demolition of 1,000 others. In addition, the city participated after 1968 in a crash federal program (Operation Rehabilitation) that provided subsidies and technical assistance for the renovation by 1972 of 2,216 units in Over-the-Rhine for low-income tenants.[1] And city council sought to reduce the cost of providing "standard" housing in Over-the-Rhine[2] by creating an "experimental overlay" zoning district in a small part of the neighborhood and by waiving building code regulations in the zone to reduce the cost of renovating residential units.[3]

The war on poverty also provided the impetus for the creation of several private, class-oriented community action organizations in Over-the-Rhine that sought to help the poor in other ways. The first of these, the Uptown Basin Council, appeared in 1965 and aimed both to help poor people and to rehabilitate the neighborhood by lobbying for better health care and improved recreational facilities, establishing a blood bank, and assisting individual residents in obtaining social services from both public and private agencies.[4] The Council also sponsored an interdenominational, interracial program that brought college students from five states into the neighborhood during the summer of 1966 to learn firsthand about the plight of inner-city residents and to help clean up and organize the neighborhood.[5]

A second community action program in Over-the-Rhine appeared in the fall of 1966. Like the Uptown Basin Council, it avoided an ethnic commitment and regarded the neighborhood as an enclave for the poor, both black and white. In this case a group of local organizers, residents, and social workers devised an agency called HUB (representing the spokes of a wheel reaching out from the axle into the neighborhood) to coordinate the work of various agencies in the area and to expedite the delivery of services. The Community Action Commission (CAC), the war on poverty's administrative agency, soon took HUB under its wing and assigned special services funds to provide it with community organizing as well as social services foundations.[6]

The special services project gave the Appalachian advocates their first official recognition by including two of them among the individuals who designed the program.[7] This group then established an ongoing advisory committee composed of representatives from every community council, block club, and service agency in HUB's target area (which included the adjacent neighborhood of Mount Auburn).[8] On their advice HUB hired Over-the-Rhine residents to canvass the neighborhood for clients, assess their needs, guide them through the network of available social service and community organizing agencies, and organize them into block clubs and tenant councils.[9]

These HUB activities built the morale of Over-the-Rhine's poverty warriors, including its Appalachian advocates, who expected to receive an even larger role when they learned about the inclusion of Over-the-Rhine in Cincinnati's application for a grant under the provisions of the federal Model Cities Act of 1966, which offered federal funds to cities interested in devising innovative ways to eliminate poverty. The act especially encouraged city governments to coordinate and concentrate in one area a broad range of federally subsidized social welfare, educational, job training, and community organizing and development programs.[10] These guidelines made it possible for cities to use ethnic consciousness and pride programs in treating inner-city neighborhoods. Cincinnati's application, however, approached the inner-city issue in terms of class by pointing to the familiar problem of suburban flight by the city's white middle class and the domination of the inner city by underprivileged and unemployed people who lacked the power to control their future. These developments, said the application, undermined the city's revenue base and burdened it with additional expenses to take care of the inner-city poor. They also explained why the city government had changed its mission from defining and meeting the needs of residents engaging people, including the poor, in processes to define their own and their neighborhoods' problems and to propose and implement solutions to them.[11]

The application contained a lengthy catalog of potential programs for this purpose but emphasized especially a participatory inner-city planning effort that would involve Over-the-Rhine for the first time in comprehensive neighborhood planning. Over-the-Rhine seemed a good target for this treatment, argued the application, because it had once been the home of "good, solid German middle-class residents" but now ranked as "the 'cheaped out' section of the city." Crime, delinquency, and "skid row type" alcoholics dominated the area, which also contained more "pre-delinquent" and battered children than any neighborhood in the city. In addition, said the application, "'hidden' oldsters" huddled in single rooms, ill, undernourished, preyed on for their social security checks, and unknown to social and health service agencies.[12]

The description of Over-the-Rhine included rhetoric that pointed to Appalachians as a special people with problems peculiar to them. It described the area as the city's premier "port of entry" for migrating Appalachian whites who now lived in a "closed" society with different customs, values, and habits than city-born and -bred people. Many refused to seek social and geographic mobility, large numbers of parents failed to participate in school affairs, and "Southern migrant mothers" balked at bringing their children to early childhood education programs. In addition, according to the application, Appalachian young adults seemed virulently racist, hanging out in the streets and mixing it up with blacks so often that the police worried about a race riot erupting from one of the frequent brawls.[13]

Yet the application's discussions of planning for who might live in a revitalized Over-the-Rhine contained no reference to an Appalachian ethnic component. The section on housing, for example, proposed the mixing of land uses, races, socioeconomic groups, and types and forms of housing through both redevelopment and rehabilitation programs, including historic preservation projects, especially in the Music Hall and Washington Park area. Another section argued for the establishment of an even broader range of services for the unemployed on the grounds that Over-the-Rhine would remain for a long time a poverty neighborhood. Still another part of the application suggested that residents themselves should decide what kind of people should live in the area.[14]

The absence in the Model Cities application of the legitimacy of Appalachian-ness as an anti-poverty tool discouraged Cincinnati's urban Appalachian advocates. But the reference to neighborhood autonomy gave them hope because community control became the keystone of Cincinnati's inner-city planning program under Model Cities auspices. The urban Appalachian advocates as a consequence launched a drive to secure official sanction for their effort to turn Over-the-Rhine into an Appalachian enclave. This campaign drew on methods that had proved so successful in gaining for militant blacks the attention and deference of both local and federal authorities. The strategy included a statement that Appalachians, like African Americans, comprised a distinct category of oppressed people who nonetheless possessed the capacity to become autonomous with a self-defined way of life and the will and ability to define and solve their own problems.

The urban Appalachian campaign attracted considerable local attention and support for several reasons. In the first place, Cincinnati's population contained a large number of second-, third-, and fourth-generation Appalachians scattered in neighborhoods throughout the metropolitan area. Second, the current migration seemed likely to persist.[15] Third, the contemporaneous rediscovery of Appalachia itself as a region set apart by its desperate poverty helped to revive nationally a dormant interest in Appalachian-ness[16] that reinforced the notion of migrant Appalachians in inner cities as a peculiar people. Indeed, these factors led one confident and assertive urban Appalachian activist to boast that the establishment of Over-the-Rhine as an urban Appalachian center would represent the first step in the ultimate recognition of Appalachian migrants as the legitimate inheritors of Cincinnati's inner city generally.[17]

In this optimistic context Cincinnati's Appalachian advocates built their case for the necessity and feasibility of developing an urban Appalachian identity and the appropriateness of anchoring it in Over-the-Rhine. They pointed particularly to the apparent inertness among Appalachians in Over-the-Rhine—not only their poverty, poor health, and low levels of attendance and achievement in the city's schools, but also their disinterest in the social and civic activism and ethnic self-consciousness that seemed so characteristic of inner-city blacks.[18] But the urban Appalachian advocates depicted the migrants as malleable, for contemporary social theory held that the decision to migrate itself, whether by Appalachians or blacks, represented a self-conscious first step toward the abandonment of old ways and a sign that mountaineers possessed the capacity to define and solve their own problems, including that of establishing a satisfying identity leading to satisfactory behavior in an urban context.

In this perspective, the problem of inertia seemed responsive to a properly framed stimulus, a situation that suggested to the Appalachianists the utility of reminding migrants of aspects of their mountain culture that might bolster their pride in themselves as a distinct people.

In this way the urban Appalachian advocates hoped both to catch the attention of migrants and to create a foundation for the development of an urban discipline, the will and ability to acquire education and jobs, build families, and become social and civic activists as part of the process of defining their own life styles. The Appalachian advocates hoped to demonstrate that both migrants and suburban Appalachians could retain a sense, but not necessarily the substance, of their Appalachian-ness, and that they could together exercise that sense in Over-the-Rhine by studying and celebrating Appalachian history, listening to mountain music, and practicing or purchasing the products of mountain arts and crafts.

Michael Maloney, a community organizer who had grown up in eastern Kentucky, took the lead during the early 1970s in selling the urban Appalachian idea. Maloney had trained as a Catholic seminarian, volunteered in the Main Street Bible Center in Over-the-Rhine, and cut his teeth as a community organizer with HUB. Now he began to build the institutional infrastructure for the urban Appalachian movement by starting an organization called United Appalachia Cincinnati to promote ethnic solidarity among all classes of urban Appalachians, outer city as well as inner city. The organization's bylaws made this explicit by committing its members to the promotion of "the self-awareness and self-activity of the Appalachian people in Cincinnati, to encourage our urban institutions to respond to the needs and interests of Appalachians, and to show the community at large the power and beauty of our culture."[19]

Maloney and his recruits also decided to push their cause by making Over-the-Rhine the anchor of urban Appalachian-ness, for which purpose they started a variety of additional organizations, some of them housed in the neighborhood and all of them active there. One of these, the Appalachian Identity Center, concerned itself principally with the problems of young Appalachians and aimed to empower them to live freely as urban individuals. Activists at the Identity Center thought that excessive high school dropout rates, high levels of unemployment and juvenile delinquency, and turf wars between blacks and Appalachian young people signaled a crisis stemming from the alienation of Appalachian youngsters from both urban society and their own roots. As a consequence the Identity Center took the form of a drop-in facility with cultural identity programs to lure young Appalachians off the streets so they could "be affirmed in their own identity, then moved toward meaningful contact with blacks, and with institutions in the city."[20]

While starting the Identity Center, leaders of United Appalachia Cincinnati also pulled together a coalition for the purpose of creating an agency to conduct research on the Cincinnati Appalachian community and to advocate its interests to the public. This group persuaded the Cincinnati Human Relations Commission (CHRC) to set up a meeting of the mayor, members of the Cincinnati Board of Education, and representatives of the Model Cities program, the Junior League, the Catholic Human Relations Commission, and the various Appalachian organizations to explore the proposal. The groups balked at the idea of creating an independent operation, but did agree to establish within the CHRC an Appalachian Committee to study inner-city Appalachians and to devise solutions to their problems, particularly the prevalence of negative stereotypes about the characteristics and behavior of Appalachians generally and inner-city Appalachian residents in particular.[21]

Some members of the Junior League wanted to do more. They decided to take the lead in educating migrants and other Cincinnatians about the positive aspects of Appalachian culture and to launch the campaign from Over-the-Rhine. League members first organized an Appalachian festival, a presentation of mountain culture through the display of handicrafts in Music Hall,[22] then established the Appalachian Community Development Association to "provide a variety of mechanisms through which the broad-based goals of social, cultural and economic development can be achieved." Association members decided to concentrate particularly on "the improvement of the migrant's self-image," first by assisting in the planning of another festival in Over-the-Rhine and then by taking over full responsibility for the event and making it a yearly affair.[23]

To supplement this annual promotion of urban Appalachian-ness in Over-the-Rhine the CHRC's Appalachian Committee established an Appalachian studies program in a "Heritage Room" in temporary quarters at Washington Park Elementary School. Staffed first by a student intern from the urban affairs division of the College of Community Services at the University of Cincinnati, the program involved parents, community organizers, and school personnel in the presentation of workshops on quilting, mining, whittling, agriculture, and music. By the end of the first year children and volunteers had organized a small library of books and slides and produced an exhibit of Appalachian culture artifacts.[24]

These small successes encouraged the Appalachian studies proponents to search for and secure a permanent home for the Heritage Room, from which they launched an extraordinary effort to get around the problem of the rising proportion of African Americans in the Over-the-Rhine population. They did this by defining blacks from Appalachia as Appalachian rather than African American and by launching a racially integrated program to validate that contention. Activities at the new site included not only cultural studies but also courses on community organization and general education, public forums on social and civic issues, and efforts to involve parents and students in addressing such problems as drug use, truancy, and dropping out of school. In addition, the staff provided legal assistance for tenants in their conflicts with landlords and aided residents in satisfying their social service needs.

These varied programs earned the lavish praise of the Heritage Room organizers. The institution, they claimed, demonstrated that blacks and whites could be brought together around the idea of urban Appalachian identity, an accomplishment of which they seemed most proud. But they stressed, too, that the Heritage Room experience validated the idea of linking community organizing to ethnic pride campaigns and that even the most desperately poor people could be reached by and would respond to the right combination of cultural, educational, and social service activities.[25]

Building on these successes the Appalachian advocates established in 1974 an independent research and public relations agency in Over-the-Rhine. Called the Urban Appalachian Council (UAC), it devoted its research, advocacy, and cultural affirmation activities to developing a distinctive ethnic identity that would persuade other urban institutions to deliver culturally specific services to Appalachians. The UAC particularly stressed the ineffectiveness of traditional casework methods in dealing with urban Appalachians, insisted that social workers should understand and empathize with Appalachian culture, and prepared a working paper on social welfare practice (written by Maloney) that described urban Appalachians as ineffectual in "collective action, personalistic when others want functional relationships, [and] traditionalistic and fundamentalistic in an age of pragmatism and relativism."[26]

The process of creating organizations and programs around the idea of urban Appalachian-ness culminated with a systematic attempt to understand the origins and persistence of poverty among inner-city Appalachians and to spread the information to a broad audience. In January 1974, Maloney, working then as a research specialist for the Cincinnati Human Relations Commission, published *The Social Areas of Cincinnati,* a "scientific" mapping of the quality of life in all the city's neighborhoods as the first step toward the development of a comprehensive plan for the provision of appropriate social services for each neighborhood. Maloney argued that the municipal government should develop such a plan, and he proposed "a Human Services Information system" to provide "mechanisms to determine need, to monitor programs, and to measure both efficiency and effectiveness."[27] As a basis for this, he attempted to determine patterns in the distribution of twenty variables—including race, poverty, housing, employment, education, and ethnicity—that defined both the quality of life in the neighborhoods and the special characteristics, including ethnic ones, of each neighborhood.

Maloney used this system to divide the city's forty-four neighborhoods into four quartiles and listed Over-the-Rhine among the thirteen most dependent on social welfare services. He also noted the interest of the Cincinnati Human Relations Commission in ensuring the distribution of services to "all elements of the population," a premise from which he argued that Appalachians should be recognized as a distinct ethnic group and that the problems of poor Appalachians ought to rank with poverty and racism as top priorities for Cincinnati's social welfare agencies. He suggested, moreover, that this would be a long-term task because poor Appalachians constituted a majority of the population not only in Over-the-Rhine but also in five other neighborhoods well removed from it.[28]

By 1974, then, activists had built a variety of institutions to organize and represent urban Appalachians and had promoted the idea of urban Appalachians as a distinct and persisting ethnic group in the metropolitan area. They had mobilized white community organizers and activists who could no longer participate in the "black power" phase of the civil rights movement of the late 1960s and recruited others who legitimated the idea of urban Appalachians among a broad range of Cincinnatians.[29] In their patronage of the Appalachian festival and support for the growing interest in bluegrass music, particularly at a nightclub called Aunt Maudie's Kitchen in Over-the-Rhine, these Cincinnatians indicated their appreciation of Appalachian culture and became willing consumers of Appalachian music and handicrafts and supporters of special programs to make Over-the-Rhine the center of urban Appalachian cultural life.[30]

Nonetheless, the prospects for making Over-the-Rhine the "mother neighborhood for the Appalachian community,"[31] as Maloney put it, dimmed in the mid-1970s, due in large part to the continued increase in the number of blacks and a decrease in the number of Appalachians in the neighborhood. One Appalachian activist attributed this setback to Operation Rehabilitation, the housing renovation program funded by HUD beginning in the late 1960s. Landlords in this program, he claimed, preferred black tenants to white Appalachians, a situation aggravated by federal housing officials who refused to track down former white occupants as their rehabilitated apartments reopened. Maloney, too, held landlords responsible for the black insurgency, but he also indicted city government, which, he asserted, consciously or not pursued policies that displaced white Appalachians from Over-the-Rhine.[32]

That may have been the case, but clearly the city government in 1974 neither acknowledged nor accepted the idea of making Over-the-Rhine the mother neighborhood for Cincinnati's Appalachians, a failure on the part of Maloney and his allies that may be best understood when compared to the position of blacks. Appalachian activists, like their black counterparts, lobbied city officials and organized demonstrations at city hall, but they could not assume that the white power structure feared Appalachians and could be intimidated by aggressive public confrontations. Moreover, Appalachian activists could not, like blacks, draw on a long history of experience in Cincinnati that stretched back into the early nineteenth century and that stressed not only their oppression but also their endurance in building a lively early-twentieth-century ghetto. Thus the Appalachian claim as the rightful inheritor of the late-twentieth-century inner city, or at least a part of it, did not carry the same authority as similar claims advanced by blacks. And the existence of several small and scattered Appalachian enclaves gave them no concentrated political base, a problem exacerbated by the rising proportion of blacks in Over-the-Rhine.[33]

In this perspective, then, the drive to make Over-the-Rhine the city's Appalachian mother neighborhood faced long odds. And the prospects looked even grimmer in 1974 when city council adopted a housing policy based on the welfare of the whole city that intended to eliminate homogeneous neighborhoods defined in either class or ethnic terms. That policy stemmed from a complaint in 1971 by the Avondale Neighborhood Association that the location of forty-eight public housing units in North Avondale would contribute to racial segregation by bringing more blacks into the racially integrated neighborhood and would also bring even more children into the neighborhood's already crowded schools.[34] City council responded by proposing the establishment of a "comprehensive strategy for the development of housing resources for all groups, and household sizes" but expressed particular concern for the problem of low- and moderate-income housing. To work out the details of the strategy the city manager appointed a large and broadly based Working Review Committee on Housing and hired Anthony Downs, a Chicagoan and a nationally prominent consultant on urban problems, to work with it.[35]

As the Committee on Housing took up its assignment, the Nixon administration decided to encourage racial residential integration and the scattering of low-income residents by mandating the dispersal of federally subsidized low- and moderate-income housing. In this context Downs and the Committee on Housing decided to develop ways of achieving a balance of racial and income groups in all neighborhoods of the city, including inner-city ones, with a plan that mandated both displacement of some poor white and black people from their neighborhoods and the racial and class integration of prosperous white neighborhoods in the outer city.

Downs's program consisted of three parts. The first included a moratorium on the creation of subsidized units in the inner city, incentives to encourage low- and moderate-income residents to move out of inner-city neighborhoods, and a program of demolition and construction to attract middle- and upper-income residents into the inner city. The second part included other proposals to make inner-city neighborhoods attractive to middle- and upper-income residents who now feared to live there, proposals that precluded the creation of "predominantly black new housing projects in or near the downtown area" while supporting the creation of predominantly white but integrated housing. The third part of the strategy called for the administration of welfare programs to prevent large numbers or high percentages of welfare families with children from concentrating on any one block or in any one school.[36]

City council responded to these propositions warily. It adopted a resolution encouraging but not mandating the development of balance in neighborhood housing, "including efforts to attract middle and upper income households into central core areas," but without passing legislation of any sort for the implementation of the policy in the city as a whole or in any of its neighborhoods. The compromise brought the city in line with the federal government's dispersal policy but created a dilemma. The resolution not only favored balance for the welfare of the whole city but also restated city council's commitment to dealing with neighborhoods through processes of maximum feasible participation for their residents,[37] processes likely to yield neighborhood programs and plans antithetical to the idea of achieving balance. And in 1974 the Model Cities program in Over-the-Rhine stood just one year short of producing a comprehensive maximum feasible participation plan for the future of the neighborhood, a plan that sought to place control of Over-the-Rhine securely in the hands of its poor and increasingly black population.

6 Empowering the Poor, 1971–1975

A S Appalachianists made their bid for control of Over-the-Rhine a contest developed among other parties over the wisdom of using historic conservation as a way to revitalize the neighborhood by bringing in more affluent residents. This conflict took shape when the city's Department of Urban Development (DUD) decided to revive and implement the idea of making Over-the-Rhine a chic downtown neighborhood, as described in the central business district plan of 1964. This proposal, of course, met stiff resistance from community organizers who advocated the right of the poor to live wherever they pleased and who adamantly objected to any Over-the-Rhine revitalization scheme that might raise rents and thereby involuntarily displace poor people. One of these advocates, moreover, held a critical position in two Over-the-Rhine planning processes, and in both he sought to postpone consideration of the development of Over-the-Rhine as a chic neighborhood until after its poor residents had been sufficiently empowered to control their own destinies and the fate of the neighborhood.

DUD, like the downtown plan of 1964, took the central business district Core as its top priority, but late in the decade it began to move into the Fringe in connection with a federally funded Pilot Cities program for the creation of a comprehensive social and employment services building in Over-the-Rhine.[1] It linked that project to the rehabilitation of the nearby Findlay Market edifice and the writing of an urban design plan to turn the surrounding blocks into a racially and socioeconomically integrated residential sub-neighborhood of Over-the-Rhine. DUD saw this not only as the first step toward making Over-the-Rhine into a chic neighborhood but also as a vehicle for establishing a model planning process for the whole of Over-the-Rhine. Consequently it set up a board of managers for the project composed of resident and business representatives from all over the district. This board then selected a planning consultant from Indianapolis (Woolen Evans Associates), which retained as its Cincinnati partner in the project Harris Forusz, a professor in the city planning program at the University of Cincinnati, and assigned him the prime responsibility for compiling the urban design plan.[2]

Forusz brought with him a passionate commitment to cultural individualism for poor people. He spent ten months engaging the residents and businesspeople of Over-the-Rhine in the preparation of a sixty-three-page urban design plan that laid out general proposals for the whole area, with special reference to a Findlay Market target area. Here the plan called for the creation of a playground and the construction of new housing north of the Findlay Market building, the construction of a new boys club building west of the market, and the installation of a parking lot south of the market. The urban design plan also proposed the use of historic preservation techniques in the rehabilitation of the Findlay Market building and in the development of both new and rehabilitated housing around and in the immediate vicinity of the market and the Pilot Center building.[3]

Forusz did not see historic conservation as leading necessarily to an influx of prosperous people. He acknowledged the diversification of the neighborhood's population as desirable from the perspective of city government but advised putting it off until it was established as a goal by the residents themselves. And he contended that this could not happen until after the residents had lived for several years in a neighborhood redesigned specifically for the purpose of empowering them, and only then if they possessed access to a suitable citizens participation governmental apparatus.[4]

Forusz, in short, wanted residents of the Findlay Market area and

Findlay Market, 1996. Photograph by Jon C. Hughes, © 1997.

Over-the-Rhine to control not only the implementation of the Findlay Market town center scheme but also any future planning and plan implementation in Over-the-Rhine. For this purpose he advocated a change in the administrative structure of the Model Cities program that in 1971 relieved DUD of responsibility for Over-the-Rhine. In the new arrangement the director of the Model Cities program reviewed all plans and development proposals for Over-the-Rhine and its parts before approving them for consideration by the Planning Commission, the last stop before their referral to city council. Forusz criticized this process because he thought that the director's review authority should have been placed in an Over-the-Rhine task force representing virtually all parties and groups interested in the process, including especially residents from the neighborhood, and chaired by a neutral party (neither a municipal official nor an Over-the-Rhine representative) with a reputation for successfully mediating disputes and working out compromises among conflicting parties.[5]

Forusz wanted to go much further in guaranteeing citizen control over future planning processes and development proposals for the Findlay Market area. He thought the most serious problem with citizen participation in poor neighborhoods was that residents and businesspeople left decision making and lobbying to professional community organizers who reinforced the powerlessness of the poor by denying them practice in defining and solving social and civic problems, skills critical to the successful exercise of cultural individualism. Forusz therefore wanted to develop indigenous leadership, but saw this as an especially difficult proposition in Over-the-Rhine, which struck him as merely "an artificial area on the map" made up of "heterogeneous envelopes" of atomized individuals,[6] not as a single area occupied by people who shared a bond such as a common racial or ethnic identity around which to build a sense of community solidarity and a participatory spirit.

Forusz therefore embellished the Findlay Market urban design plan with additional proposals to attack the problem of heterogeneity and powerlessness—not by homogenizing the population along racial or ethnic lines, however, but by inculcating neighborhood civic pride, solidarity, and activism. He placed at the heart of this scheme the establishment in the target area of a town center anchored by the improved Findlay Market and the new Pilot Center building across the street, each of which he saw as contributing to both neighborhood and citizen revitalization. Forusz argued, for example, that the rehabilitation of Findlay Market would not only stimulate investment in related commercial facilities but also promote confidence among residents in the future of the neighborhood and in their ability to shape that future. Similarly, he contended that the Pilot Center would assemble in one place a multitude of social services that would attract and intermingle diverse people from the various "envelopes" and provide them with resources useful to impoverished civic activists. And he proposed new and rehabilitated housing and recreation facilities around the town center to promote neighborliness and a strong sense of local pride and vitality.[7]

Forusz topped off his town center conception by proposing the establishment within it of an information agency. Forusz contended that Over-the-Rhine residents stood helpless in part because they lacked knowledge for making informed judgments on issues confronting the community and the political savvy to influence the resolution of those issues. An information agency could meet those needs in a variety of ways, Forusz said. It could disseminate information about events, issues, and meetings of common concern to Over-the-Rhine residents. It would retain a receptionist to advise individuals on questions related to welfare rights, civil rights, tenant rights, job opportunities, educational and training programs, rodent control, loans and grants, and health care. It would assist block clubs and development corporations by supplying information about incorporation procedures, about how to petition local government agencies, and about how to secure federal funds for housing, recreation, and education programs. And it would keep a registry of experts in various fields willing to counsel groups in Over-the-Rhine.[8]

Yet even the most ably designed and staffed town center seemed insufficient to Forusz for the daunting task of building a sense of solidarity and power among the neighborhood's poor, powerless, and diverse residents. That would require in addition the creation of civic and social service sub-centers in sub-neighborhoods throughout Over-the-Rhine. Forusz conceived of this network as "perhaps the strongest stimulus to citizen participation" because each component would be "clearly recognizable as community turf around which community organization can grow." Each would be a meeting place for block clubs and a headquarters for citizen action groups attacking specific problems. Each would be highly visible and project an image of a neighborhood concerned about its self-improvement. And each would provide a forum for the discussion of neighborhood affairs and the formulation of criticism and advice for the Pilot Center staff, the Over-the-Rhine Community Council, the Over-the-Rhine task force, the Model Cities administration, and city, state, and federal government agencies.[9]

Forusz in this plan gave DUD officials much more than they requested, and they responded by implementing its Findlay Market and Pilot Center aspects while ignoring the rest, including the recommendation to postpone historic conservation and the addition of prosperous residents until after the poor had been empowered by their experience of living in a neighborhood designed to inspire and teach civic activism. Instead, DUD hired John C. Garner, Jr., executive director of the Miami Purchase Association, Cincinnati's major historic preservation advocacy organization, to write development guidelines and design regulations for a historic district around the Findlay Market. Garner's plan placed top priority on historic preservation as a means of shoring up property values and luring visitors to the area, rather than Forusz's preference for empowering the poor before deciding the issue of who else should live in the neighborhood.[10]

But Garner's plan implicitly addressed the question of a desirable social composition for Over-the-Rhine. Like the writers of the Avondale-Corryville conservation plan, Garner embellished his with a culturally individualistic social history that stressed processes by which individuals in the past made choices about their life styles. In Garner's hands this interpretation depicted Over-the-Rhine not only as a historic staging ground for socioeconomic and geographic mobility but also as a place in which some members of each ethnic group accumulated. As a consequence the neighborhood's population "even today reflects its ethnic development by the Germans, southern Appalachian and Black groups still living there."[11]

Garner's plan, then, suggested that prosperous and poor people had in the past, and therefore could in the future, live together comfortably in Over-the-Rhine's old physical fabric, some of them occupying it for decades because that suited their life-style choices and others using it as a first step up the ladder of mobility because that suited *their* life style choices. But neither Garner's history nor his historic preservation renewal plan raised the issue of the involuntary displacement of the poor as the result of efforts to improve the area and to add prosperous people to its population mix. This, however, was precisely the possibility that most concerned the parties who put together Cincinnati's Model Cities program. Indeed, the city manager had approved in 1971 a Model Cities first-year action plan that reserved Over-the-Rhine for impoverished individuals and, like Forusz's Findlay Market plan, sought to improve citizen participation. As the Model Cities document put it, the poor should "become instruments in the solution of problems and share responsibility for the renewal of the community" through a "people-directed process" based on the "people's perceptions of their own needs."[12]

The Model Cities program particularly wanted to engage Over-the-Rhine residents in defining their own needs and solving their own problems by securing their participation in a task force charged with the preparation of a comprehensive plan for the area. Such a plan, said the program, should treat the root causes of the difficulties of the neighbor-hood and its residents, namely racism, "exclusion," lack of access to re-sources, and an "inadequate" and unhealthy environment. To help assure that outcome, the Model Cities program said the Cincinnati Plan-ning Commission should provide planning services but hire an outside professional to conduct the citizen participation planning process.[13]

Not surprisingly, the Planning Commission chose Harris Forusz, a planner with impeccable citizen participation credentials and the one most knowledgeable about Over-the-Rhine, to oversee the development of the Model Cities comprehensive plan for the neighborhood. Forusz regarded himself as the employee of the people of Over-the-Rhine and involved himself in a variety of tasks on their behalf, including commu-nity organizing.[14] In 1971 and 1972 he helped organize the Over-the-Rhine Planning Task Force, which he then served as secretary. He also established other vehicles for citizen participation, including block clubs, sub-neighborhood associations, and a recreation committee for the en-tire area, all of which he helped keep going as he consulted with them on the problems and prospects of their areas of concern and the Over-the-Rhine district generally.

Forusz finally completed in 1975 a comprehensive plan for the entire area that, like his Findlay Market plan, established what he called a "pro-cess" rather than a blueprint. He laid this out in a 350-page document consisting of detailed and complicated proposals designed to create a physical, social, and civic environment that would assist the residents in becoming more effective and independent citizens. In addition, he pro-posed a planning and development review mechanism to give a strong voice in deciding which proposals should be adopted and when and how they would be implemented.[15] And as in the Findlay Market plan, he left the issue of who should live in the area as the last item for resolution, after the residents had secured control of themselves and the neighborhood.

As if responding to Garner's historic preservation plan, Forusz also prepared a history of Over-the-Rhine that reinforced his plan's position on the neighborhood's population composition. Forusz, like Garner, stressed the importance of immigration/migration and ethnicity in un-derstanding the history of Over-the-Rhine. And like Garner, Forusz posited the choice of life styles by individuals as the dynamic factor in that history. But Forusz's account described a pattern of ethnic group succession, rather than ethnic group accumulation. As a result, it left Germans out of the neighborhood's recent past and suggested that its future belonged either to blacks or Appalachians, or both.[16]

The plan itself prescribed neither a black nor an Appalachian future but instead proposed ethnically neutral programs to build neighborhood civic pride, loyalty, and activism, after the accomplishment of which residents would decide both the ethnic question and the issue of whether to admit more affluent persons as residents and participants in the continuing discourse about the neighborhood's future. Indeed, the Forusz plan contained an astonishing range of housing, human services, educational, and economic development proposals to provide residents with a maximum degree of control over their destinies and that of their neighborhood. For example, he advocated the creation of twenty-three sub-neighborhoods (he now called them "environmental areas"), each differentiated by types of people, zoning, topography, visual form and character, physical facilities, land uses, and myriad other factors. He proposed to focus each on a small town center comprising a complex of commercial and human services and community organizing agencies located at "nodes" where pedestrian and vehicular traffic met. Through these small town centers, Forusz contended, the routine of daily sub-neighborhood life would bring people together and create skilled citizens freed of their dependence on professional community organizers.[17]

The plan anticipated that this liberating process would take about fifteen years, after which Over-the-Rhine's future, including the question of opening the area to prosperous people, would rest safely in the hands of its poor residents. In the interim, however, the residents would require assistance in fulfilling their responsibility for monitoring the implementation of the plan. This would not be easy, Forusz warned, because most residents had little time to look beyond the daily burden of finding food, shelter, medical attention, and other basic necessities. They might rally to fight an issue obviously important for their survival, but it would be difficult to persuade them to participate in the tedious and never-ending neighborhood development process without "the help of professional organizers." This, said the plan, both justified the provision of staff support for block clubs and sub-area councils and accounted in part for the environmental areas scheme, which gave each sub-area a "mini-plan" and resources with which to work for its implementation.[18]

Forusz by this time had also developed proposals to improve the city's citizen participation procedures, which he characterized as racist, paternalist, and ineffective in sustaining neighborhood representation throughout lengthy planning and plan implementation efforts. He thought, for example, that citizen representatives, like city officials, should be paid for attending meetings. In addition, the plan advocated the creation of a direct link between citizens and government agencies by bringing their representatives together on a permanent rather than the ad hoc Planning Task Force formed in 1971–72. It also recommended the use of the Over-the-Rhine Community Council as the reviewer of policies proposed by sub-neighborhoods and other citizens' groups for consideration by the permanent Planning Task Force.[19]

Forusz's attack on city government complained especially about the "insidious" procedure by which city council referred neighborhood grievances to bureaucrats who returned their advice directly to council. This procedure resulted, he charged either in "no-change" or the adoption by council of the bureaucracy's recommendations, a process that removed citizens from participation in discussions after the grievances left the neighborhood. Forusz proposed to correct this deficiency by urging city council to appoint an impartial citizens mediation commission to hear all neighborhood proposals to city government and to let it, rather than the city's bureaucracy, make the final recommendation to council. Under this arrangement a grievance would pass from the community council to city council, which would review and refer the problem to the bureaucracy and the mediation commission for their review. The commission would then consult with all groups concerned with the problem and make a recommendation to council for action, after which council would make a ruling and direct the bureaucracy and the Community Council to cooperate in implementing it.[20]

The next part of the section on citizen participation moved to the problem of educating residents on issues concerning the improvement of community services and plan implementation. The plan suggested that information centers in each of the community sub-centers should disseminate bibliographies and written analyses of the problem at hand.

The plan also proposed the formation of community radio and television stations and community newspapers, and the use of a few tall buildings and several ground-level locations as electronic bulletin boards on which information such as dates and locations of meetings could be projected. The last item on the list suggested the use of a portable projector to cast on the sides of buildings images powerful enough to be seen even at night under "the most brilliant street lighting," a service, the plan said, that could be used at different locations at different times.[21]

The plan then offered advice to professional planners on how to get all parties concerned to recognize both the particular character of each community and the fact that certain principles applied to all of them. Suggestions included learning the cultural norms of each group in the neighborhood before doing anything; identifying the agendas, including hidden ones, of all groups; suggesting alternative physical layouts that responded to the community's specific sociodemographic character; and developing an aversion to the "appalling redundancy" in the physical environment that flowed from the conventional planning practice of fitting populations into "an environment prefabricated on the power structure's perception for the reality."[22]

Forusz presented this plan as a compendium of steps necessary for the revitalization of an inner-city neighborhood and its residents.[23] It sought to combine new development with rehabilitation and design control for the creation of a poor neighborhood that resembled in some respects nineteenth-century city life, a city of unsorted land uses, a city with a lively street life that mixed vehicles with pedestrian activities, a city of buildings that contained both apartments and small business enterprises. While preserving the neighborhood's physical character and ambiance, the plan sought to update, modernize, sanitize, and beautify it, to make it clean, green, uncluttered, rich in open space, safe, and aesthetically stimulating.

Through its social welfare, educational, and citizen participation provisions, moreover, the plan sought to give each of the residential subcommunities a maximum degree of control over its own destiny. These provisions, if fulfilled, would have established a modern version of the fabled nineteenth-century urban political machine, which not only provided jobs and social welfare but also gave citizens access to the elected officials and bureaucrats who made decisions affecting their lives. This new machine, however, would not have a boss, for its constituency would be composed of autonomous individuals who through citizen participation would provide the personnel for staffing the community and neighborhood organizations that dealt with elected officials and bureaucrats (although the plan did not say so, this scheme implied that political parties possessed no legitimate roles in the coming order of things).

Viewed in this perspective Forusz's plan hewed to the parameters of the post-1950 discourse about treating old inner-city neighborhoods. It attributed to Over-the-Rhine a distinctive past and drew on it as a resource for shaping its future. It also focused on who would occupy the neighborhood in the future and on ways of deciding that issue as democratically as possible. And the plan contended that cultural individualism could be delivered to inner-city poor areas only by a policy that improved the quality of life and empowered poor people, who once empowered might or might not decide to bring more prosperous persons into their neighborhood.

The plan's commitment to empowering the poor matched the prime objective of Cincinnati's Model Cities program. Nonetheless, Forusz's handiwork received short shrift from the no-nonsense Model Cities director, Hubert Guest, an African American with a bachelor's degree in architecture from the University of Kansas and a master's degree in community planning from the University of Cincinnati. While finishing his master's, Guest had lived in the West End, where he met and worked with the black community organizers who put together the West End Task Force and produced the Queensgate II plan for racial separatism. Guest himself also participated in the Queensgate II project as the Planning Commission's liaison with the citizen participants, with whom he spent long evenings as a translator of technical terminology and planner's jargon.[24]

From these West End experiences Guest had developed a taste for working with well-organized and forcefully led communities capable of putting together in a relatively brief time short planning documents for small chunks of large neighborhoods. Forusz's plan fell far short of this ideal, and Guest tried to condense it into a shorter and less complicated form before sending it to the Planning Commission. That proved impossible without violating its integrity, however, and Guest finally dismissed the plan as so difficult to understand and so expensive to carry out that it stood no chance of clearing the Planning Commission, let alone city council. Forusz in self-defense conceded that it might cost $3 billion to implement the scheme in its entirety but emphasized that it should be applied piecemeal. Guest, however, wanted not only a less costly but also a clearer plan that sifted, sorted, and prioritized for the Planning Commission and city council the vast number of development proposals in the massive document, not one that merely laid out a host of alternatives for consideration by representatives of twenty-three sub-areas, the Over-the-Rhine Community Council, and the Planning Task Force before they reached city hall.[25]

7
Integration through Historic Preservation, 1972–1980

THE failure of the Model Cities experiment to produce an acceptable plan for Over-the-Rhine coincided with the arrival in the neighborhood of a new cadre of community organizers, most of them highly religious former members of the middle class who deeply distrusted government and drew support from Protestant and Catholic churches inside and outside of Over-the-Rhine. They also knew and took advice from Harris Forusz, but unlike him they did not seek to empower Over-the-Rhine residents so that they could define and pursue their own life styles. Instead, the new community organizers pushed the idea of cultural individualism to its extreme by contending that the residents had already been empowered and made their choice. On these grounds the new community organizers fought any proposal to racially or socioeconomically integrate, gentrify, or otherwise "improve" the physical design of the neighborhood or the culture of its residents, including not only its poor and predominantly African American inhabitants but also its growing population of homeless people, including especially its alcoholics.

These views created trouble, for the arrival of the new community organizers coincided with an attempt by the city government to make Over-the-Rhine a chic neighborhood with a racially and socioeconomically mixed population. This conformed, of course, with city council's resolution of 1974 in favor of balance in all of Cincinnati's neighborhoods. But city officials reluctantly pushed the idea in Over-the-Rhine in response to heavy pressure from the Miami Purchase Association (MPA), the city's major historic preservation advocacy organization, and several other civic organizations for the designation of many parts of the city, including some inner-city locales such as Over-the-Rhine, as historic conservation zoning districts.

Some of the impetus for this conservationist pressure came from the U.S. Historic Preservation Act of 1966, which had helped shift the focus in historic preservation from authentic restoration and national patriotism to the "adaptive reuse" of rehabilitated old buildings and neighborhoods and the stimulation of local and neighborhood patriotism.[1] As the act put it, historic preservationists wanted to make the commonplace physical legacy of the past "a living part of our community life and development in order to give a sense of orientation to the American people."[2] The act also strengthened the hand of the MPA and other preservationists in additional ways. It provided federal funds for the establishment of state historic preservation offices to conduct surveys of historic resources and to inflate the volume and accelerate the rate of processing nominations to the National Register of Historic Places. And while the act did not prohibit the demolition of historic resources, it sought to deter their rash destruction in projects involving federal funds by instituting a review process to assess the impact of such projects on potential or designated historic resources and to seek ways of mitigating any adverse impact, not merely demolition, on such resources.[3]

The movement of Cincinnati historic preservationists toward Over-the-Rhine may be traced to December 1964, when the Planning Commission defined open spaces and hillsides, including those on the northern boundary of Over-the-Rhine, as resources for preservation and enhancement because of their aesthetic and psychological value, a definition qualifying them as subject to zoning for the health, safety, and welfare of residents. The next year the Park Board and the Planning Commission set down a schedule by which the Park Board would purchase hillside and hilltop land for use as parks, a scheme that sparked an increased interest among private developers of such land. That in turn intensified efforts to control private hillside developments, including the design of such developments. City council responded to this pressure in 1972 by appointing a Citizens Task Force on Environmental Quality to make recommendations to protect the right of every citizen to "clean air, pure water, the scenic, natural and aesthetic qualities of his environment, and freedom from excessive noise."[4]

In the meantime the Planning Commission took on a related but somewhat narrower project, the preparation of an overlay zoning ordinance to control the design of hillside developments, neighborhood business districts, areas of high public investment, and historic areas. Between 1970 and 1973 the Commission drew up several drafts of ordinances, including one for historic conservation and one for environmental quality zones covering hillsides, high public investment areas, and neighborhood business districts for which city council had adopted an urban design plan. The Citizens Task Force on Environmental Quality endorsed such a dual approach in its report of 1973, but spent the next three years wrangling with opponents of environmental quality zones instead of working out the language for new historic preservation legislation.[5]

By 1973, however, the MPA and several civic organizations in favor of historic preservation had grown dissatisfied with the historic area protection ordinance of 1964 because it provided no way to cover individual buildings. The concern climaxed in 1972 and 1973 after the Southern Railway announced its intention to demolish the concourse at the rear of the forty-year-old Union Terminal rail passenger station, which, like the front part of the building, contained enormous mosaic tile murals. City council responded in two ways to the public furor over this matter. It negotiated an agreement with the Southern Railway to remove the murals before demolishing the concourse and then adopted an ordinance to protect from demolition or inappropriate alteration three kinds of properties: buildings significant in the history of the city's neighborhoods, the city itself, the state of Ohio, and/or the United States; properties of notable architectural character or of special character because of some other feature, such as landscaping; and properties noteworthy because of public investment for the improvement of their quality or value.[6]

This, of course, did not satisfy the MPA and other advocates of historic conservation zoning districts, whose continued pressure on the Citizens Task Force on Environmental Quality finally paid off. The Task Force's report, released just after the passage of the listed properties ordinance, supported the idea of environmental quality overlay zoning districts and also proposed the consolidation of the city's protected areas ordinance, the listed properties ordinance, and the proposed historic preservation zoning overlay district ordinance into a new and comprehensive historic landmarks ordinance modeled on the New York City landmarks legislation.[7]

Director of city planning Herbert Stevens responded unenthusiastically to the Task Force's call to overhaul the city's historic preservation legislation. He argued that any action on historic preservation zoning should await the passage of environmental quality zoning district legislation, which might or might not provide for historic conservation zoning. He also contended that the area and listed property ordinances seemed to be functioning satisfactorily.[8]

Stevens did not oppose all design control innovations, however, for he took this occasion to push for the adoption of Interim Development Control (IDC) district zoning, which became law in December 1974. This kind of zoning regulated demolition and development in IDC districts for periods of three months (extendable) while the Planning Commission and city council considered zoning changes affecting the districts. The enabling legislation authorized the Planning Commission to approve only work in IDC districts deemed consistent with proposed amendments to the zoning code and with the prevailing land use, building, and structure patterns in the surrounding neighborhood and community, with the planning policies of the neighborhood, city, metropolitan area, region, or state, and with "sound" planning principles, including physical, social, and economic considerations.[9]

The IDC device gave the Planning Commission a chance to become a major player in the fight to control Over-the-Rhine's future in connection with the Findlay Market/Pilot Center project.[10] As part of that project the director of the Department of Urban Development tried to persuade Stevens to designate the Findlay Market area as a historic district under the city's protected areas ordinance and to nominate the area for a place on the National Register to qualify it for federal subsidies for historic preservation projects. Stevens refused both requests. He claimed that the plans for the project inadequately described the historic characteristics of the area and contended that the Dayton Street protection area stood first in line for National Register designation.[11]

Nonetheless, Stevens and the Planning Commission stood ready to protect the Findlay Market area through the IDC device because of the anticipated passage of an environmental quality enabling ordinance, the consideration of which made it possible to set up temporary IDC districts to protect potential environmental quality districts. The Planning Commission approved the creation of such an IDC district for Findlay Market in December 1974, instructed the staff to secure the support of community organizations in the area, and held a public hearing on the proposed IDC in March 1975. No one at the hearing opposed the IDC, and several participants, including representatives of the Findlay Market Association and the Over-the-Rhine Planning Task Force, spoke in favor of the proposed IDC regulations,[12] which cleared the Planning Commission and city council without opposition.[13]

At this point, however, the environmental and historic preservation district issue in Over-the-Rhine became more controversial because the focus shifted from Findlay Market to the Music Hall–Washington Park area. This shift occurred in the context of the rush by big cities in the 1970s to create mixed-use performing arts centers. To compete in these "amenities" sweepstakes, the Music Hall Association, which managed Cincinnati's hundred-year-old Music Hall for the city government, decided to undertake an expensive refurbishment of the three buildings making up the facility. To raise money for the project and to protect and enhance the prestige of Music Hall, the Association in short order entered it on the National Register, secured its designation as a listed property under the city's listed property ordinance, and in 1975 got it designated as a National Historic Landmark under the National Historic Landmark Act of 1935.[14]

The drive to secure historic status for Music Hall represented merely one event in a general upsurge of nominations to the National Register, including many buildings in Over-the-Rhine. This created confusion and consternation in city hall, where the issue became not pro- or anti-preservation but why so much of it.[15] To answer that question the Planning Commission contracted with the MPA for a new and "professional survey and ranking" of Cincinnati's historic resources. The MPA saw this as a golden opportunity to identify and document the thousands of buildings it regarded as eligible for the National Register, but the Planning Commission saw it as a first step toward stemming the proliferation of nominations. The next step would be finding some way to secure an agreement between MPA and the city on which historic sites, buildings, and areas should be nominated to the National Register, which might be considered for local designation under the city's protected area legislation, and which might be left unconsidered and unprotected.[16]

Well before the completion of the survey, the Department of Urban Development (DUD) started work on a historic preservationist urban design plan for the revitalization of the Washington Park area of Over-the-Rhine as part of its downtown development activities. In the early 1970s DUD conferred with representatives from Over-the-Rhine and with their approval prepared a proposal for a new construction residential development in Garfield Park, which sat four blocks south of Central Parkway, as a complement to a future residential development around Washington Park.[17] The urban design plan for Washington Park (1977) called not only for the refurbishment of the park but also for historically compatible new residential construction on vacant lots and the renovation of old residential buildings to create a neighborhood with a historic ambiance.[18]

The Washington Park plan failed to specify the income and racial composition of the population that it proposed to accommodate, but several people assumed that implementation of the plan might lead to a mixed-income neighborhood and eventually to higher rents that would displace poor persons. Indeed, the announcement of the Washington Park plan provided the occasion for the first public outcry against displacement from rehabilitation in Over-the-Rhine since the Model Cities planning effort. This time it came from Jack Towe, the holder of a Harvard law degree (but not a practicing lawyer), a white resident of Over-the-Rhine, and one of the new activists on its Community Council. He referred to inner-city neighborhood rehabilitation as "gentrification," by which he meant "rich people moving poor people out" and inflicting on them as a result "psychological, social, and economic stress and family strains." He also called gentrification a major problem in Mt. Adams, Mt.

Auburn, Over-the-Rhine, and the West End, all neighborhoods on the edge of downtown, and quoted approvingly Carl Westmoreland, a young and dynamic black Mt. Auburn community organizer, who contended that neighborhood residents must "own the dirt" or be moved out by owners seeking higher profits.[19]

These outbursts ended for a time the serious consideration of the Washington Park revitalization plan but did not slow the MPA's drive to put on the National Register many Over-the-Rhine buildings, including several in the Washington Park area. By the end of 1977 these included not only Music Hall but also the Apostolic Bethlehem Temple Church (formerly known as St. John's German Evangelical and Reform Church). In 1978 the Ohio Valley Chapter of the Victorian Society in America added another, the Hamilton County Memorial Building, constructed in 1908 just south of Music Hall to commemorate soldiers, sailors, marines, and pioneers.[20]

Stevens opposed none of these nominations publicly, but their announcement led him to take the second step in his effort to regulate the nomination of buildings to the National Register. For this purpose he proposed a preservation planning program in which he hoped all parties with an interest in historic preservation would participate and ultimately agree on three things: a list of "excellent" buildings and districts that the city would take the initiative in preserving, a list of marginal buildings and districts that would be considered for preservation on a case-by-case basis by all parties concerned, and a list of buildings and districts that might qualify for the National Register but that would not be nominated by anyone except the owners of the buildings.[21]

Stevens could not be sure of the outcome of such a participatory planning process. But he pressed on nonetheless and persuaded both the MPA and the Planning Commission, which contained a few preservationist members, to go along. He included the idea in his request for federal Community Development Block Grant money for 1978[22] and worked hard to keep the proposed preservation planning project alive. In February 1978, for example, he presented to the Planning Commission a report on the U.S. Reform Tax Act of 1976, which provided tax reduction incentives for the rehabilitation of National Register properties for commercial uses, including residential ones. This law, explained Stevens, comprised "a serious threat to the local government's ability to control and direct the redevelopment of its own communities," for it applied not only to listed properties but also to historic resources eligible for but not yet nominated to the National Register.[23]

At this point Stevens received critical assistance in his effort to develop a comprehensive historic preservation plan from Fred Mitchell, an ardent preservationist who believed the city's Department of Economic Development (formerly Urban Development) had not complied adequately with the impact review procedures of the Historic Preservation Act of 1966. Mitchell checked city hall for documentation of such procedures, found none, and informed the federal Department of Housing and Urban Development (HUD). HUD officials then told city manager William V. Donaldson that the failure to comply could lead to a cutoff of urban renewal and Community Development Block Grant funds, and that the responsibility for compliance rested with the city government.[24]

Donaldson responded to this news by backing Stevens's efforts to secure city government control over historic preservation. Stevens then took to the Planning Commission the recently completed MPA survey of historic resources, which he had hoped to use as the basis for developing the comprehensive historic preservation plan.[25] But the staff report on the inventory noted with dismay that its ranking system classified as "significant" 1,000 properties and 209 districts, including all of Over-the-Rhine (the city's inventory of 1960 identified as significant just 350 sites and nine districts). Stevens found the list appallingly long and persuaded the Planning Commission to accept the inventory merely as a "resource document."[26]

Stevens next gave the Planning Commission a memo from Donaldson that endorsed the idea of developing a preservation plan to establish a priority system to create a "reasonable and manageable list of buildings and districts we want to protect." Stevens and his staff then drew up a preservation planning program to work out compromises between the city government, which wanted to restrict preservation to the protection of a few architectural or historical gems, and preservation advocates, who wanted protection for anything that met National Register criteria for significance. The proposal sought to bridge the gap by creating an Urban Conservation Task Force made up of representatives of city council, the Planning Commission, the city's manager's office, the Department of Economic Development, the Department of Buildings and Inspections, the Division of Community Assistance, the Environmental Advisory Council, the MPA, the local chapter of the American Institute of Architects, the Greater Cincinnati Chamber of Commerce, real estate developers, and other persons with expertise related to the issue.[27]

City council endorsed this strategy in August 1978, but it took two years for the Urban Conservation Task Force to complete its work, largely because it used the occasion to work out the details of new historic preservation legislation and to draft ordinances embodying those details. During this time new actors intensified the preservationist pressure on both the Music Hall–Washington Park area and Over-the-Rhine generally. In 1977 sixteen chief executive officers of major Cincinnati-area businesses organized as the Cincinnati Business Committee (CBC) to assist local governments in solving problems, especially downtown problems, that might threaten the economic viability of greater Cincinnati.[28] City manager Donaldson shortly thereafter approached the CBC for assistance in developing neighborhood housing, a proposition that Fred Lazarus III, a CBC member, soon focused on the Music Hall–Washington Park area of Over-the-Rhine,[29] although Hubert Guest, the former head of the city's Model Cities program and now director of the city's Department of Buildings and Inspections, and Susan Utt, the head of the city's Revolving Loan Fund, told him that the Over-the-Rhine Community Council had failed to unify various factions in the neighborhood and probably would not offer effective cooperation.[30]

Nonetheless, the CBC organized a complicated operation not merely to develop housing in the Washington Park area but also to make it the first phase in the revitalization of all of Over-the-Rhine and to use historic preservation as a key renewal treatment. It first delegated several of its members to form a charitable company, the Queen City Housing Corporation, to raise and distribute money to a housing developer, and then assessed all of its members to provide Queen City Housing with seed money of $38,250 for the first year of a three-year commitment to the Washington Park project. As developer, Queen City Housing selected Cincinnati Neighborhood Housing Services, Inc., the director of which was Carl Westmoreland. The staunch opponent of gentrification came on board because he believed Lazarus's vow to avoid the involuntary displacement of poor people from Over-the-Rhine.[31]

Queen City Housing, however, soon altered this arrangement after it learned that city, state, and federal law required representation by neighborhood residents on the board of any development corporation operating on their turf, something Westmoreland's organization could not provide. To solve the problem Queen City Housing set up the Heritage Preservation Development Corporation as the not-for-profit agency with which Westmoreland would work most directly,[32] and placed on its board three members of the Queen City Housing board, including Lazarus and W. Joseph Dehner, a young lawyer in one of the city's largest and most prestigious law firms. These three selected six other people, including the president of the Over-the-Rhine Community Council and enough other residents of Over-the-Rhine to give them a majority on the board.[33]

By May 1979 this interesting coalition of corporations and Over-the-Rhine insiders and outsiders had formulated intentions to integrate the Washington Park area racially and socioeconomically. Specifically, it aimed to tap federal historic preservation subsidies and other government programs as well as private sector funds to build new housing and rehabilitate old structures for the creation of a residential area containing blacks and whites and people of low, middle, and upper incomes. It intended also to minimize displacement in the Washington Park area by starting with low-income housing rehabilitation and to avoid forcing anyone out of Over-the-Rhine by raising $2 million to $3 million to purchase from the city's largest low-income housing developer some 1,500 housing units, 80 percent of them in Over-the-Rhine and 1,238 of which qualified for federal rent subsidies. And it proposed to start new construction within eighteen months and to complete the other phases of the Washington Park program in five years.[34]

This seemed a fair, democratic, and practical proposition to Hubert Guest, who steered it through city hall despite the protests of a faction of the executive committee of the Over-the-Rhine Community Council.[35] The leadership of this faction came from Buddy Gray, who had recently won a well-publicized battle with the city's Department of Health to keep open his Drop-Inn Shelter for alcoholics, a Main Street agency which provided food, clothing, and shelter but not treatment of the conventional sort to homeless alcoholics. Before the end of the fight Gray had earned a sympathetic hearing from city council, which deferred to him out of its commitment to community control, despite the opposition of city manager Donaldson and other members of the city administration. Gray also secured city council support, again over the opposition of the city administration, when he moved the Drop-Inn Shelter to quarters a block south of Music Hall. The location not only offended major patrons of Music Hall, including Lazarus's wife, Irma, but also put the Drop-Inn Shelter within the Washington Park area project, the director of which, in Gray's view, wanted to clear him and his shelter out of the neighborhood.[36]

Despite this opposition, Queen City Housing and its allies, which now included the MPA, pushed ahead with the Washington Park project.[37] The MPA, which Joe Dehner served as a board member, completed in the fall of 1979 a nomination to the National Register for an Over-the-Rhine historic district encompassing 350 acres and 1,300 buildings, and the Ohio Historic Preservation Office and the Planning Commission decided to hold in 1980 a public hearing on the nomination jointly with the Ohio Historic Sites Preservation Advisory Board,[38] the citizens participation agency of the state preservation office. Prospects for approving the nomination brightened in November 1979 when Carl Westmoreland informed the Queen City Housing board that he had conducted a number of successful meetings with Gray and other members of the Over-the-Rhine Community Council at which they expressed dislike for the Washington Park project but seemed willing to discuss plans for the area.[39]

That willingness soon faded, in part because Joe Dehner failed to consult formally with the Over-the-Rhine Community Council when he pushed for the establishment of an emergency IDC district for the Washington Park area in the expectation that the neighborhood would soon become a local historic district under legislation being drafted by the Urban Conservation Task Force. Dehner felt he had to take this hasty step to prevent the Central Park YMCA from lopping off the top six floors of its building, space that Heritage Preservation hoped to convert into apartments for low-income residents of the Washington Park area and Over-the-Rhine.[40]

The Planning Commission considered the IDC request,[41] which as an emergency measure required no public hearing, at a session that featured a stern warning from Barbara Lichtenstein, a member of the city government's Community Assistance Team for Over-the-Rhine. She announced that the Over-the-Rhine Community Council had recently gone on record against historic preservation (a sign of Gray's growing strength in the organization) because of its belief that such activities would lead to gentrification regardless of Heritage Foundation's pledge to avoid displacing the poor, and she stressed that the Community Council had not been informed of the proposal. Describing Over-the-Rhine as a "very sensitive community," Lichtenstein said, "I'm afraid you are going to be stormed if you enact an IDC without even notifying them. I'm not saying you're not going to be stormed anyway because they're opposed."[42]

That plea did not sway the Planning Commission or, as it turned out, city council, which was not stormed and which promptly voted for the emergency IDC district.[43] Nor was that all. The Planning Commission sent a grant proposal to the U.S. Department of the Interior to fund the writing of a historic conservation plan for the Washington Park area that, it hoped, would placate the Over-the-Rhine Community Council and especially Gray, to whom the staff sent a description of the project and an invitation to participate. The proposal called for an "unparalleled" level of neighborhood involvement in a process that would involve a committee of residents and a community organizer in writing "a plan for the neighborhood . . . largely generated by the neighborhood."[44]

By this time the Urban Conservation Task Force had virtually completed its work, which produced city council approval of a new chapter (35) of the zoning code that established historic conservation zoning and passage of supplementary legislation to give the city government control over both National Register and local designations. These laws created a Historic Conservation Board to recommend to the Planning Commission historic resources, including districts, for local designation, to review and approve building and demolition permits involving historic properties, to replace the MPA as the Cincinnati liaison to state and federal historic preservation agencies, and to carry out for city departments environmental and historic reviews required by federal law. In addition, the legislation created the position of urban conservator as an assistant to the director of city planning to work with the Historic Conservation Board and to supervise the staff assigned by the Planning Commission to the Board.[45]

In anticipation of this outcome Over-the-Rhine activist Jack Towe, who was representing the neighborhood on the Urban Conservation

Task Force, began a drive to protect Over-the-Rhine through the enact-ment of an anti-displacement ordinance and developed in the process an effective twist to the anti-gentrification argument that connected it to the widely discredited urban redevelopment policies of the 1950s and early 1960s. Towe argued that large stocks of nineteenth- and early-twentieth-century residential buildings in the inner city would soon be purchased at low prices for private development projects that would displace mas-sive numbers of poor people. This, he contended, would result in an enormous intracity migration of blacks that would transform once white neighborhoods and yield the re-ghettoization of blacks, a phenomenon, he asserted, that had set off days of rioting by blacks in Avondale during the summer of 1967. To back this up he claimed that gentrification had already driven working-class whites out of Mt. Adams and both whites and poor African Americans out of Corryville near the University of Cincinnati and the Liberty Hill neighborhood immediately north and northeast of Over-the-Rhine. In this context Over-the-Rhine appeared to be next in line for massive displacements.[46]

That argument attracted attention in city hall and so disturbed the city manager that he appointed a committee of seven people from vari-ous agencies of city government to assess the extent of displacement since the mid-1960s and consider what might be done to prevent or mitigate it. The group concluded that not much displacement had occurred or could be expected in Cincinnati, not enough to adopt rent controls and other anti-displacement devices of the sort suggested by Towe. Instead, the group recommended continued monitoring of the situation, both to keep track of the movement of middle- and upper-class people into old poverty neighborhoods and to gauge the extent of involuntary displace-ment of poor people from their homes and neighborhoods.[47]

The report never reached city council, but a Planning Commission staff member sent a copy to Towe.[48] Shortly thereafter, People Against Displacement, a new Over-the-Rhine organization, asked John Schrider of the Cincinnati Legal Aid Society to draft an anti-displacement ordi-nance. In the spring of 1979 Schrider completed a draft that provided for rent controls on federally subsidized housing and the payment of re-location benefits of up to $4,000 to people forced out of their dwellings by rehabilitation.[49] Schrider then persuaded Tecumseh X. Graham, a black clergyman and city council member, to ask city solicitor Thomas A.

Luebbers to use Schrider's draft in preparing an ordinance that Graham might bring before council.[50] Luebbers responded with a draft closely resembling Schrider's, but warned Graham that it contained expensive and currently unfunded relocation benefits,[51] including benefits for persons displaced by private sector investments unaided by city assistance.

Luebbers also sent the ordinance to the city administration, including various department heads, all of whom objected to it. As a result Sylvester Murray, the city's new and first black city manager, prepared a draft that lacked rent controls and that applied only to cases of involuntary displacement caused by housing activities involving city assistance. Murray circulated it among his top administrators, most of whom did not like this version either, then sent it to city council with a cover letter noting that he found little support among department heads "for any aspect of the proposed ordinance" and that "different Departments disagree with different sections." Murray concluded by observing that any "final ordinance on displacement will be one the City Council specifically dictates and City Departments will simply have to accept."[52]

Murray's willingness to endorse anti-displacement legislation over the objections of his department heads suggested two things. It implied city council support for an anti-displacement ordinance as well as historic preservation and intimated that the revitalization of Over-the-Rhine would proceed along lines and through means worked out in the 1970s. No one had objected to the rehabilitation of older buildings, though Buddy Gray led a faction of the Over-the-Rhine Community Council that had registered its opposition to the use of historic conservation techniques and subsidies as a means of achieving that goal. The rehabilitation of the Findlay Market area had begun, and a powerful and resourceful coalition with a special interest in the viability of downtown had secured city government support for a Washington Park historic conservation project to create a neighborhood of mixed land uses and mixed peoples as the next major step in revitalizing Over-the-Rhine. That commitment also conformed with the spirit of the city council resolution of 1974 in favor of integrating racially and socially all the neighborhoods of the city.

But the idea of creating a city of integrated neighborhoods in the era of cultural individualism and community control created a potential dilemma for the city's bureaucrats and council members. It left no place for racial and economic separatists,[53] including neighborhood leaders in

Over-the-Rhine who might prefer to preserve it as a pocket of poverty rich in social services, charitable agencies, cheap housing, bars, and homeless shelters for people who had allegedly chosen a life style congruent with such conditions, despite the crime and vice that accompanied them. And confronting that dilemma seemed unavoidable if Gray, who wanted to preserve the status quo in Over-the-Rhine, secured control of the Community Council, unified, eliminated, or mitigated factionalism in its jurisdiction, and demanded that city government adhere to its long-standing commitment to neighborhood autonomy and maximum feasible participation by the poor.

8
The Separatist Counterattack, 1980–1982

THE patchwork of proposals worked out in the late 1970s for the revitalization of Over-the-Rhine by creating a racially and socioeconomically integrated neighborhood around Washington Park moved forward in 1980. The federal Department of the Interior in April 1980 funded the Planning Commission's proposal for the development of a Washington Park historic preservation plan, and a month later city council adopted the new historic conservation legislation recommended by the Urban Conservation Task Force, a sign of support for Lazarus of the Cincinnati Business Committee, the Miami Purchase Association, and their allies. A month after that, council also approved an anti-displacement ordinance that contained elements of both the city manager's and the Legal Aid Society's drafts,[1] a gesture of sympathy both for the manager, who had forwarded his draft over the opposition of his department heads, and the new community organizers in Over-the-Rhine, who applauded its passage but felt that it did not go far enough in the fight against gentrification.

Progress toward the development of the Washington Park plan stalled, however, because Buddy Gray emerged as the acknowledged leader and spokesperson for the Over-the-Rhine Community Council and skillfully manipulated the historic conservation/gentrification issue to build support for the separatist cause, the preservation of the neighborhood as an enclave for its poor and increasingly black population. Ironically, Gray, like most of Over-the-Rhine's other new community organizers, came from a white, middle-class background. He grew up on a small farm with a swimming pool near a town in Cincinnati's eastern suburbs called Mt. Carmel, a name associated in the Old Testament with Elijah, the zealous prophet of the one true God, a healer of ordinary people, a political as well as a religious figure. Stanley (Gray's given name) grew up in a Methodist family, attended Sunday school regularly, and earned a reputation among his adult neighbors as a "model boy—polite, intelligent, considerate."

That mild disposition turned hostile when, as a scholarship student in engineering at Purdue University, he participated in protests against the war in Vietnam. After two years of college he dropped out and returned to Cincinnati, where he moved to Over-the-Rhine in the 1970s to tutor poor children at Prince of Peace Lutheran Church. There he came under the tutelage of the young Reverend Joel Hempel, a trained community organizer and an exponent and practitioner of confrontational tactics. In this context Gray let his beard and hair grow long and befriended two of the neighborhood's street alcoholics, both of whom froze to death one night while they slept unattended in an abandoned building. The incident haunted Gray and inspired him to make a career of alcoholic shelter work and community organizing on behalf of the poor, which in Over-the-Rhine in the late 1970s and after meant especially the African American poor.[2]

Gray described himself as "a hard-nosed radical, a street fighter for street people" who believed, no matter what city administrators, council members, or historic conservationists said, that they really wanted to run him, his alcoholic shelter, and the poor out of Over-the-Rhine and turn it into an "artsy-craftsy" neighborhood for the "urban gentry." He identified his Drop-Inn Shelter and "the struggle for low-income housing" as the "basic things" in his life, but refused to elaborate on the source of either his motivation or his income. When queried about his reticence he replied, "When you're out there punching in the front lines of social struggle, you have to expect to be attacked, and you have to draw a clear line of defense."[3]

Gray and his allies put on one of the first displays of their new strength in February 1980 when they rallied some 250 protestors to a public hearing on the nomination of Over-the-Rhine to the National Register of Historic Places. The session began with introductory remarks from planning director Herb Stevens. A staff member of the Miami Purchase Association presented a slide show defining the boundaries of the district and illustrating its architectural and historic significance. Then seven diverse persons testified to the proposed district's eligibility for listing and stressed that designation would make available tax breaks as incentives for the production of low-income housing. These people included Joe Dehner and Mary Heller, executive secretary of the MPA, and also an officer of the Findlay Market Association, a member of the teamsters union, and representatives of the Over-the-Rhine Business Association, who described the neighborhood as a "natural extension of downtown" and an "irreplaceable architectural and historic resource" threatened by the kind of urban redevelopment that had flattened much of the city's West End and displaced thousands of people.[4]

The opposition featured twelve speakers, including Laura Goodell, a Gray ally and the new head of the Over-the-Rhine Community Council. Gray himself also spoke and, like all the speakers on his side, emphasized social problems and ignored the issue of the district's eligibility for inclusion on the National Register, the only criteria of concern under federal historic preservation legislation. Gray attacked Mitchell's slide show for ignoring "human issues," such as the closing of schools, poverty, alcoholism, poor housing, and unemployment. Joel Hempel then asked why Mitchell had not shown pictures of the 15,000 residents of the area and contended that the listing of Over-the-Rhine would bring gentrification and an urban renewal program that would yield "negro removal."[5]

One of the most dramatic speakers against the nomination was the Reverend Maurice McCrackin, a pacifist, a well-known veteran Cincinnati defender of the downtrodden, and since the 1940s the pastor of a Protestant community church in the then white Dayton Street area of the West End. In that capacity McCrackin sought to integrate his congregation racially, participated enthusiastically during the 1950s in the fight against racial segregation elsewhere in the city, and acquiesced in the adoption of historic preservation legislation for the Dayton Street area. Now, however, he came down against efforts both to assure the success of racial integration in Over-the-Rhine and to use historic preservation as a means of accomplishing it. To proponents of these ideas he offered an eleventh commandment, "Thou shalt not manipulate thy brother or sister," and added for good measure that "the faces of people, not the facades of buildings" should be the major concern.[6]

In the midst of these passionate protests a representative of the state historic preservation office, Gretchen Klimoski, tried vainly to calm the fears of the dissenters. She contended that preservationists *prevented* displacement by using conservation grants and tax credits to provide low-income housing, and she argued that more displacement took place from deterioration and abandonment than from revitalization, with or without historic designation. She noted, too, that developers found historic areas of cities *before* their listing on the National Register and that displacement sometimes occurred without designation and did not invariably follow after designation. And she added that National Register listing, unlike local designation, did not establish design or demolition controls, and referred the audience to a preservationist handbook on anti-displacement strategies.[7]

Nonetheless, the anti-preservationist barrage persisted. Three letters opposed to the nomination brought new voices, all of them respectably religious, to the fray. The pastor of St. Francis Seraph Roman Catholic parish in Over-the-Rhine condemned the nomination as an effort "to preserve the past without concern for current residents" and excoriated it as "a crime and a moral injustice." Ted W. Sippel, president of the Prince of Peace church council, more calmly claimed that historic designation would reduce the number of rental units and increase rents in Over-the-Rhine and explained that his organization preferred to improve housing for residents "rather than providing either a face lift or transforming the area into an elite neighborhood."[8]

The third new voice of opposition came from a source representing the largest single religious constituency in the Cincinnati area, the Social Action and World Peace Commission of the Roman Catholic archdiocese, an advisory body composed of lay and religious men and women in various fields of work. Its director, Archie Brunn, noted that Catholic social teaching called on all members of the church to speak and act on behalf of the poor and powerless, and that he wrote not out of simple opposition to historic preservation, "a value which the Commission in fact affirms." Brunn described the nomination as ill-timed because it would add to the threat of involuntary displacement of poor residents, but stressed that the Commission had consistently supported the poor of Over-the-Rhine, most recently by publicly endorsing city legislation to prevent the involuntary displacement of low-income residents.[9]

Clearly, Gray and his allies scored humanitarian points on culturally individualistic grounds in this debate by painting a picture of poor people about to be uprooted from their chosen homes against their wishes. But their case sounded compelling not only because of the emotional, religious, and cultural charge of their presentations but also because the historic preservationists made no concentrated, systematic, coordinated response based on higher principles than architectural and historical significance. No one observed, for example, that wealthy whites, unlike the residents of Over-the-Rhine, possessed the economic resources to live anywhere they wanted and chose not to live in Over-the-Rhine or areas like it. None of the historic preservationists brought up the city administration's study of gentrification that discounted it as a threat anywhere in the city, which lost population between 1970 and 1980, just as it had between 1960 and 1970. No one noted that retaining Over-the-Rhine as a separatist racial and low-income enclave violated federal law and city council's resolution in favor of racial and class balance in all neighborhoods. And no one remarked that the metropolis offered rich pickings for people who chose to live in neighborhoods segregated by race and/or class but only a small and dwindling number of localities integrated by race and/or class for people who preferred that style of living.

By trumping architectural and historic significance with the gentrification card, moreover, Gray and his allies caught the attention and sympathy of planning director Herb Stevens, who decided to strengthen Gray's political position in the planning process. Gray now contended that the Washington Park planning program, like the Findlay Market renovation and the recent agreement by the city government to help the Verdin Bell Company rehabilitate St. Paul's Church for commercial use, represented part of a scheme to divide and gentrify various parts of Over-the-Rhine on a piecemeal basis. He proposed instead that the Washington Park planning effort be folded into a process for developing a plan for all of Over-the-Rhine. Stevens picked up on this idea, sold it to both the Planning Commission and the city administration, and then persuaded the state historic preservation office to accommodate the new planning program by postponing for six months a decision on the nomination of Over-the-Rhine to the National Register.[10]

This change in the process for dealing with Washington Park gratified Gray but exacerbated the growing concerns of Fred Lazarus about the lack of progress on the Washington Park plan, the timely completion of which the Queen City Housing Corporation regarded as crucial for its continued support for the effort to revitalize the area as a neighborhood with a socially and economically mixed population. Lazarus met with city manager Sylvester Murray about this problem and reiterated Queen City Housing's intention to avoid displacement by developing housing for low-income residents until all of the residents of the area had been located in properly rehabilitated and maintained housing. Murray replied "emphatically" that Queen City Housing should stay in the Washington Park arena and promised to meet with Lazarus in "a couple of weeks" to outline specifically what he would do.[11]

Gray and his allies responded to Murray's renewed pledge of support for Queen City Housing's treatment for Washington Park by trying to discourage Lazarus and the Cincinnati Business Committee about their prospects for success in integrating the area by using historic preservation subsidies and techniques. Jack Towe, now a member of the Housing Committee of the Over-the-Rhine Community Council, started the campaign by inviting Lazarus to a meeting. Lazarus agreed to come in the hope that he could secure the support of the Community Council, or at least of some key members of it. But Towe did most of the talking and delivered three decidedly negative messages. First, the Housing Committee would not accept any plan unless the Committee had been involved from the beginning in preparing the scheme, even if it approximated what the Committee wanted for the area. Second, the Housing Committee wanted to provide low-income housing in Over-the-Rhine not only for current residents but also for other low-income people who might want to move into the neighborhood. Third, Towe suggested that Queen City Housing and the Heritage Preservation Development Corporation should get out of Over-the-Rhine and that the Cincinnati Business Committee and the city should instead support a development corporation directed by the Over-the-Rhine Community Council.[12]

When Lazarus refused to back down, Towe set up another meeting and brought along the Reverend Joel Hempel, Buddy Gray's mentor in confrontational community organizing practices. Hempel announced that he distrusted the motives of the Cincinnati Business Committee and that he thought Lazarus himself had unidentified "ulterior motives" for his work in the area. Hempel then said that he opposed the provision of new and rehabilitated housing for middle-income people because it would attract more of the same and eventually drive out the poor. Hempel objected particularly to middle-income housing near the Drop-Inn Shelter because "middle income people would object to the derelicts from the Drop-Inn Shelter wandering around in the area." He concluded with a general attack on "wealthy people" and their power and proposed that Queen City Housing form a new corporation "governed by a board of directors appointed by the Over-the-Rhine Community Council," the only group that represented "the sentiments of the people of the area."[13]

This session shook Lazarus, who now wondered if he could count on the city in the face of protests from an apparently united Community Council. He raised the question with city manager Murray and planning director Stevens at a meeting on what to do next to help Queen City Housing in its Washington Park project. In the course of the discussion Stevens indicated that it would take two to three years to develop a plan because the Community Council distrusted both Queen City Housing and the city due to a "lack of communication." Lazarus doubted that lack of communication explained the Community Council's attitude and reminded Stevens that Heritage Preservation could not wait two years to rehabilitate buildings it had already purchased on Race and Pleasant Streets, let alone to secure federal support for the creation of housing units for the elderly on the upper floors of the YMCA building on Central Parkway.[14]

Murray responded by pledging his continued support to Lazarus. Specifically, he asked Heritage Preservation to continue its low-income housing work on Race and Pleasant Streets and with the YMCA. He also told Stevens that he should proceed promptly with the plan for the Washington Park area. And Murray said that he would attend the next meeting of the Over-the-Rhine Community Council and offer it an opportunity to create its own development corporation, which the city would provide with financial planning assistance but not with funds to pay staff members.[15]

Murray subsequently made a strong effort to placate the leaders of the Over-the-Rhine Community Council. He not only encouraged them to start the development corporation (which they did, naming it Owning the Realty, Inc.) but also gave them favorable terms in drawing up the comprehensive plan for the neighborhood. Murray agreed to create an Over-the-Rhine Planning Task Force and to charge it with both writing a plan and reviewing all other planning activities in Over-the-Rhine, including work already started for the Findlay Market and Washington Park areas, the Mohawk area in the northwestern section, and the Pendleton area in the eastern section of Over-the-Rhine. The Task Force would consist of nineteen representatives of Over-the-Rhine residents and businesses—ten of them recommended by the Over-the-Rhine Community Council and at least eight of them residents of Over-the-Rhine—and nine persons appointed by the city manager, at least two of them residents of Over-the-Rhine. The distribution gave a one-seat majority to residents of Over-the-Rhine.[16]

Gray now controlled both the Over-the-Rhine Community Council and the Planning Task Force. These positions, given city council's long-standing deference to neighborhood autonomy, forced others also to try conciliation with Gray in hopes of working out a compromise between him and the historic conservation advocates. The Ohio Historic Sites Preservation Advisory Board took a step in this direction by postponing action on the Over-the-Rhine nomination for an additional six months but requested in return the extension of some form of protection for the neighborhood's historic resources.[17] City council obliged by extending the Interim Development Control district protection for Findlay Market and Over-the-Rhine from three months to an additional nine months,[18] and by adopting an ordinance extending the Washington Park IDC district for six months (to May 1981), by which time it thought the Task Force would have completed the Over-the-Rhine comprehensive plan.[19]

But the Over-the-Rhine Planning Task Force soon bogged down in controversy. At its first meeting the Task Force decided that city hall officials could not speak at its meetings until granted permission by the Task

Force. Then a nasty squabble developed between resident and business members over the makeup of a committee to help select a consultant for the planning process. After the resolution of that problem the resident faction not only expressed its opposition to the designation of Washington Park as either a national or local historic district, but also persuaded the Task Force to establish a Housing Subcommittee, chaired by Father William Schiesl of St. Mary's Catholic Church, to seek alternatives to historic preservation for financing, protecting, and increasing the number of low-income housing units in Over-the-Rhine.[20]

That rocky session set the tone for the planning process, which bumped along slowly and contentiously thereafter. During the winter and spring of 1981 the Task Force spent a great deal of time and debate on the Findlay Market area plan, particularly a dispute over what to do about the intention of Catanzaro & Sons to demolish residential structures so it could expand its food produce warehouse. The Task Force also wrangled with city officials over which agency would report on which sub-area planning activity, when the Task Force should review plans for sub-areas, and the status of a three-year-old Community Council request for community development funds for low-income housing. The Task Force seemed especially determined to find a way to both protect and encourage the development of additional low-income housing without using historic preservation subsidies and regulations.[21]

In April, a frustrated Sy Murray tried to speed up the process. He sent the Task Force a memo asking it to focus exclusively—and more effectively—on planning.[22] To expedite matters in city hall he directed Charlotte T. "Tommie" Birdsall, the Planning Commission's staff coordinator on the project, to push the appropriate city departments and agencies to quickly prepare statements of policies and goals for the Task Force's consideration. The Task Force, Birdsall told her city hall colleagues, might modify some of the goals but they would at least provide a framework for her dealings with Buddy Gray and his allies.[23]

At this point what had been an in-house spat became a public issue that deepened divisions all around. A *Cincinnati Enquirer* reporter learned about the Task Force's slow progress and interviewed two of its members. Kathy Laker, a commercial developer in eastern Over-the-Rhine, pinned most of the blame on low-income housing advocates who refused to consider parking, zoning, street improvements and lighting, or housing for "young professionals" until after the settlement of the low-income housing question. But Buddy Gray blasted city administrators as "tiny power brokers, each vying to develop Over-the-Rhine on a piecemeal basis" by pouring millions of dollars of local and federal tax revenues into the creation of apartments and townhouses for middle- and high-income persons—"the Music Hall crowd," as Gray put it.[24]

That same day, coincidentally, a new actor, Genevieve Ray, the city's first urban conservator under the recently adopted historic conservation legislation, tried to break the logjam on the Task Force. Ray was a former VISTA volunteer organizer in Harlem, newspaperwoman, and executive director of a not-for-profit development corporation in York, Pennsylvania. She and Mary Asbury of the Legal Aid Society met with the Housing Subcommittee of the Over-the-Rhine Planning Task Force to discuss historic conservation issues. The subcommittee still associated gentrification with historic districts, so Ray and Asbury unveiled a low-income "housing preservation" ordinance from Seattle, Washington, that seemed a way of preventing that outcome and asked the city solicitor to draft a version of it for review by the Over-the-Rhine Planning Task force.[25]

The city solicitor, however, expressed reservations about applying the Seattle ordinance to Cincinnati and Over-the-Rhine. Part of the difficulty stemmed from the preamble to the ordinance, which justified the law on the basic of a severe housing shortage. The solicitor doubted that such a condition could be demonstrated for Cincinnati and especially in Over-the-Rhine, where the population had dropped by 60 percent in twenty years while the number of housing units had decreased at less than half that rate. He expressed concern, too, about the feature of the ordinance that established a fee for the demolition of low-income housing units to generate funds for the construction or rehabilitation of replacement housing. Ohio law provided that fees could be used only to cover the cost of administering a law, and the idea of loosely interpreting that restriction remained untested in Ohio courts. The solicitor thought, however, that the city might issue certificates to rehabilitators of low-income housing that then could be sold to other developers seeking demolition permits for other purposes, the proceeds from which could be used only for the creation of new or rehabilitated low-income housing.[26]

The solicitor's cautious response to the Seattle ordinance produced more discussions in the Task Force, annoying Murray, who once more pressed it to focus exclusively on the business of planning. This time, moreover, he sent along the city's goals for the area, including the preservation of subsidized housing units, the creation of new subsidized and market-rate housing, the establishment of a socially and economically mixed population, the application of local historic conservation zoning to parts of the neighborhood, and the development of new commercial and industrial ventures at appropriate locations. Murray described these goals as a response to those Task Force members who ascribed to the city a hidden agenda, but he emphasized that he wanted the Task Force to come up with its own "final goal statement," which, he said, "you can do . . . with or without referring"[27] to his list.

This initiative by the city manager did not inspire the Task Force to either step up its pace or change its direction. Instead it recessed for July and August and instructed the Housing Subcommittee to hold brainstorming sessions during the summer months on legislating to protect low-income housing.[28] At the first of these sessions the subcommittee noted that the Washington Park IDC district would expire in six months and asked Birdsall to secure support in city hall for the Seattle ordinance. She came back with bad news. She reminded the subcommittee of the solicitor's reservations and reported that the city manager did not like the idea because it involved additional bureaucratic regulations. And she indicated that the Planning Commission doubted that it could secure in six months the passage of an ordinance of such "magnitude."[29]

Genevieve Ray, however, saw this plea for support from city hall on the Seattle ordinance as an opportunity to hold talks between preservationists and Buddy Gray's forces in an effort to work out a compromise. She persuaded planning director Stevens to sponsor an Over-the-Rhine charette, a two- or three-day conference of all parties to the conflict supervised by a professional facilitator to negotiate an agreement on replacements for expired IDC districts in Over-the-Rhine, especially the Washington Park district.[30] The Community Council approved the idea in July and agreed to participate, although it reserved the right to oppose whatever proposal might emerge from the charette and indicated that it wanted the process to produce an ordinance protecting low-income housing in the area.[31]

Meanwhile, Ray's charette organizers, a steering committee that included members of the Housing Committee of the Over-the-Rhine Community Council, sent out invitations to representatives of twenty-four organizations and agencies in real estate and finance, government, and social service work, and to all members of the Over-the-Rhine Planning Task Force. The organizers called the charette a "Meeting of the Minds" and defined its objective as compromise. They also described the problem as the desire to replace the IDC districts with something to prevent the demolition of buildings and to encourage their use for low-income housing, and to discourage the displacement of current residents of Over-the-Rhine. The solution, said the organizers, had to take those goals into account but also recognize that business and "historic preservation people" had goals that would affect the solution and the decision of city council.[32]

The charette itself lasted three lively days and produced no meeting of the minds.[33] But it inspired a sustained effort by Ray and her staff to devise legislation for a new kind of zoning district, one that would combine historic conservation techniques with regulations to preserve low-income housing units and financial incentives to create more of them. The legislation went through several drafts and at one point contained a demolition fee for tearing down low-income housing.[34] By the time it emerged from negotiations involving Legal Aid Society lawyers, the Planning Task Force, and Stevens, this provision had been replaced by the certificate scheme suggested by the city solicitor. The proposed law also set up stiff criteria for granting demolition permits and banned rehabilitation projects that would lead to "significantly increased" rents. In addition, the ordinance contained historic design review regulations and established a building permit review board consisting of two representatives of the community (one a resident and the other a property owner in the district) and three representatives of the city (one from the Historic Conservation Board, one from the Department of Neighborhood Housing and Conservation and one appointed by the city manager).[35]

The proposal got a cold shoulder everywhere. Gray refused to accept its historic preservation provisions, which prompted Ray and the Historic Conservation Board to withhold their support.[36] The Planning Task Force then suggested that Stevens reintroduce demolition fees and strip the legislation of its historic conservation content, which he did.[37]

But Sy Murray rejected this version of the law, now called the neighbor-hood housing retention enabling ordinance, as too complicated and too stringent.[38] In addition, the Planning Commission staff discovered that the proposed ordinance violated the city's Housing Allocation Policy (HALP) for the dispersal of low-income housing and would require the passage of five amendments to that policy to permit additional subsi-dized low-income housing in areas already containing concentrations of such housing.[39]

The Planning Commission reacted to this confusing situation by ap-proving the neighborhood housing retention enabling ordinance and postponing the question of weakening the city's policy for the dispersal of low-income housing. Stevens defended these steps by noting that fed-eral officials under President Ronald Reagan interpreted loosely the reg-ulations on dispersing low-income housing and by invoking the name of Anthony Downs, the consultant who helped the city devise both its bal-anced neighborhood and HALP strategies. Downs, said Stevens, had now changed his mind and regarded "slums" as necessary for providing low-income people with decent housing.

Trouble developed when the Planning Commission considered the application of the neighborhood housing retention enabling ordinance to the Washington Park area, a step that required separate legislation. Only four members attended the meeting and two of them, including Murray, voted against it, which killed the motion. That infuriated the Over-the-Rhine Planning Task Force, which urged Murray to call for a reconsideration of the question so all Planning Commission members could vote on the issue. Murray agreed to this, and both the motion to reconsider and the law itself passed (the ayes picked up two and the nays but one additional vote).[40]

These actions cleared the way for city council's consideration of both the neighborhood housing retention ordinance and the proposal to make the Washington Park area the first such district. In an effort to pla-cate as many sides as possible, council amended the legislation to give de-molition review authority to the Planning Commission and eliminated the certificate scheme and the ban on significantly increasing rents. This version of the law went back to the Planning Commission, which voted it down. That forced council to pass it by a two-thirds vote, which it did, although the enactment of this version of the law disappointed Buddy Gray, who complained that it gave him only half of what he wanted, stiffer anti-demolition rules but no incentives to create more low-income housing.[41]

Council's action also displeased some advocates of racial and socio-economic integration, who saw the ordinances as additional steps toward legal separatism, the de facto definition of Over-the-Rhine as an enclave for poor African Americans, alcoholics, and their community organizers. Under these rules persons who demolished low-income housing had to pay a fee of $25 per unit up to a maximum of $250 per building, wait a year after filing an application for a demolition permit, demonstrate that they tried to secure a subsidy to rehabilitate the dwelling for low-income occupancy, and show that denial of the application would deprive them of economic return on the real property. And the ordinance rested on the explicit premise that many low-income residents preferred to live in pockets of poverty for social, economic, or aesthetic reasons, although no one had done a scientific opinion survey of the residents of the city's low-income areas on this issue or conducted a study of voluntary geographic mobility out of the neighborhoods.[42]

9 The National Register Controversy, 1982–1983

THE end of the battle over the neighborhood housing retention legislation suggested that the Over-the-Rhine Planning Task Force, now known as "Stevens's folly" among department heads with projects in the neighborhood,[1] would at last concentrate on completing its work. Odds for this seemed even better in light of two contemporaneous events. First, internecine squabbling on the Task Force ceased after six business representatives walked out in disgust, contending that they supported low-income housing as the plan's top priority but complaining that only one-fourth of the group's members attended meetings, that the group had not even discussed land uses, and that resident representatives dominated the body and used it principally to promote low-income housing.[2] Sy Murray responded to the boycott by leaving the business seats vacant and by promising Buddy Gray and his allies that he would not sanction the establishment of a separate business group as a planning body to work in tandem with the Task Force.[3]

The retirement of planning director Herbert Stevens, who sided almost from the outset with Gray and who never pressed the Task Force to pick up the pace of its work, provided the second reason for optimism about expediting the plan. It gave Murray the chance to replace[4] Stevens with Hubert Guest, the same man who a decade earlier had helped write

125

in fairly short order the Queensgate II plan; who then served as Model Cities director, in which job he derailed Harris Forusz's long and complicated plan for Over-the-Rhine; who next became director of the Department of Buildings and Inspections, where he supported the now stalled Lazarus effort to diversify Over-the-Rhine's population; and who most recently worked directly with Murray as assistant to the city manager. In all these posts Guest earned a reputation for getting things done as simply and quickly as possible, and he deplored as much as if not more than Murray the embarrassingly slow progress of the Over-the-Rhine Planning Task Force.

Instead of quickly completing the plan, however, the Task Force held it hostage in a renewed and protracted fight over the nomination of Over-the-Rhine to the National Register of Historic Places. This took shape in February 1982, when W. Ray Luce, the state historic preservation officer, informed the city government and the Over-the-Rhine Community Council that the National Register had reopened after being closed in 1981 to allow federal officials to work out procedures to handle a congressional mandate prohibiting the listing of a district if a majority of property owners objected.[6] The Over-the-Rhine Planning Task Force immediately voted its opposition to National Register listing "in recognition of the current planning process in the neighborhood" and urged the city administration and the city's Historic Conservation Board to take the same stance.[7]

Stevens might have backed the request, but Guest, who knew the Conservation Board supported the nomination, as did he, told the board to prepare and approve a report for the Planning Commission.[8] Genevieve Ray, the city's urban conservator, wrote the report, which in the context of the earlier debate on the issue took an unavoidably defensive tone. Ray labeled National Register listing as irrelevant to the planning process because the decision one way or another would not affect either land use planning or the establishment of neighborhood boundaries for planning purposes. She also argued that further postponement of the listing would discourage reinvestment under the Economic Recovery Tax Act of 1981, which provided major tools both for the creation of low- and moderate-income housing and for stimulating rehabilitation of higher-income housing. She then attacked the "myth" that displacement automatically followed National Register listing, asserted that displacement flowed from disinvestment, not reinvestment, and observed that Over-the-Rhine in any case contained room for some middle- and upper-income housing because of its 24 percent vacancy rate.[9]

The Historic Conservation Board reviewed Ray's report, unanimously endorsed the nomination,[10] and sent the issue to the Planning Commission, where Guest supported the listing. Predictably, Buddy Gray objected vehemently, but not on architectural or historical grounds. He conceded that Murray acknowledged low-income housing as the top priority for Over-the-Rhine but complained that the city government had made no such commitment "on paper" and contended that city council had not gone on record in favor of "any type of development action" in Over-the-Rhine. Council member Thomas Brush (C) responded that the city council needed a "clear and concise plan" on which to act, pointed to an immediate need for incentives for developers, especially in view of the high interest rates, and added that historic designation provided "the only mechanism that offers some hope" and that it would not "result in any worse condition than what now exists in Over-the-Rhine." With that, the Planning Commission unanimously endorsed the nomination.[11]

City council consideration came next, just two days before the issue went before the OHSPAB, the Ohio Historic Sites Preservation Advisory Board. Here, however, the attempt to line up a united front for the listing failed. Four people, including Gray and Jack Towe of the Over-the-Rhine Community Council and Planning Task Force, spoke against the measure, after which Mayor David Mann (D) transmitted to council various communications and petitions from residents of Over-the-Rhine objecting to the nomination. These pleas elicited some sympathy, for city council member Charlie Luken (D) moved to request the state advisory board to defer action. The vote yielded a three to three tie,[12] which left the state board without guidance by city council.

By this time, moreover, the state historic preservation office had been bombarded with letters against the listing, some of them from powerful people. These included three black members of the Cincinnati delegation to the state legislature, Representatives William L. Mallory (D) and Helen Rankin (D) and Senator William F. Bowen (D), two of whom (Rankin and Bowen) referred to earlier incidents of displacement stemming from other governmental actions, including expressway construction and urban redevelopment in the West End.[13] Other letters of opposition came from the Reverend James Willig of St. Joseph Catholic Church on Ezzard Charles Drive just west of Over-the-Rhine; Andrew Fox, O.F.M., publisher of the *St. Anthony Messenger;* Buddy Gray; and Grace Raines, speaking for People Against Displacement.[14]

Proponents of the listing comprised a large and diverse group,[15] but they could match neither the clout of the opposition nor the show it put on at the hearing before the OHSPAB. Buddy Gray and his allies brought to the hearing a busload of forty residents of Over-the-Rhine, many of whom testified in passionate terms about the gentrification and displacement that they claimed would follow from historic designation. Once again the advisory board voted to delay consideration of the nomination, this time for a year, to permit the Over-the-Rhine Planning Task Force to complete the comprehensive plan and the city to make all of Over-the-Rhine a neighborhood housing retention district.[16]

This did not settle the matter, for Luce soon received inquiries from Cincinnati about the procedure for appealing decisions by the state board directly to the keeper of the National Register, Carol Shull. In response Luce warned Buddy Gray that interested citizens could appeal directly to the keeper, who might then either bypass the state review process or require the consideration of the nomination by the state board "at an earlier date than scheduled." Luce reported too that Shull had gone on record as favoring the listing of the proposed Over-the-Rhine district and added, "I think you can see the need for haste in completing the process you are involved in at the local level," by which he meant both completing the plan and securing protection for low-income housing in all of Over-the-Rhine.[17]

Diane Smart, chair of the twenty-five-member Over-the-Rhine Property Owners Association, doubted that the Task Force would speed up and decided to pursue another strategy. She demanded that Luce exercise his right to override the advisory board and forward the nomination to Shull. She threatened to appeal the nomination directly to Shull if he did not. And she claimed that OHSPAB acted in response to "propaganda" from a "small but vocal group of alleged residents," not on the basis of the architectural and historic merits of the proposed district.[18]

Luce, however, refused to cooperate. He acknowledged the frustration of Smart and other property owners, and described the advisory board's action as "unprecedented." Yet he said he could not grant Smart's request to bypass OHSPAB because federal regulations permitted him to forward a nomination to Shull only when he disagreed with a decision by his advisory board. And the board, he explained, had delayed the consideration of the nomination to encourage "local planning decisions," not because it judged the proposed district ineligible for listing under the National Register criteria.[19]

Smart and her allies nonetheless persisted in their efforts to get around OHSPAB. Late in May 1982 they filed an appeal with Shull that accused the advisory board of having acted on the basis of "local political and social issues . . . totally irrelevant" to historic designation criteria. The appeal also claimed that the delays had not only encouraged the demolition of many of the historic buildings in the proposed district but also had "caused more displacement than they prevented" by permitting the continued deterioration of housing units. It closed by requesting Shull to instruct Luce to send the nomination to her "forthwith."[20]

Shull considered this request for two months, during which time low-income housing advocates sought to protect all of Over-the-Rhine with a low-income neighborhood housing retention district. Mary Asbury of the Legal Aid Society and Jim Bower, chairperson of the Over-the-Rhine Planning Task Force, persuaded the Planning Commission staff to prepare such an ordinance,[21] and the Planning Commission approved it on a five to one vote, despite the opposition of city manager Murray. Murray said the creation of the district would not produce low-income housing and contended that the ordinance would "put a hold on development in Over-the-Rhine for the next 20 years." He then challenged the Task Force and "members of the community" to produce a plan that specifically ranked low-income housing as its top priority instead of always saying "don't do, don't do."[22]

City council disagreed with Murray, in part because of an optimistic report on the housing retention district and the Task Force's progress by Charlotte Birdsall, the Planning Commission staff liaison with the Task Force. The Task Force had been working for eighteen months, she noted, and "frequently . . . in the spotlight—not always favorably." Nonetheless, she predicted the Task Force would present "a product" for city council consideration within six months or less. In the interim, she argued, the creation of an Over-the-Rhine housing retention district would support the work of the Task Force and contribute to the orderly development of the area without significantly impeding development opportunities.[23]

This sanguine plea impressed most members of city council, although Mayor Mann tried but failed to secure the passage of an amendment to reduce the duration of the district from two years to six months. Another member then offered an amendment reducing its duration to one year, a motion that passed by a six to one vote (two members absent). Council next offered the privilege of the floor to Birdsall and Buddy Gray, both of whom spoke in favor of the revised legislation, after which council passed the amended ordinance by a six to one vote.[24]

Planning director Guest stayed out of the issue but intensified efforts to speed up the Over-the-Rhine planning forces. He assigned staff members to the preparation of a new zoning district to accommodate businesses in the basements and on the first floors of apartments in older areas of the city, such as Over-the-Rhine.[25] That same month, increasingly frustrated with the lack of progress by the Over-the-Rhine Planning Task Force, he ordered the consultant on the project to prepare a land use plan without waiting longer for the Task Force to adopt goals and objectives for land uses in Over-the-Rhine.[26]

At this juncture the Task Force shifted its focus back to the nomination of Over-the-Rhine to the National Register. Carol Shull, the keeper of the Register, had finally responded to Diane Smart's demand that Luce circumvent his advisory board and send the nomination to the keeper. Shull stopped short of this, recommending instead that Luce schedule the nomination for reconsideration by his advisory board as soon as possible.[27] Luce ignored the advice until Smart sent him a telegram demanding action.[28] He then told Smart he would ask his board to consider the nomination on September 17 and requested the city manager, the Over-the-Rhine Property Owners Association, and the Planning Task Force to provide him evidence of "good prospects for a timely implementation of an effective plan."[29]

Guest and Charlotte Birdsall responded for the city manager to Luce's request, but sent contradictory messages. Guest said that the Historic Conservation Board and the Planning Commission still supported the nomination, regarded it as an important tool for the provision of low- and moderate-income housing in the area, and urged the advisory board to approve the nomination "at the earliest possible date."[30] Birdsall, however, asked the advisory board to defer action on the nomination until December 1982, by which time, she said, the plan would be ready for consideration by the Planning Commission and city council and would recommend the "designation of National Register and local historic districts."[31]

Two persons acting as representatives of Over-the-Rhine residents also requested a delay of the reconsideration of the listing. Catherine Howard, vice president of the Over-the-Rhine Community Council, urged the state board to defer action for a year,[32] and Jack Towe offered a surprising reason for such a delay: the highly unlikely possibility of amending the city's new neighborhood housing retention law so that it included historic design controls, fees for significantly increasing the rents for low-income housing, and certificates that low-income developers could sell to developers of higher-income housing.[33] These, of course, were features stripped from the law to secure its passage, and the Planning Task Force itself had eliminated historic design controls before submitting the proposed ordinance to city council.

The Over-the-Rhine Property Owners Association wanted immediate action on the nomination. It reminded Luce and the advisory board in a letter that the nomination process had started in December 1979, that the Task Force had failed to meet its original deadline of December 1981 for completion of the plan, and that it still had not completed it despite repeated goading by Luce and the city administration. In the meantime, said the letter, Over-the-Rhine was "self-destructing," citing as evidence its declining population, surplus housing stock, increasing demolition rate, infestation by vagrants and "fire-starting thrill seekers," and rising incidence of rape, theft, and murder.[34]

These and other entreaties for prompt consideration did no good, for the board once more put off its consideration of the nomination, this time until December 3, 1982. Before that session, Luce met with the Over-the-Rhine Planning Task Force to make the case for historic designation,[35] and letters from the usual suspects supporting and opposing the nomination poured in to the state historic preservation office.[36] These included deputy city manager Philip A. Hawkey's description of the planning process as "almost complete."[37] Birdsall, however, was less reassuring. She indicated that the Task Force had voted on two of the

three components of the plan and predicted that the third vote would occur in mid-December. After that, she observed, would come "clean-up"
work, an official review of the plan by the departments of city government and the Planning Commission, and the submission of the plan to
city council in the spring of 1983,[38] the date suggested by Towe for completion of the planning process.

The state historic preservation advisory board took up the Over-the-
Rhine nomination on December 3, although it had to move the session
from its regular conference room to an auditorium because more than a
hundred Over-the-Rhine residents and their allies traveled to Columbus
to oppose the nomination. As in the past, opposition speakers ignored
historic preservation criteria and focused on the threat of gentrification
and displacement. One of the most effective presentations came from a
young and very angry black man who used confrontational language
more common in the 1960s. The other came from Buddy Gray, who
spoke calmly but passionately about the potential innocent victims of displacement, such as the young girl standing quietly by his side. Genevieve
Ray ranked the presentation as a very good show, beautifully choreo-
graphed, complete with priests in their cassocks and lots of emotion—
"You almost expected candles to be lighted and a choir to be singing in
the background. . . . They beat us cold."[39]

The anti-nomination demonstration also impressed a narrow majority of the board members, several of whom had received phone calls and
visits from opponents of the nomination before the hearing. After the
vote the tally showed eight against and seven in favor of the nomination,
after which the crowd shouted down the use of a proxy to create a tie that
would permit the chair, who favored designation, to break the deadlock
and carry the nomination for the preservationists. With the nomination
dead, the board approved by a margin of fourteen to one a recommendation that both sides consider the possibility of nominating to the National
Register smaller districts within Over-the-Rhine.[40]

The defeat of the nomination seemed to the victors to assure the future of Over-the-Rhine as a predominantly black and poor neighborhood and produced jubilation among the foes of historic preservation,
who as they left the hearing sang "We Shall Overcome,"[41] the anthem,
ironically, of the racial integrationist civil rights movement of the 1950s
and 1960s. On returning to Cincinnati the leaders of the anti–historic

preservation cause vowed to continue to fight, in part because such historic districts as Dayton Street to the west and Prospect Hill to the east of Over-the-Rhine consisted of "monuments and mansions" that presented a world inhabited by "masters, but no servants, owners, but no workers." As a corrective, Mike Henson, another of the new, white Over-the-Rhine activists, sketched an alternative history of the neighborhood, "the story of one wave after another of immigrants who came into the city from Europe, then from Appalachia and the Deep South" to live in "overcrowded brick apartments" with no running water, dim gas lights, and outhouses in back. These strong and courageous people, wrote Henson, "Germans, Italians, Jews, Appalachians, and Blacks—each managed to improve their lives by creating their own cultural networks and by fighting against the landlords and bosses for better conditions." "We" need "our" history, Henson concluded, one to "give us, the people . . . lessons for changing history."[42]

Father William Schiesl also celebrated the victory by picking up the theme of struggle, but he complained bitterly about the planning process and predicted that the outcome of the Task Force's work would prove inconclusive. He alleged that planning director Guest and his staff made decisions "behind the scenes" for review and "*input*" by the Task Force, instead of letting the Task Force make the choices. He contended, too, that the Task Force had to fight with the staff and consultants over virtually every detail of the plan to keep low-income housing in the forefront on every issue, including the zoning of particular plots of land. And he predicted that the plan, when adopted, would provide a basis for protecting low-income housing but would contain no management strategies for implementing any aspect of it, a weakness that would leave to the Community Council the task of finding other ways to perpetuate Over-the-Rhine as a poverty neighborhood.[43]

Schiesl and the Housing Committee of the Community Council had given this question some thought, and in January 1983 they announced six proposals to protect and increase the number of low-income dwelling units in Over-the-Rhine and to keep out more prosperous people. The first proposal asked city council to adopt an ordinance guaranteeing the establishment of a minimum of 5,520 low-income housing units in Over-the-Rhine, a figure almost identical to the existing number of unoccupied and occupied units, almost half of which ranked as substandard.

The second called for financial and technical support from the city for Owning the Realty, Inc., and Sign of the Cross (Towe's development corporation) to enlarge their capacity to produce low-income housing in the neighborhood. The third asked the city to sponsor the establishment of a "major multi-million start up package" by private interests for low-income housing in Over-the-Rhine. The fourth proposed a commitment by the city to bring one hundred apartments up to code standards. The fifth called for the rehabilitation of boarded-up HUD properties for low-income housing. And the sixth asked the city to withhold money from the Heritage Preservation Development Corporation until it set up "a fair, public election through the Over-the-Rhine Community Council for a majority" of seats on its board of directors.[44]

Action on these ideas had to wait, however, because the fight over the National Register nomination was not quite over, as Buddy Gray and his allies should have known. Luce had earlier explained to Gray the process of appealing decisions of the state advisory board to the keeper of the National Register. Others knew about these procedures, too, and three days after the meeting in Columbus, Joe Dehner, acting for Heritage Preservation, asked Luce to forward the nomination to the keeper, preferably accompanied by his professional comment in support of the nomination. Dehner said no one at the meeting had objected to the nomination on the basis of historical or architectural criteria, contended that without the listing Heritage Preservation would lose $50,000 in proceeds from two syndications for low-income housing in Over-the-Rhine, and threatened further action (presumably a lawsuit) against those responsible for the loss. That same day, Mary Heller, executive director of the Miami Purchase Association, also asked Luce to forward the nomination to Washington and informed him that Shull had assured her that federal regulations required state historic preservation boards to make their judgments on nominations on the basis of historical and architectural criteria exclusively.[45]

Luce responded to this pressure on December 22, 1982, by informing his advisory board that he had forwarded the nomination of Over-the-Rhine to the National Register because the architectural and historic criteria established by law compelled him to do so.[46] He attached to the nomination a long letter to Shull describing Over-the-Rhine and exploring the question of displacement, which he portrayed as an issue that played a sufficient role in the consideration of the nomination to warrant some discussion. Luce claimed that no one could predict what would or would not happen with or without listing, but asserted that two things stood out clearly. First, additional displacement would occur if the area continued on its current course, which had yielded the demolition of sixty-one rental units in the past two years. Second, National Register listing provided one of the few sources of funds for subsidizing low-income housing, and such subsidies had in fact been tapped extensively across the country for such ventures. Indeed, Luce observed, half of the new housing units created in the United States using historic preservation tax act subsidies consisted of low- and moderate-income housing projects. This fact, in addition to the commitment of the city of Cincinnati to low-income housing in Over-the-Rhine, brought Luce to the conclusion that listing would not lead, as opponents claimed, to widespread displacement in the area.[47]

Buddy Gray may or may not have seen a copy of the letter, but he was outraged by Luce's decision to forward the nomination. "What's the point of having a public board if a bureaucrat can overturn [its] decision?" Gray fumed. After all, he argued inaccurately, a "majority on the state board opposed this district and voted by a 14 to one margin to send the matter back to the neighborhood. We are furious," Gray concluded, "and we're not going to give up."[48]

Indeed, Gray and his allies fought back desperately. First, they appealed to Shull to ignore the nomination because minutes of the state advisory board didn't record the vote sending the matter back to Cincinnati for a solution. This move failed when Luce, at Shull's request, sent her a copy of the minutes, which showed both the motion and the vote on it.[49] Gray and the Over-the-Rhine Community Council then asked Shull to reject the nomination by alleging that city officials had not heeded the advisory board's recommendation to consider the nomination of smaller districts in Over-the-Rhine to the National Register (something already established as a goal by the city administration); and they delivered to her letters protesting Luce's action from organizations in Over-the-Rhine, several labor unions, state representatives Rankin and Mallory, state senator Bowen, and U.S. congressman Thomas Luken (D).[50]

Before the National Register office could review these pleas, the battle over the future of Over-the-Rhine took an unusual turn. On April 6, an assistant to the recently elected governor of Ohio, Richard F. Celeste (D), sent a telegram to the National Register indicating that the governor's office had received "a number of credible complaints" about the procedures followed in the nomination of Over-the-Rhine and requested the return of the nomination for its reconsideration by the governor's office. The National Register office complied and called the intervention by a governor in the nomination process an "infrequent occurrence" that left the matter "up to the state."[51]

While proponents of the nomination, including Cincinnati mayor Thomas Brush (C) and top city administration officials, lobbied the governor[52] to return the nomination to Washington, Gray and his allies finally aired their views on the eligibility of Over-the-Rhine for National Register listing. They asserted that buildings in Over-the-Rhine did not represent German architecture, contended that German Americans had maintained their culture in Cincinnati but had abandoned Over-the-Rhine, and claimed that parking lots, demolitions, and new construction had destroyed the architectural integrity of the proposed historic district, all of which rendered the idea of a physically and culturally cohesive German Over-the-Rhine a "fiction, a racist and ethnically biased myth" that overlooked black and Appalachian cultures. "We would prefer," they added, "that those who pretend to be saviors of our neighborhood would choose instead to support what the neighborhood is trying to build and to respect our right as a people to decide our future."[53]

This assault on the preservationists changed no minds, however. The governor's office concluded that all applicable historic conservation laws and procedures had been followed and returned the nomination to Washington on May 6, 1983.[54] The National Register office promptly listed the nomination, which provoked one last effort to overturn the decision. The Over-the-Rhine Community Council asked the keeper to cancel the listing because 600 residents of Over-the-Rhine had each purchased a share in a building at 1421 Republic Street, thereby creating more Over-the-Rhine property owners opposing the nomination than supporting it.[55]

That did not work either. George Kyle, public affairs officer for the National Park Service, announced that objections to a listing by a majority of property owners in a proposed district had to come *before* the listing. Jerry Rogers of the cultural resources division of the Department of the

Interior confirmed that judgment in a letter to Gray,[56] a letter that finally ended the dispute over the nomination of Over-the-Rhine to the National Register of Historic Places.

But in this last phase of the National Register contest the opponents of the nomination averted total defeat. They not only delayed the decision on historic designation but also secured the passage of a low-income neighborhood housing retention district for the entire area, garnered abundant publicity for their cause, and secured promises from the city government that at least some low-income housing would be preserved in Over-the-Rhine. Now the focus of the fight returned to the question of *how much* low-income housing, a process that took two more years and culminated with the completion and adoption of an Over-the-Rhine plan.

10 Separatists Victorious, 1983–1985

THE end of the National Register controversy shifted the focus in Over-the-Rhine to the planning process but failed to accelerate it. The continued drag on progress toward a plan stemmed in part from the emergence of James Tarbell, an entrepreneurial celebrity in the local entertainment business, as the most adamant and voluble opponent of Buddy Gray's racially and socioeconomically separatist attempt to commit the city to maintaining Over-the-Rhine as a predominantly black and overwhelmingly poor enclave. But Tarbell also framed the case for historic preservation in a new way and a manner characteristic of the most vocal advocates of the cause at this stage of the game.

Tarbell's emergence proved important for several reasons. He appeared at the most critical point in the long debate about the future of Over-the-Rhine, the moment for final decisions about a comprehensive plan for its future. In addition, he now dominated the anti-Gray side of the debate; other historic preservationists faded into the background as if convinced that city council would defer once more to Gray, as it had so often in the past. But Tarbell framed his arguments in a way that facilitated a victory for Gray and the racial and socioeconomic separatists.

Tarbell displayed an open disdain for the "sloppy" poor, the homeless, alcoholic, and other underemployed or unemployable people who made up such a large and visible part of the Over-the-Rhine population. Yet Tarbell, like Gray, refused to make the question of poverty itself a prime civic and political issue and especially a part of the problem in Over-the-Rhine. Tarbell's positions gave the preservationist cause in the 1980s a conservative cast and also reinforced the resolve of those who saw Gray as a charitable humanitarian friend of the homeless rather than as a builder of the second ghetto, a champion of poverty and social and civic fecklessness as life-style choices.

Tarbell proved adept at securing publicity, in part because he, like Gray, struck print and electronic journalists as a quintessential cultural individualist, a person who had "done his own thing" by devising a life style quite different from the middle-class Catholic family into which he had been born.[1] Tarbell, like Gray, wore his hair long and sported a beard. Tarbell, like Gray, moved to Over-the-Rhine in the late 1970s to help the poor and homeless. And Tarbell, like Gray, came out early against the listing of Over-the-Rhine on the National Register of Historic Places because of the fear of gentrification. Tarbell, however, changed his mind, and in so doing emerged as the most striking leader on the integrationist and historic district side after 1983.

Tarbell's family moved from a small Ohio town to Cincinnati in 1946 and settled in the generally affluent neighborhood of Hyde Park. Tarbell grew up there and attended St. Xavier High School in downtown Cincinnati, a few blocks south of Over-the-Rhine. After graduating he secured a job with Jewish Hospital in Cincinnati, then went to Boston, where he worked first in a hospital and then as a commercial fisherman. He returned to Hyde Park in 1967 to run a community youth center (a nongovernmental operation to keep teenagers off the streets), then opened a drug-free nightclub for young rock music fans in a renovated automobile garage in Clifton, a neighborhood close to the University of Cincinnati.

The club soon folded, leaving Tarbell disappointed, broke, and looking for inexpensive housing in a conveniently located and interesting neighborhood. In 1971 he chose Over-the-Rhine, which he remembered from his high school days and which he had revisited in the 1960s

Buddy Gray, September 1985. Courtesy of the *Cincinnati Enquirer.*
Photograph by Michael E. Keating.

to see his sister, one of the many youngsters from Cincinnati's outer-city neighborhoods and suburbs who served as volunteers in the Main Street Bible Center run by the Roman Catholic archdiocese. Tarbell himself tackled social problems in Over-the-Rhine by renovating low-income housing for low-income residents (and his family), and he earned a living by turning a nineteenth-century saloon a few blocks south of Over-the-Rhine into a combination bar-restaurant-nightclub that attracted a young white crowd, people in their late teens to their early forties served by employees who lived in Over-the-Rhine.[2]

Tarbell at first, as he put it, carried "a lot of anger for the landlords, businessmen and politicians who were ripping off the poor." After several years in the low-income housing field, however, he divided the poor into two classes: people who cared, and "sloppy people" who "threw garbage out of windows, played loud music night and day, got drunk in the street, and let small children roam the streets unattended." Now he wanted to save the neighborhood, in part by getting other middle-class people to help him assist the responsible poor who were "doing their part" by paying rent on time, picking up litter in front of their apartments, working instead of relying on welfare, and disciplining their children.[3]

Tarbell also now expressed disdain for those social activists he described as naively sympathetic to the "sloppy people." These kinds of activists, thought Tarbell, made wrong-headed "assumptions about who are the oppressed, and the oppressor," acted as if "they've cornered the market on devotion and self-sacrifice," and so distrusted "the establishment" that they presented "a terrible barrier to getting things done for poor people. What they don't see is that it doesn't make it any better to pat them [the careless poor] on the back and say, 'It's okay, we know you've been exploited.'"[4]

Tarbell's framing of the issues dominated the debate about the proposed comprehensive plan for Over-the-Rhine, and economic and demographic conditions at the time seemed to tip the odds in his favor. Cincinnati, like other American cities, still suffered from a stagnant national economy, high energy prices, capital shortages, and diminishing federal support for low-income housing. These factors not only exacerbated an already serious shortage of safe and sanitary dwelling units for poor and moderate-income people but also inhibited the production of

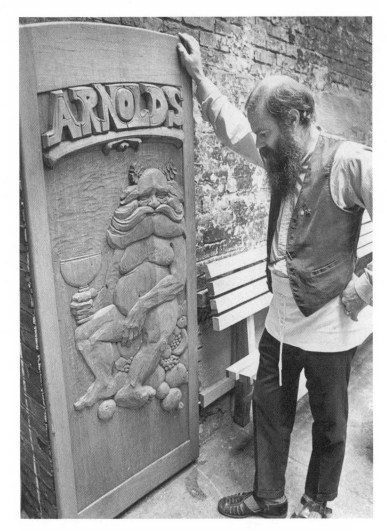

Jim Tarbell, June 1978. Courtesy of the *Cincinnati Enquirer.* Photograph by Dick Swaim.

new and rehabilitated market-rate housing. At the same time, the population of the city continued to drop—by almost 15 percent between 1970 and 1980—and the city government continued to compete with the suburbs and other metropolitan areas for residents and businesses to shore up its shriveling tax base.

These conditions, as in the 1950s and 1960s, threatened to swamp in a sea of deterioration and despair all of the city's neighborhoods and their metropolitan serving institutions (including hospitals, universities, and cultural and other recreational facilities) and helped attract key city administrators in support of historic preservation. These administrators saw National Register districts as one source of funds to subsidize the creation of low- and moderate-income housing. And they backed local historic districts as a means both to control the demolition of low- and moderate-income housing units and to assist in stemming and/or reversing the suburban exodus by preserving features of metropolitan life that made Cincinnati attractive to many prosperous blacks and whites. But the outcome of the Gray/Tarbell struggle over the comprehensive plan for Over-the-Rhine depended on city council,[5] an uncertain element in the planning and historic preservation calculus because its consideration of the neighborhood's nomination to the National Register in the early 1980s had concluded with a decision split evenly on both sides.

Yet council could not act on the question until and unless planning director Hubert Guest put a plan on its agenda, something now high on his list of priorities. In the spring of 1983 Guest launched an effort to wrap up the plan by the end of the year and to include within it an integrationist historic preservation component and a set of development policies he wrote one night during a bout of insomnia while on business in Columbus. Now Guest cleared this scheme with city manager Sylvester Murray and the heads of relevant departments in city hall and informed Murray that he might reject the plan prepared by the Over-the-Rhine Planning Task Force even if the Planning Commission approved it. With that, Guest turned over to the Task Force's consultant his development policies and told the consultant to finish the job within six months.[6]

The consultant followed Guest's orders but also produced a draft of the plan that bore the clear imprint of the residents on the Task Force. It called, for example, for the creation and maintenance of 5,520 low-income housing units and contained another effort to replace the low-income housing retention ordinance, which required periodic review and renewal when applied to a particular neighborhood, with a law that would protect low-income housing on a permanent basis. The proposal, called the Redevelopment Management Strategy, suggested the adoption of an enabling ordinance authorizing the creation of overlay zoning "development districts." Each of these would be provided with strict regulations for new or rehabilitated non-subsidized housing to prevent such projects from having a "negative" effect, such as the involuntary displacement of residents, and the proposal laid out thirty-three "policies" for use by city staff in grading projects, including one that called for the reservation in each project of at least one-half of the dwelling units for persons of low or moderate income.[7]

The Task Force, led by Bonnie Neumeier, tore the plan apart. Neumeier complained that the plan failed to prescribe specific solutions to problems it outlined and pointed out that the consultant deleted an "education overview" prepared by the Task Force. She added that the Task Force had not voted on criteria for defining proposed architectural resource clusters or on the plan's development policies, which, among other deficiencies, devoted too much space and detail to historic districts and too little to low-income housing. She also observed discrepancies between the text and the maps in the zoning recommendations.[8] Neumeier then wrote recommendations for consideration by the Task Force[9] (twenty-two typed pages of text, ten pages of revised land use and zoning maps, and two short attachments) that advanced from an assumption of the normality, legitimacy, and vitality of predominantly low-income neighborhoods, including Over-the-Rhine, and proposed that the physical environment of the whole area should remain cheap and plain as long as the residents liked it that way.

This view appeared at the beginning of the critique in its review of the draft plan's history of Over-the-Rhine, which presented poverty as something to be eliminated. Neumeier said the story would have to be rewritten by the residents as a history that made "more of a positive statement of who we are" and that gave a more upbeat account of housing rehabilitation for the poor since the late 1970s, when Buddy Gray and his allies became important players in the Over-the-Rhine drama. Similarly, Neumeier disliked the plan's use of the term "vagrants," which she called a "slander on our homeless people," and proposed to amend a section on current planning efforts to give residents (rather than former planning commissioner Herb Stevens) the credit for initiating the Planning Task Force.[10]

Neumeier also disliked the "value judgments" in the next section of the draft. She proposed to change a reference to "poorly educated women" into an observation that low levels of education among women typified low-income neighborhoods. She also proposed to explain the difficulties confronting such women, including the absence of equal opportunities for education and jobs and the fact that they often had sole responsibility for raising their children. She defended the desire of Task Force members to place high-density residential land uses near and around warehouses and industries as a practice befitting the mixed land uses of Over-the-Rhine, even though conventional planning wisdom and the draft plan condemned such "spot zoning."[11]

Neumeier then came down hard on the draft plan's "Visual Analysis," lambasting it even as she proposed its deletion. This chapter, said Neumeier, represented only the consultants' point of view, gave a "bleak, depressing view of the community," neglected "people oriented conceptions," and too often cited the "attractiveness" of views of the city as seen from Over-the-Rhine rather than views inside the area. Residents of Over-the-Rhine should decide "what looks good, feels good and is valued and positive and attractive, . . . particularly as it relates to the planning of *our* community," Neumeier said.[12]

The next part of the draft plan, "Architectural Resource Clusters," received even rougher treatment. Neumeier said the consultant and the city's Historic Conservation Office and Planning Commission staff drew up the section without the participation or approval of members of the Task Force, who objected to its goals and objectives and the local historic districts recommended in it. Neumeier wanted this chapter deleted too, but nonetheless wrote a denunciation of both national and local historic districts, said the residents would never even consider local historic districts until all low-income residents in the area had secured housing, and climaxed the assault with a page and a half criticism of specific aspects of the chapter, including its failure to point out "neighborhood efforts" to prevent the demolition of old buildings, such as the passage of the interim development control districts and the neighborhood housing retention ordinances.[13]

Finally, Neumeier proposed to amend extensively part of the last chapter of the draft plan. This section included land use and zoning recommendations as well as neighborhood improvement policies, to which she offered eight pages of proposed changes, including the deletion of all references to "historic" characteristics or districts. She also dismissed the neighborhood improvement strategies as unacceptable because the Task Force had played no part in devising them and because they failed to relate specifically to the plan's emphasis on low-income housing. In addition, the neighborhood improvement strategies offended Neumeier because they seemed likely to attract more prosperous "outsiders" into the area by promising new "infill" housing and "pie-in-the-sky" design ideas, such as "dreams about cobblestone pavements," a "village commons look, and bicycle/pedestrian paths."[14]

The Task Force revised slightly Neumeier's revision of the plan, adopted it in February 1984,[15] and then offered to work out with Murray a compromise version of the draft. This uncharacteristically civil move came not as a gesture of conciliation, but in response to a rumor that Guest would reject the Task Force's handiwork. Murray fielded this request by arranging for talks between Guest and Gray in which Guest managed to wring some concessions from Gray by threatening to walk out of the negotiations. Gray, for example, approved the inclusion of Guest's development policies but at the price of altering the historic preservation proposal to state that such action might be considered in the future. Gray also wanted to eliminate—but finally agreed to relegate to an appendix—a proposal to preserve the architectural "clusters" that could not pass muster as historic districts. But the two reached no agreement on how to zone the area around the Drop-Inn Shelter, which Gray preferred to designate for high-density residential (R-7) and Guest for office use.[16]

After these negotiations the Planning Commission amended the city's housing allocation policy to permit additional low-income units in Over-the-Rhine, and Birdsall and Gray revised the draft plan according to the compromise worked out between the Task Force and city administration representatives. The Task Force took under consideration and approved this version of the plan in September 1984 at its thirty-sixth and, as it turned out, final meeting, one year after Guest's target date for completing the plan.[17] This took time, however, because Task Force members made thirty-four corrections covering errors of fact and omission, typographical mistakes, and out-of-date information in the last revision of the draft plan.[18]

At this point the pace of planning for the future of Over-the-Rhine picked up, but only slightly. Jim Bower, chairman of the Planning Task Force, formally delivered the comprehensive plan—an inch-thick document composed of 190 pages—to the Planning Commission and city manager Murray,[19] who met on February 6, 1985, with a contingent from the Task Force and pledged his support for the Task Force's comprehensive plan. Gray thanked Murray for that, but also registered with him a complaint about Guest's idea of office district zoning around the Drop-Inn Shelter. Gray contended that such zoning would jeopardize the future of the facility in what he depicted as an ideal location "near our people, on the edge of downtown, on the edge of Over-the-Rhine, a couple of blocks away from the nearest bars, and in a section with a small residential population."[20]

By this time, however, Guest had adopted a strategy for dealing with the next step in the planning process that put him in opposition to both the city manager and the Task Force. Guest did not think the Task Force's comprehensive plan would be approved by either the Planning Commission or city council because it, like the Forusz plan of 1975, was too long, too complicated, and loaded with non-essential details, such as the history of the community. As planning director, however, he felt responsible for securing the approval of some kind of plan. So he proposed to give Buddy Gray "everything he wanted," but in a more succinct package.[21]

Guest did not formally reject the comprehensive plan. Instead, he recommended that the Planning Commission accept it, which meant "recognizing that it exists without approving or disapproving it," and then adopt a two-part package prepared by Guest. The first part selected from the comprehensive plan twenty-five goals, six categories of development policies, and twenty-two land use maps for approval as parts of the Coordinated City Plan. The second advocated the preparation of a short urban renewal plan for adoption by the Planning Commission and city council, a document necessary to authorize the city to expend funds to acquire property through eminent domain (if necessary) and to carry out federally subsidized projects in the area.[22]

Guest's report came before the Planning Commission for its initial public hearing in May 1985. It was a long session that opened with a blistering attack on Guest's recommendations by Task Force chairperson Jim Bower, who insisted on the adoption of the Task Force's comprehensive plan in its entirety. So, too, did several other speakers, including former planning director Stevens and Buddy Gray. But James Tarbell, as a representative of the Over-the-Rhine Chamber of Commerce, denounced both the comprehensive plan and the Guest proposal. Tarbell claimed that both lacked balance, discouraged housing renovators and business developers, and contradicted city council's policy of distributing low-income subsidized housing throughout the city. The proposal for giving top priority to low-income housing, he charged, rested on a "ghetto mentality" and amounted to "saying high-income housing should be the top priority of Hyde Park" (one of the city's wealthiest neighborhoods).[23]

The Planning Commission's second hearing on Guest's proposals on May 17 lasted five hours and proved even livelier. Bower again backed the comprehensive plan, a position supported by the testimony of twenty-two others, not counting five people who talked only about "saving" the Drop-Inn Shelter from the threat of office zoning and one person who used the occasion to denounce historic preservation as leading invariably to the involuntary displacement of the poor. The commissioners then listened to the eighteen speakers who opposed the adoption of the comprehensive plan, the last of whom, Tarbell, not only pilloried both the comprehensive plan and the Guest alternative but also called for the appointment of a new Task Force to write a plan capable of commanding a consensus of support.[24]

At this point Murray, who had not attended the first public hearing, spoke out to encourage the Planning Commission and city council to approve the comprehensive plan. He chastised those who called it "the Buddy Gray Plan," which struck Murray as an affront to the many "citizen volunteers" who put so much time and work into the effort. But he also addressed several particular criticisms of the plan, especially the charge that the supporters of 5,520 low-income housing units wanted to create a perpetual slum by excluding upper-income residents. He contended instead that "we want rich and poor people" in Over-the-Rhine, which he described as capable of containing 11,000 housing units, all of which, above 5,520, could be reserved for upper-income people, if necessary by amending the plan.[25]

Murray also attacked those who thought that approval of the plan would prevent the city from spending money on anything except low-income housing. He described the plan as a guideline, "not a Bible," the goals and objectives of which did not subordinate commercial and industrial development to housing, all of which could "receive money at the same time." The plan merely intended to say, insisted Murray, that "where housing is concerned, public moneys will be allocated to meeting the 5,520 low income housing goal as a priority before . . . upper income housing." He closed by warning low-income housing proponents that such housing required federal government aid that was "drying up" to such an extent that "our goals may not be met. Nonetheless," he added, "we should try as genuinely as possible."[26]

Murray in these remarks offered the Planning Commission an easy way out of the argument: mollify the Gray faction by adopting the comprehensive plan and placate the Tarbell faction by persuading it that the plan's top priority could not be fulfilled. The commissioners, however, got into a wrangle. Marion Spencer, city council's representative on the Planning Commission (and the city's first female African American council member), moved the approval of the comprehensive plan, which fell to a tie vote. Commissioner Donald J. Mooney responded by proposing to pursue Guest's urban renewal/Coordinated City Plan approach and to review and perhaps revise his specific recommendations for each. This passed, but the Planning Commission put off working out the details because of "considerable confusion" over what would be considered for transfer into the Coordinated City Plan and what should be considered for insertion into the urban renewal plan.[27]

While Guest and his staff clarified these details Murray conferred privately with the commissioners about the Over-the-Rhine situation. He hoped to patch up the rift between Mooney, Spencer, and himself, which seemed likely after Mooney showed Spencer and Murray the latest version of his scheme. But Murray also lobbied successfully for the insertion of language to make clear the city's dedication to commercial and industrial development in Over-the-Rhine because of his previous commitment of support to the Verdin Bell Company's efforts to rehabilitate a nineteenth-century Catholic church and school complex (St. Paul's) in the Pendleton neighborhood for use as a market for religious goods.[28]

Meanwhile, Mooney made additional efforts to build a consensus for his scheme both on the Planning Commission and among the followers of Gray and Tarbell. First, Mooney, fellow commissioner Estelle Berman, and urban conservator Genevieve Ray went over the goals, objectives, and development policies for transfer from the comprehensive plan to the Coordinated City Plan and drafted amendments and alternative language for consideration by the Planning Commission (they changed the proposed zoning around the Drop-Inn Shelter from office to public or quasi-public). Mooney opened the public hearing on these items by announcing that the Planning Commission had spent eight hours discussing the plan—"a lot of discussion," interjected city manager Murray—after which it agreed to hear no more testimony on the issue.[29]

Mooney and Berman then unveiled their revisions—a dozen minor changes, almost all of which aimed at mollifying Tarbell and his allies but none of which removed low-income housing as the top priority for the future of Over-the-Rhine or eliminated or reduced the target of 5,520 low-income units. The proposals received mixed reviews.[30] Buddy Gray complained that the Planning Commission had watered down the previous version of the plan because of "pressure from the urban gentry that has moved into the neighborhood" but admitted to "a good feeling" because the compromise represented a step forward that put "the city on record for low-income housing." Tarbell, however, denounced the Planning Commission for not going far enough in encouraging commercial projects and residential developments for people of all income levels. He also scoffed at Murray's expression of hope for commercial and industrial development as "a self-serving statement to appease critics" and claimed that the low-income housing priority set the neighborhood on a "tragic" course, which he described as a "serious mistake" both "symbolically" and "practically."[31]

After these remarks the Planning Commission approved Guest's revised package and sent the urban renewal plan[32] to city council's Urban Development Committee. The chair of this committee, former mayor David Mann, made clear very early his support for the document by describing it as a collection of goals and objectives to guide decisions rather than as a legally binding blueprint, and by emphasizing that the plan could be changed if it failed to produce desirable results. Advocates of the plan dominated the subsequent floor discussion, and a dozen of them testified before Buddy Gray took the floor to make a closing plea. He characterized the plan as an assemblage of compromises, some of which he disliked. But he praised the low-income housing features while contending that they would not prevent the moving in of higher-income people. Gray also pointed out that the plan represented merely guidelines rather than commandments, but promised to watch implementation decisions closely and on a case-by-case basis because "we want low income housing protected."[33]

The Urban Development Committee approved the plan and took it in August to city council. Mann there described it as a plan that offered commercial and residential balance, respect for "historic resources," and a chance for persons of all income levels to live in Over-the-Rhine while protecting the right of current poor residents to remain, a point he especially emphasized. He also repeated his depiction of the plan as a statement of "desire and hope" providing guidelines for the actions of city government without restricting private development activities. After hearing statements for and against by Gray and Tarbell, council approved and adopted the Over-the-Rhine urban renewal plan by an eight to one count.[34]

Buddy Gray had called the urban renewal plan a compromise, although he might more accurately have called it a victory for racial and socioeconomic separatism. The chances of its yielding a significant level of mixed-income residential and commercial development looked slim because of the low-income housing priority, because of the existence of the Over-the-Rhine low-income neighborhood housing retention ordinance, and because Gray and his allies expected to (and did) control the implementation of the plan. Gray and his allies, that is, held to and realized a vision of an Over-the-Rhine dominated by an ideologically homogeneous people—themselves and the mostly black, low-income people they had chosen to represent and reside among—who wielded sufficient influence to control economic and residential development and redevelopment, social service and religious agencies, and acceptable life styles in Over-the-Rhine. The Gray faction sought from outsiders not toleration—a term that connoted the patronizing of an inferior—but recognition as equals and as the sole representatives of the poor from a territorial base under its control.

This stance, ironically, put the Gray faction in league on a variety of scores with the experts who wrote the Cincinnati metropolitan plans of 1925 and 1948. The Gray faction, like the metropolitan planners, loved homogeneous neighborhoods. And like the metropolitan planners, Gray and his allies objected to the idea of maximum feasible participation of all those concerned with the area, a form of planning that engaged not only local residents but also city government, its consultants, and non-residents with a stake of some sort in the future of the sub-community as part of the larger social, cultural, and civic entity. Instead, the Gray faction preferred community control, a form of minimal feasible participation that eliminated outsiders as players by reducing them to meeting organizers, clerks, research assistants, and copy editors, and by casting city council members as rubber-stampers.

Yet the Gray faction had not returned entirely to the past. The metropolitan planners had deplored the mixing of commercial, industrial, and residential land uses, a practice warmly endorsed by Gray and his allies. And the metropolitan planners had identified the public interest with the welfare of the metropolis, an interest they put before and above the particular interests of the various groups and parts that comprised the metropolis. The Gray faction (like others after the mid-1950s) did not talk about the metropolis and said little about the welfare of the city, which it implicitly viewed as a collection of liberated local communities free to pursue goals, objectives, and life styles chosen by their residents. To the Gray faction the city did not resemble an organically related system of groups and parts but an agglomeration of self-determining entities, a balkanized collection of mutually suspicious and competitive local enclaves. This conception of the city ruled out compromises that might jeopardize the control of a community by the leaders of its majority (which by definition identified the chosen life style for the neighborhood) and made community control the key element in a politics of separation and isolation for each enclave.

Because of these views, the Gray faction, unlike the metropolitan planners, did not worry about nurturing cooperative and coordinative intergroup relations based on mutual understanding, empathy, and cordial coexistence. Instead, its members—and especially Gray—earned reputations as not only tenacious but also extraordinarily tough partisans who treated opponents with an incivility bordering on intimidation and who impugned the motives and disputed the veracity of anyone professing to care about the poor of Over-the-Rhine while seeking to integrate them with other kinds of individuals.[35] The Gray faction, that is, assumed that the poor residents of Over-the-Rhine had chosen that place and poverty as their life style and for that reason deserved differentiation and segregation from others, poor or otherwise, who might prefer integration and who therefore deserved the right to pursue *their* life styles in some other neighborhood. By this reasoning people who sought to integrate Over-the-Rhine seemed either hypocrites ("they say they believe in choice but seek to integrate this neighborhood to change the life style of its residents and our ideology of separatism for the poor") or liars ("they do not really believe in choice for poor persons and seek to drive them out and take over the neighborhood"). In either case, the integrationists struck the Gray faction as subversives who sought to undermine the integrity of a neighborhood that poor residents and their representatives had selected as their own and started to shape into a no-frills social and physical environment appropriate for their aspirations. And the poor, like the wealthiest of racially and socioeconomically separatist suburbanites, claimed the Gray faction, should continue to enjoy that right of self-definition and self-determination.[36]

Tarbell and his allies did not characterize the plan as a compromise but as a capitulation to racial and socioeconomic separatism. Yet they shared many of the views of Gray and his allies. The Tarbell faction also condoned the mixing of land uses and accepted the assumption that individuals should exercise a choice of life styles and of appropriately arranged and designed neighborhoods in which to pursue them. Tarbell objected to the Over-the-Rhine plan, however, because he thought it inhibited prosperous individuals from exercising their right to choose a neighborhood (and to help arrange and design it) and because it isolated the poor residents of Over-the-Rhine, a step that denied them ready access to alternative life styles and ideologies that they might mimic, adapt, or reject.

Tarbell also assumed that poverty itself denied the poor an effective choice of life style and no choice of residence except in predominantly low-income neighborhoods. Indeed, Tarbell thought of Over-the-Rhine as a ghetto for the underclass, a locality virtually abandoned by the working poor and now populated by the poorest of the poor, most of them demoralized and functionally if not literally illiterate people under the control and manipulation of a well-intentioned but misguided group of soft-hearted, hard-headed, white middle-class drop-outs. Such a ghetto by definition restricted its residents, especially younger people, in their choice of life styles to those varieties pursued by their underclass neighbors or to those represented by Gray and the other white advocates for the homeless who resided in Over-the-Rhine, people who *had*, argued Tarbell, decided to live in the neighborhood, and a faction that insisted on ideological and life-style homogeneity.

Tarbell, that is, objected not so much to the presence of the Gray faction in Over-the-Rhine (at least in principle) as to its efforts to deprive poor people of day-to-day exposure to examples of alternative ways of thinking and living. He objected especially to the Gray faction's willingness to welcome large numbers of demoralized and irredeemable residents (such as "sloppy people" and "drunks," as Tarbell described them) whose behavior would not be tolerated in other neighborhoods, including those of the working poor. Yet neither Tarbell nor the other integrationists talked much about the destiny of the presumably irredeemable poor, including deinstitutionalized mental patients. He and the others eschewed gentrification, a position suggesting that they thought the irredeemables would get along as well if not better after the integration of the neighborhood and would not require additional improvement efforts by government or philanthropists, which would have been futile gestures on behalf of people who could not be changed or change themselves.

The Tarbell faction also differed from Gray and his allies on the question of the planning process. Tarbell favored maximum feasible participation of all parties concerned with the area and thought the plan's defects derived from a defective process. The Tarbell faction contended that the Gray faction abandoned this ideal by dominating the Planning Task Force and by frustrating many business representatives into resigning. As for the city planners, Murray, and city council, Tarbell thought they simply but hypocritically went along with Gray out of deference to "community control."[37]

Yet the city administration and Planning Commission, like Gray, regarded the Over-the-Rhine urban renewal plan as a compromise. Mooney secured at least some rhetorical movement in adding balance to the plan on the issues of residential and commercial development. Murray sent a message to commercial and industrial interests that he retained his commitment to the promotion of such developments and regarded the land use provisions of the urban renewal plan as satisfactory tools with which to get things done in small, targeted areas, the mode of operation he preferred from the beginning. But their sense of the urban renewal plan as a compromise also stemmed from their sharing of assumptions with other participants about individual choice and from their commitment to Tarbell's views about the ideal planning process.

Murray, Guest, and the planning commissioners, that is, felt also that individuals should make choices about their life styles and neighborhoods of residence, the basis on which rested the idea of participatory planning that involved representatives of residents of the area. And they supported a form of participatory planning involving the maximum feasible participation of all parties concerned, the rationale for their view of the active role of representatives of city government in making the final version of the plan. When this process seemed tilted too far in the direction of the residents, Murray and Guest intervened more forcefully in the process. The Planning Commission did the same thing by voting merely to accept rather than to adopt the comprehensive plan and by then amending the work of the planning staff on the entries to the Coordinated City Plan and the provisions of the urban renewal plan.

City council seemed also to regard the plan as a compromise, a stance registered by its approval of the Planning Commission recommendation. This vote in addition endorsed implicitly the validity of the planning process as an exercise involving the maximum feasible participation of all parties concerned. And council in discussing the plan as a guide to balance in the mixture of land uses and people sought to disarm critics by emphasizing that it constituted not a blueprint but a collection of goals, objectives, and recommended policies that might be interpreted loosely during implementation and even, as Mann pointed out, changed if necessary to assure the realization of the promise of balance.

City council in this way seemed to embrace both the idea of the plan as a compromise and the idea of balance (integration) as the ideal policy in the age of individual choice in life styles and neighborhoods. Yet the record in Over-the-Rhine since 1950—including the plan of 1985, which touted balance while making low-income housing, not balance, its top priority—left unclear the meaning of the city's commitment to this and other neighborhoods. Did council intend to designate balance as the appropriate policy for all the neighborhoods of the city? Or did it intend to leave the issue of balance versus homogeneity to the choice of residents of each neighborhood, a policy that might yield the status quo, a city divided into white and black turfs overlain with several havens for the separatist poor, many havens (mostly white ones) for the separatist non-poor, and just a few havens for integrationists—a formula that gave more choice in neighborhood design and arrangement to the separatist non-poor than to the other two groups.

This ambiguity, moreover, stemmed largely from the fact that no one in the Over-the-Rhine planning debate discussed the relationship of various proposals to the public interest defined as the welfare of the city as a whole, a characteristic void in public discourse in the age of autonomous neighborhoods.[38] Such an assessment would surely have condemned the Over-the-Rhine plan of 1985, which seemed likely to sustain the status quo, despite the talk about balance during its adoption by city council. The policy of standing pat, especially under conditions of no white population growth by natural increase or in-migration, seemed more likely to yield a continuation of conditions that in the 1950s prompted the long search for new treatments for the inner city: an expanding black ghetto, a growing black underclass, and racially fixated and fleeing white middle- and upper-income classes. That search soon stalled, and almost no one after the early 1970s focused the Over-the-Rhine debate on poverty as a problem and on socioeconomic and racial residential integration as a way to both mitigate that problem and reduce the corrosive effect of the persisting ghetto on African American morale and interracial relations.

EPILOGUE

Eclipsing the Public Interest

THIS book covers two eras in the history of American cities, each of them characterized by a mode of thinking about urban society that suggested distinctive ways of defining and treating old neighborhoods close to downtown. The first understanding of the city subordinated particular interests to the public interest and defined the latter as the fulfillment of the social mission of the city, that is, the organization of the physical and social environment to promote cosmopolitanism, the sharing of traits among socially determined cultural groups without erasing any group's sense of its distinctive identity. This mode of thought drew a sharp distinction between the central business district and its surrounding "slums" and prompted efforts to eliminate the latter, either by razing and rebuilding or by zoning them for non-residential land uses as the first step toward their gradual absorption into the central business district.

Attempts to implement these treatments yielded varied consequences, including the survival of some white slums, particularly, in this case, Over-the-Rhine. Yet here as elsewhere the slum eradication program thinned out the inner-city population and scattered some of its residents, especially African Americans. Some of these displaced persons left the city, but most of them joined in-migrants from the South to form black enclaves that spilled into Over-the-Rhine and other white neighborhoods farther out, a process that produced the second African American ghetto, heightened interracial tensions, intensified "white flight," and generated resentment among African Americans that sparked a black separatist movement focused on the surviving but dying neighborloods of the first ghetto.

These conditions in the context of the mid-century revolt against the social determinism of culture produced a new understanding of the city that differed fundamentally and dramatically from that of the cosmopolitan epoch. The new understanding subordinated the public interest to individual interests and defined the social mission of the city as the promotion of individual self-fulfillment through self-actualization. Implementation of this mission yielded efforts to organize individuals into self-constructed groups for the purposes of defining their own life styles and cultures and designing physical and social environments compatible with the life style and culture preferred by the dominant self-constructed neighborhood group.

We have called this approach cultural individualism and noted that it unleashed in the 1950s a long contest for control of inner-city residential areas, especially Over-the-Rhine. This contest focused on various proposals for the revitalization of Over-the-Rhine and some other parts of the inner city as chic neighborhoods on the edge of downtown to attract as residents middle- and upper-income persons regardless of ethnicity or race. These proposals prompted tenacious opposition, the leaders of which varied from time to time but included social workers, black racial separatists, urban Appalachian advocates, and white community organizers of the poor and homeless. These varied factions often disagreed about the appropriate treatment for Over-the-Rhine, but they united in opposition to the idea of the racial and class integration of the area on the grounds that such a policy, like slum clearance and redevelopment before it, would drive rents up and poor people out.

This racial and socioeconomically separatist strategy proved an effective means of keeping more prosperous people out of Over-the-Rhine, but it also contributed to the continued shrinking of its population. Low-income advocates, that is, stopped one kind of revitalization program without agreeing on another. Under these circumstances city council waited for the emergence of a common front among the squabbling factions, a stance that prevented it from adopting either an integrationist treatment or applying in Over-the-Rhine the sort of concentrated conservation and rehabilitation schemes that stabilized the populations of the West End and Avondale-Corryville without altering markedly their racial and class makeup.

The most spectacular episode in the fight for control of Over-the-Rhine started in the 1970s and involved a new treatment for inner-city neighborhoods, the use of historic conservation techniques and subsidies both to protect low-income housing and to attract to the neighborhood more prosperous people, regardless of their race and ethnicity. In the course of this conflict Buddy Gray emerged as the dominant voice in Over-the-Rhine. Gray captured control of its Community Council, committed it to the idea of racial and socioeconomic separatism, and played upon city council's commitment to neighborhood autonomy to secure in 1985 a plan for the neighborhood that took as its top priority the protection and enlargement of the neighborhood's stock of low-income housing. James Tarbell, the chief opponent of the plan, warned that it guaranteed the persistence of Over-the-Rhine as a predominantly black enclave of poverty and despair, despite the claims of its city hall defenders that the plan contained nothing to prevent either the development of balance in the racial and class composition of the neighborhood's population or commercial and industrial initiatives.

In the next seven years the plan of 1985 neither produced balance in the residential population nor moved Over-the-Rhine in that direction. Buddy Gray had promised to watch closely the implementation of the plan with the goal of securing 5,520 units of low-income housing before permitting city action on the few balance elements in the plan, including especially the creation of a few historic districts. Gray and his allies kept that promise, and city council followed their lead. In addition, the Gray faction persuaded council to renew the Over-the-Rhine neighborhood housing retention ordinance.

Grumbling about Gray's reign in Over-the-Rhine by Tarbell and other historic preservationists persisted into the 1990s, but no one seriously challenged it until 1992, when Karla Irvine, executive director of Housing Opportunities Made Equal (HOME), called for a reconsideration of the future of the neighborhood. She noted that the adoption of

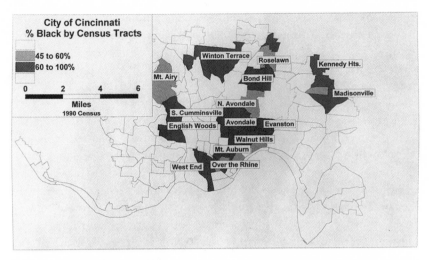

Racial residential segregation by neighborhood. Map by Noel Morgan, courtesy of Housing Opportunities Made Equal. The West End became Cincinnati's first central ghetto during the early twentieth century. Between 1940 and 1960 the city's second central ghetto took shape to the northeast of Over-the-Rhine, and by 1990 it had absorbed all or parts of the neighborhoods of Mt. Auburn, Walnut Hills, Avondale, Bond Hill, and Roselawn. Over-the-Rhine's population turned predominantly black after 1960 and became the link between the first and second central ghettos. The heavily black neighborhoods to the east of the central ghetto spread out from small, nineteenth-century African American enclaves, and most of those to the west from twentieth-century housing projects subsidized by the federal government at the request of the city. Considerable variation exists in the spatial distribution of the races within census tracts containing a black population of 45 to 60 percent, which appear on the map (misleadingly) as uniformly integrated.

the plan of 1985 had not yielded balance in the composition of Over-the-Rhine's population or produced significant commercial and industrial development in the area. She stressed, however, that city government had not only extended the Over-the-Rhine neighborhood housing retention district but also had supported and continued to support the creation of additional low-income housing units in the area.[1] Meanwhile, the African American population of Over-the-Rhine grew steadily, as it had since 1960.

Population and Housing in Over-the-Rhine, 1970–90

	1970	1980	1990
N assisted occupied units	0	1,900	2,500*
% assisted of all occupied units	0	34	60
Total population	16,363	12,355	9,572
% decrease		25	3
Black population	6,783	7,869	6,835
% of total population	42	63	71
N dwelling units	8,515	7,312	5,655
N occupied units	6,658	5,558	4,200*

Source: Housing Opportunities Made Equal, "Over-the-Rhine: A Permanent Ghetto?" typescript, July 1, 1991, p. 3.
*Estimated.

These circumstances bothered Irvine, who contended that Over-the-Rhine stood on the verge of becoming a "permanent low income, one-race ghetto—a stagnant, decaying 'reservation' for the poor at the doorstep to downtown." In support of this view she estimated that the number of government-subsidized low-income housing units in Over-the-Rhine had risen from virtually none in 1970 to 2,500 in 1990 (60 percent of all occupied units in the area), while the population decreased from 16,363 to 9,572 and the black proportion of the population jumped from 42 to 71 percent (see table).[2]

To stem these trends Irvine suggested that city council adopt a new and citywide policy on balance, one that suggested the racial and class integration of some but not all the neighborhoods of the city as a way of preserving choices of neighborhoods for both integrationists and separatists. But Irvine concentrated her fire on Over-the-Rhine and challenged especially the assertion of the Gray faction that the poor there had chosen a life style of poverty and picked that neighborhood as a good place to pursue it. She not only thought some of those people wanted to move up the socioeconomic ladder but also argued that moving to a better neighborhood would make such mobility easier for poor parents and their children. Such people should receive assistance in exercising their

Counties in the Cincinnati metropolitan area. Courtesy of the University of Cincinnati, Institute for Policy Research.

rights of socioeconomic and geographic mobility, Irvine said, both when they opted for residential integration and when they selected residential segregation. To accomplish this she proposed that the city government do three things. First, it should acquiesce in the persistence of some black and white low-income enclaves for those who desired such a life style and said so themselves. Second, it should discourage the expansion of those enclaves by eliminating or limiting the placement of additional subsi-

Black Population by County in the Cincinnati Metropolitan Area, 1990

County	Population	Black Population	% Black
Boone, Ky.	57,589	361	0.6
Butler, Ohio	291,479	13,134	4.5
Campbell, Ky.	83,866	851	1.0
Kenton, Ky.	142,031	4,158	2.9
Clermont, Ohio	150,187	1,291	0.8
Warren, Ohio	113,909	2,415	2.1
Dearborn, Ind.	38,835	252	0.6
Hamilton, Ohio (Cincinnati)	866,228	181,145	20.9

Source: Table prepared by Bill Berger, Housing Opportunities Made Equal.
Note: Blacks living in the city of Cincinnati made up 68 percent (138,110) of all black residents in the metropolitan area, and 38 percent (340,000) of the population of the city.

dized low-income housing in neighborhoods already surfeited with such housing. Third, it should offer a choice of subsidized housing in more prosperous neighborhoods to low-income residents who might like to move out of low-income enclaves and into integrated settings.[3]

This citywide strategy intended to accomplish several things. It pointed to poverty as a continuing and major problem, rather than to homelessness, a symptom of poverty made worse by the deinstitutionalization of mentally ill persons. And it stressed racial residential integration as a way both to mitigate the problem of poverty and to reduce the corrosive effect of the persisting and expanding ghetto on African American morale and interracial relations. Specifically, this approach aimed to encourage both class and racial residential integration in neighborhoods outside the inner city and to facilitate the movement of non-poor whites into Over-the-Rhine and other inner-city neighborhoods of their choice. However, both types of racially integrative moves (poor and black to more prosperous white neighborhoods and more prosperous whites to poor and black neighborhoods) would come as the free choice of individuals in a broad arena and under government regulations that did not prohibit separatist choices by either blacks or whites, rich or poor.[4]

This proposition for the universalization of the right of neighborhood choice represented an attempt to compromise the argument over the future of Over-the-Rhine by altering the rules of the game without violating the culturally individualistic social mission of the city. It endorsed prevailing assumptions about the virtue of the individual pursuit of self-fulfillment by defining a life style, choosing a neighborhood in which to live it, and participating in the design of that neighborhood. It also rested on the idea of maximum feasible participation in decision making of all parties concerned with a problem, including the departments and divisions of city government, neighborhood residents, and outsiders, such as HOME.

But it proposed to modify the past practice of maximum feasible participation by calling on city council to do more than merely approve or disapprove of schemes developed on a neighborhood-by-neighborhood basis. Instead, it conceived of city council as the representative of all the participants and called on it to stand above them as the steadfast guardian of the public interest defined as a city composed of a diverse population living in a mix of heterogeneous and homogeneous localities under a strong central government that guaranteed to all individuals the right to live in a neighborhood of their choice and design, regardless of race, income, or ideology (life-style preference).

Irvine's proposal asked a lot of city council. Could it as a matter of practical politics champion her version of the public interest while retaining the neighborhood-by-neighborhood planning process and adhering to the principle of maximum feasible neighborhood autonomy? The Over-the-Rhine experience suggested that it could not, despite the existence of a housing allocation policy designed to protect the welfare of the whole in ways compatible with Irvine's proposal. The outcome of the Over-the-Rhine planning process suggested instead that council would promote a compromise among participants in neighborhood-by-neighborhood planning that gave the best deal to the most persistent and best organized faction speaking through the neighborhood's community council.

City council in any case did not accept Irvine's proposition. But she had not asked for the impossible. Neighborhood-by-neighborhood planning on the principle of maximum feasible participation might have turned out differently if all the participants had been challenged first to focus on the public interest by defining their vision of the *whole* city as a social and physical environment.[5] They may or may not have agreed on the vision implicit in Irvine's proposal, but they might have created a compromise on the public interest useful in negotiating a broader consensus on a compromise about the future of Over-the-Rhine. Instead, the Over-the-Rhine urban renewal plan of 1985 left the Gray and Tarbell factions locked in bitter hostility that virtually assured the perpetuation of the conflict in the same uncompromisable terms with which it began, an all-out contest for complete control of the territory in the name of the right to individual choice of life style and an appropriately designed social and physical environment in which to live it. In such a contest, city council could only designate one side as the winner and hope that the losers would merely protest their failure as a violation of their human and civil rights instead of taking their case to the courts.[6]

Such a situation carried profoundly anti-political, anti-governmental, and anti-democratic implications, for it left the losers in a state of civic alienation. But it also removed from elected officials the ability to influence significantly the future of Over-the-Rhine (or the outcome of any contested policy) because it undermined the possibility of working out compromises satisfactory to all sides, an ideal realizable only when the claims of disputants can be measured against some greater good, such as the public interest. The Over-the-Rhine story suggests, then, that citizen participation might function more effectively and democratically if the process began with an argument among all parties concerned over their visions of the welfare of the city as a whole, not the welfare of a neighborhood or of other kinds of self-constructed groups. If not, the revolt against social determinism may continue to yield bitter and implacable conflicts just as corrosive of democracy as those feared by the social deterministic planners of cosmopolitanism in the second quarter of the twentieth century.

The revival of the idea of the public interest[7] defined as the welfare of the city as a whole involves an exaltation of our sense of civic identity and the cultivation of our willingness to make sacrifices for the welfare of the whole. This may strike some as naive. Indeed, it may seem impossible in an age of cultural individualism, when few of us would quietly relinquish our liberation, our right to life-style choices. But we need not go that far in our pursuit of civic virtue and the recovery of the idea of the public interest. We need only relax our quest for self-actualization and more deeply engage in the struggle to reinvigorate the human capacity for empathy on which rests the willingness to strike viable compromises.

In this connection it may be useful to remember that our obsession with neighborhood planning without reference to other neighborhoods, the anti-government animus that undergirds and drives that process, and the eclipse of the public interest defined as the welfare of the whole stemmed from our mid-twentieth-century fears of social determinism, totalitarianism, and conformity in the context of World War II and the Cold War, all of which now lie behind us. It may now be easier to nourish and fortify our capacity for empathy and engage ourselves in citywide participatory planning from neighborhood bases on the old-fashioned premise that democratic governments can safely deliver some things better than the private and voluntaristic sectors, especially in an age of cultural individualism that exalts civil rights and liberties as bulwarks against state-sanctioned cultural engineering. As Vaclav Havel recently put it, in today's multicultural world "the truly reliable path to peaceful co-existence and creative cooperation must start from what is at the root of all cultures, and what lies infinitely deeper in human hearts and minds than political opinion, convictions, antipathies or sympathies: it must be rooted in self-transcendence."[8]

This may or may not be easier in Cincinnati today because of the tragic end of the story for Buddy Gray. The conclusion of his long fight came at the hands of Wilbur Worthen, a once homeless African American with a long crime record and history of mental illness whom Gray had befriended and helped, and who lived in one of Gray's rehabbed buildings. On the morning of November 15, 1996, Worthen barged into Gray's office at the Drop-Inn Shelter and killed him with a burst of three bullets from a .357-caliber Magnum revolver.[9]

The killing sparked immediate reactions. It added, of course, to Over-the-Rhine's grim reputation as the city's most dangerous neighborhood, one that in the first eight months of 1996 had recorded 1,452 incidents of murder, rape, and robbery, an increase of 17.2 percent over the same period for 1995.[10] And it provoked rumors from Gray supporters that it was an "assassination" and "hate crime" inspired by a recent anti-Gray pamphlet and phone campaign. However, police could not connect

Mourning Buddy Gray at his Drop-Inn Shelter. Photograph by Jon C. Hughes, © 1996.

Worthen to the campaign effort, just as they could not identify any other motive for his action.[11]

Gray's death prompted an outpouring of eulogies for him as a passionate and persistent friend of the poor,[12] most of which proved misleading, however, because they agreed with Jack Towe's assessment of the meaning of Gray's work. Gray, wrote Towe after the shooting, tried to keep Over-the-Rhine from remaining a slum, a locality that Towe defined in strictly physical and narrow terms. For him a slum consisted of a neighborhood "where buildings are indecent, unsafe and unsanitary."[13] Towe's definition blithely dismissed the grim social, economic, and racial dimensions of inner-city life, the problems they created for residents of Over-the-Rhine and other parts of the city, and the failure of either the public or private sector to offer neighborhood choices to those striving but poor inhabitants of Over-the-Rhine who regarded themselves as involuntary occupants of a dangerous and demoralizing place.

Towe's and Gray's definition of the Over-the-Rhine problem as a housing issue defined the question as a single-focus matter confined to a particular locality. It also rested on cynical assumptions appealing to social conservatives as well as to charitable humanitarians. The focus on bad housing and homelessness presumed both that the poor will always be with us and that the city government should do no more than provide them with decent, safe, and sanitary dwelling units and shelters.

But the social, economic, and racial questions dismissed by Towe and Gray exist and will not go away. Worse still, they will not even command our attention unless we define the Over-the-Rhine problem as a multidimensional issue with ramifications for every neighborhood in the city. Such an approach will not catch on unless we decide to exercise our capacity for self-transcendence, not to escape reality but to generate the empathy required to accommodate cultural individualism while also taking into account the public interest, the welfare of the whole city as an entity with a social mission encompassing the ideals inscribed in the Declaration of Independence and the Constitution of the United States.

This kind of commitment to the public interest was the message embedded in Karla Irvine's eulogy for Buddy Gray. Irvine said she shared some values with Gray but her strategy for Over-the-Rhine "differed like night and day" from his.[14] Irvine wanted to attack the social, economic, and racial as well as the housing dimensions of the Over-the-Rhine problem. And in working to a solution that addressed those questions, she considered both the welfare of the whole and the welfare of individuals and self-constructed groups. From this perspective she concluded that only a citywide policy could improve conditions of life in Over-the-Rhine and make it a safer place for everyone—insiders and outsiders, the homeless, the working poor, and more prosperous individuals who might choose to reside or remain there.

APPENDIX

The Major Housing Goal of the Over-the-Rhine Urban Renewal Plan, 1985

Goal 1: Provide Decent and Diverse Housing Opportunities for All People Who Live in Over-the-Rhine.

Objectives:

1. Expand low-income housing opportunities for existing and displaced Over-the-Rhine residents.

2. Stabilize the base of decent, safe, and sanitary low-income housing at a minimum of 5,520 units.

3. Maintain an equitable distribution of low-income housing units in each sub-area of Over-the-Rhine.

4. Expand assisted housing opportunities for persons of low income.

5. Develop policies to encourage home ownership opportunities for all-income-level citizens in Over-the-Rhine.

6. Housing opportunities should include city-owned property, HUD boarded-up buildings, and incentives for businesses that provide housing above their storefronts.

7. Increase housing equity opportunities for low-income persons through W.D.C.s, nonprofit housing associations, co-ops, home ownership, etc.

8. With city support, develop new and innovative policies and programs for securing low-income housing.

NOTES

Introduction

1. The origins and meaning of the term *Over-the-Rhine* remain obscure. But see Alan I Marcus, *Plague of Strangers: Social Groups and the Origins of City Services in Cincinnati, 1819–1870* (Columbus: Ohio State University Press, 1991), p. 227; and Donald Heinrich Tolzmann, "The Survival of an Ethnic Community: The Cincinnati Germans, 1918 through 1932" (Ph.D. diss., University of Cincinnati, 1983), p. 48 n. 8.

2. Daniel W. Young, *Over-the-Rhine: A Description and History* (Cincinnati: Historic Conservation Office), pp. 18–19.

3. Outsiders worried too. See, e.g., Jeff Shrimpton, "Historic Preservation and Low-Income Housing," *Ohio Preservation* 12 (January–February 1992): 1, 6; and Charles Bolton, "Will Over-the-Rhine Make It Over the Top? Cincinnatians Fight Chronic Erosion of Their Inner-City Neighborhood," *Historic Preservation News,* March/April 1992, p. 10.

4. *Cincinnati Enquirer,* April 17, 1996, B2. The ad listed eight names under soliciting prostitution and seventeen under drug-related offenses.

5. Ibid., June 25, 1996, A1, and June 26, 1996, B1. The Over-the-Rhine Community Council opposed the ordinance as "a police license to harass residents" backed by business owners, while one of the city's leading civil rights lawyers disputed the law's constitutionality. *Cincinnati Enquirer,* September 21, 1996, A10.

6. Richard C. Wade, "Urbanization," in C. Vann Woodward, ed., *The Comparative Approach to American History* (New York: Basic Books, 1968), p. 202; Douglas S. Massey and Nancy A. Denton, *American Apartheid: Segregation and the Making of the Underclass* (Cambridge: Harvard University Press, 1993). For a recent piece on the anger of the black middle class, see George M. Frederickson, "Far from the Promised Land," *New York Review of Books* 43 (April 18, 1996): 16–20; Donald

R. Kinder and Lynn M. Sanders, *Divided by Color: Racial Politics and Democratic Ideals* (Chicago: University of Chicago Press, 1996); Carl T. Rowan, *The Coming Race War in America: A Wake-up Call* (Boston: Little, Brown, 1996).

7. For a different approach to the history of inner-city treatments (and one that omits historic conservation) see Robert Halpern, *Rebuilding the Inner City: A History of Neighborhood Initiatives to Address Poverty in the United States* (New York: Columbia University Press, 1995). The concept of an African American ghetto is a controversial one. By such a ghetto we mean an area containing an involuntary and high concentration of people with varied interests, religions, occupations, incomes, and behavioral and physical traits who share one attribute, their identification by whites as African American based on their skin color.

Prologue

1. Peter M. Harsham, "A Community Portrait: Over-the-Rhine, 1860," *Cincinnati Historical Society Bulletin* 40 (Spring 1982): 63–72; Zane L. Miller, *Boss Cox's Cincinnati: Urban Politics in the Progressive Era* (New York: Oxford University Press, 1968), pp. 29–30.

2. Miller, *Boss Cox's Cincinnati,* p. 11. See also Fannie Hurst, *Back Street* (1930; New York: Pyramid Books, 1974), chap. 1. This novel, which opens with a seduction scene set in turn-of-the-century Over-the-Rhine, became a best-seller that inspired three movie versions (1932, 1941, and 1961) of the story.

3. Henry D. Shapiro, "The Place of Culture and the Problem of Identity," in Alan Batteau, ed., *Appalachia and America: Autonomy and Regional Identity* (Lexington: University Press of Kentucky, 1983), esp. pp. 109–28; Zane L. Miller, "The Rise of the City," *Hayes Historical Journal* 3 (Spring and Fall 1980): 73–83; Zane L. Miller, "Pluralizing America: Walter Prescott Webb, Chicago School Sociology, and Cultural Regionalism," in Robert B. Fairbanks and Kathleen Underwood, eds., *Essays on Sunbelt Cities and Recent Urban America* (College Station: Texas A&M University Press, 1990), pp. 151–65; Rivka Shpak Lissak, *Pluralism and Progressives: Hull House and the New Immigrants, 1890–1919* (Chicago: University of Chicago Press, 1989); Zane L. Miller, "Race-ism and the City: The Young DuBois and the Role of Place in Social Theory," *American Studies* 30 (Fall 1989): 89–102; Hamilton Cravens, "Child Saving in Modern America, 1870s–1990s," in Roberta Woolens, ed., *Children at Risk in America: History, Concepts and Public Policy* (Albany: State University of New York Press, 1993), esp. pp. 3–12; Adna Ferrin Weber, *The Growth of Cities in the Nineteenth Century: A Study in Statistics* (1899; Ithaca, N.Y.: Cornell University Press, 1965), esp. pp. 149–50, 155–83; 368–409.

City planners in this era acted as if a defective group or part affected adversely the functioning of the whole but did not threaten the vitality of all the other groups and parts. This notion of mechanical interdependence led them to devise particular solutions to particular problems rather than to comprehensiveness as defined in the 1920s. See, e.g., Alan I Marcus, "Back to the Present: Historians' Treatment of the City as a Social System during the Reign of the Idea of Community," in Howard Gillette, Jr., and Zane L. Miller, eds., *American Urbanism: A Historiographical Review* (New York: Greenwood Press, 1987), pp. 13–20; Alan I Marcus and Howard P. Segal, *Technology in America: A Brief History* (San Diego: Harcourt Brace Jovanovich, 1989), esp. pp. 180–216, 255–70.

Biological determinism seems also to have characterized thinking about class and gender cultures in the late nineteenth and early twentieth centuries, an issue beyond the ken of this book but one worthy of exploration by urban and planning historians. For the ubiquity of "racialism" in American social sciences and its fading by the 1920s, see Dorothy Ross, *The Origins of American Social Science* (Cambridge: Cambridge University Press, 1991), parts 2–4, esp. pp. 106, 129, 146–47, 154–55, 157–58, 219–56, 319, 442–43. For the definition of race in racialism as "an indivisible essence that included not only biology but also culture, morality, and intelligence," see Peggy Pascoe, "Miscegenation Law, Court Cases, and Ideologies of 'Race' in Twentieth-Century America," *Journal of American History* 83 (June 1996): 48.

4. Daniel H. Burnham and Edward H. Bennett, *Plan of Chicago* (Chicago: Commercial Club, 1908), p. 124.

5. Miller, *Boss Cox's Cincinnati.*

Part One: Introduction

1. On cosmopolitanism in this period, see David A. Hollinger, "Ethnic Diversity, Cosmopolitanism, and the Emergence of the American Liberal Intelligentsia," *American Quarterly* 27 (May 1975): 133–51; Zane L. Miller, "Pluralism, Chicago School Style: Louis Wirth, the Ghetto, the City, and 'Integration,'" *Journal of Urban History* (May 1992): 251–62; and Julian Huxley, "The Education of Primitive Peoples," *Progressive Education* 9 (February 1932): 122.

2. Robert S. Lynd and Helen Merrell Lynd, *Middletown: A Study in American Culture* (New York: Harcourt, Brace, 1929), pp. 478–502; Winfred Ernest Garrison, *Intolerance* (New York: Round Table Press, 1934), esp. pp. 257–70; Robert E. Park, "Succession, An Ecological Concept," *American Sociological Review* 1 (April 1936): 171–79, and "Human Ecology," *American Journal of Sociology* 42 (July 1936): 1–15; M. C. Otto, "Intolerance," in Edwin R. A. Seligman, ed., *Encyclopedia of the Social Sciences* (New York: Macmillan, 1937), pp. 242–45; George G. Galloway and Associates, *Planning for America* (New York: Henry Holt, 1941), esp. pp. vi–vii; Roy Franklin Nichols, *The Disruption of American Democracy* (New York:

Macmillan, 1948), esp. pp. viii–ix, 513–17; David Edgar Lindstrom, *American Rural Life: A Textbook in Sociology* (New York: Ronald Press, 1948), esp. pp. 148–87; Avery Craven, *The Coming of the Civil War* (1942; Chicago: University of Chicago Press, 1966); Kenneth M. Stampp *The Imperiled Union: Essays on the Background of the Civil War* (New York: Oxford University Press, 1980), pp. 199–209; Warren I. Susman, *Culture as History: The Transformation of American Society in the Twentieth Century* (1973; New York: Pantheon, 1984), pp. 99–104, 122–49. See also the primary sources on the "metropolitan mode of thought" in Zane L. Miller, *Suburb: Neighborhood and Community in Forest Park, Ohio, 1935–1976* (Knoxville: University of Tennessee Press, 1981), pp. 248–49. Park, it should be noted, stressed explicitly that human ecology (social determinism) differed from the older plant and animal ecology (biological determinism). On biological determinism and planning, see the prologue.

3. The so-called city and neighborhood planners of the late nineteenth and early twentieth centuries in America did not engage in this kind of planning. See, e.g., Zane L. Miller, "The Role and Concept of Neighborhood in American Cities," in Robert Fisher and Peter Romanofsky, eds., *Community Organization for Urban Social Change: A Historical Perspective* (Westport, Conn.: Greenwood Press, 1981), p. 8–11; Marc A. Weiss, *The Rise of the Community Builders: The American Real Estate Industry and Urban Land Planning* (New York: Columbia University Press, 1987), esp. pp. 53–78; Patricia Mooney Melvin, *The Organic City: Urban Definition and Neighborhood Organization, 1880–1920* (Lexington: University Press of Kentucky, 1987); William H. Wilson, *The City Beautiful Movement* (Baltimore: Johns Hopkins University Press, 1988), esp. pp. 78, 80–82, 84–86, 88, 89, 91–93, 286–90; Stanley Schultz, *Constructing Urban Culture: American Cities and City Planning, 1800–1920* (Philadelphia: Temple University Press, 1989), esp. pp. 213–17; Mansel G. Blackford, *The Lost Dream: Businessmen and City Planning on the Pacific Coast, 1890–1920* (Columbus: Ohio State University Press, 1993); Stanley Buder, *Visionaries and Planners: The Garden City Movement and the Modern Community* (New York: Oxford University Press, 1990), esp. pp. 71–73, 76, 96, 157–65. The standard survey remains Mel Scott, *American City Planning since 1890* (Berkeley: University of California Press, 1971).

4. Edward A. Filene, *The Way Out: A Forecast of Coming Changes in American Business and Industry* (Garden City, N.Y.: Doubleday, Page, 1924), esp. pp. 51, 53–54, 60, 96–104, 110–11, 160–62, 226–31, 234–35, 284–306; Robert A. Walker, *The Planning Function in Urban Government* (Chicago: University of Chicago Press, 1941), pp. 140–43; Seymour Freedgood, "New Strength in City Hall," in William H. Whyte, ed., *The Exploding Metropolis* (1957; Berkeley: University of California Press, 1993), esp. pp. 87–93; Ralph A. Straetz, *PR Politics in Cincinnati: Thirty-Two Years of Proportional Representation* (New York: New York University Press, 1958);

Barry D. Karl, *Charles E. Merriam and the Study of Politics* (Chicago: University of Chicago Press, 1974), esp. pp. 118ff.; Kathleen L. Barber, *Proportional Representation and Election Reform in Ohio* (Columbus: Ohio State University Press, 1995).

Chapter 1

1. See Robert E. Park, Ernest W. Burgess, and Roderick McKenzie, eds., *The City* (Chicago: University of Chicago Press, 1925); and Ernest W. Burgess, ed., *The Urban Community: Selected Papers from the Proceedings of the American Sociological Society* (Chicago: University of Chicago Press, 1926).

2. Robert E. Park, "Community Organization and Juvenile Delinquency," pp. 115–16, 119ff., and Ernest W. Burgess, "Can Neighborhood Work Have a Scientific Basis?" pp. 144–55, esp. pp. 146–47 and 153–55, in Park et al., *The City*.

3. Wirth first laid out these notions in *The Ghetto* (Chicago: University of Chicago Press, 1928). Also see Zane L. Miller, "Pluralism, Chicago School Style: Louis Wirth, the Ghetto, the City, and 'Integration,' " *Journal of Urban History* 18 (May 1992): 251–79; and Robert E. Park, "Magic, Mentality, and City Life," in Park et al., *The City*, pp. 123–44.

4. The Chicago school sociologists suggested these political tendencies in the 1920s without discussing them explicitly. Later, however, Wirth articulated them in "Urbanism as a Way of Life," *American Journal of Sociology* 44 (July 1938): 1–24.

5. Park, "Community Organization," p. 109. See also James Ford, *Slums and Housing with Special Reference to New York City*, vol. 1 (Cambridge: Harvard University Press, 1936), "What Is a Slum?" pp. 3–14.

6. Andrea Tuttle Kornbluh, " 'The Bowl of Promise': Civic Culture, Cultural Pluralism, and Social Welfare Work," in Henry D. Shapiro and Jonathan D. Sarna, eds., *Ethnic Diversity and Civic Identity: Patterns of Conflict and Cohesion in Cincinnati since 1820* (Urbana: University of Illinois Press, 1992), pp. 180–201.

7. Robert A. Burnham, "The Cincinnati Charter Revolt of 1924: Creating City Government for a Pluralistic Society," in Shapiro and Sarna, *Ethnic Diversity*, pp. 202–24. The new system did not eliminate two-party politics. Instead, reform Republicans, regular and reform Democrats, and the independents and "radicals" who created the new charter organized the Charter Committee (a political party, in fact), which they portrayed as a pluralistic political and civic association dedicated to the welfare of the city as a whole. From the mid-1920s into the 1950s the Charterites' opposition came from the Republicans, who reorganized themselves on pluralistic principles, touted the GOP as the best representative of the welfare of the city as a whole, and accepted all the features of the new city charter except PR, which they tried frequently but not successfully (until 1957) to eliminate on the grounds that ward representation could more accurately reflect the

pluralistic nature of the city. Both parties, moreover, engaged in ethnic, racial, religious, gender, and class balancing of slates. See Zane L. Miller and Bruce Tucker, "The New Urban Politics: Planning and Development in Cincinnati, 1954–1968," in Richard M. Bernard, ed., *Snowbelt Cities: Metropolitan Politics in the Northeast and Midwest since World War II* (Bloomington: University of Indiana Press, 1990), pp. 91–93; and Zane L. Miller, "Corruption Ain't What It Used to Be: City Politics, Ethics, and the Public Welfare," *Queen City Heritage* (Summer 1991): 21–29.

8. On the comprehensive planning movement in Cincinnati, see Robert B. Fairbanks, *Making Better Citizens: Housing Reform and the Community Development Strategy in Cincinnati, 1890–1960* (Urbana: University of Illinois Press, 1988), pp. 41–43; and Andrea T. Kornbluh, "The Cultivation of Public Opinion: The Women's City Club of Cincinnati, 1915–1925" (M.A. thesis, University of Cincinnati, 1983), pp. 51–79.

Comprehensive planners and housing reformers worked hand in glove in Cincinnati. This leads one to suspect that the secondary literature, which has tended to focus on national professional organizations rather than on people on the line in particular cities, has exaggerated the differences between the planners and the "housers."

9. For Segoe's account of his employment by TAC and his work in Cincinnati in the 1920s, see Sydney H. Williams, "The Recollections of Ladislas Segoe," in Donald A. Krueckeberg, ed., *The American Planner: Biographies and Recollections* (New York: Methuen, 1983), pp. 301–17.

10. Technical Advisory Corporation, "Program for a City Plan for Cincinnati, Ohio," March 1922, typescript, pp. 2, 18, 20–21, 26–30, 183–84. The report noted that the city's population rose from 363,591 to 401,207 between 1910 and 1920. The metropolitan population stood at 707,581 in 1920.

11. Ibid., pp. 158–59.

12. Ibid., pp. 11–13, 21–22, 27–31, 141–42, 149. The report called specifically for the creation of local civic centers containing churches, firehouses, branch libraries, police stations, hospitals, and other public buildings as "the hubs of the respective [residential] communities" (p. 141).

13. Cincinnati City Planning Commission [hereafter cited as CPC], *Official Plan of the City of Cincinnati* (1925), pp. 8, 17, 52, 210–11.

14. On the ruralness and southernness of native migrants to the city, see ibid., p. 24.

15. Ibid., pp. 50–51.

16. For the four previous proposals see Technical Advisory Corporation, "Program for a City Plan," p. 132.

17. CPC, *Official Plan,* pp. 199–207.

18. TAC, "Program for a City Plan," CPC, *Official Plan,* p. 202.

19. See, e.g., CPC, *Official Plan,* pp. 7, 8, 10, 25, 38, 42, 46, 57, 69, 85, 98, 130, 144, 146, 150–51, 159, 161, 163, 167, 168, 170–71, 174–75, 177, 203, 206, 209, 215, 219, 220–21, 225, 226.

20. Ibid., pp. 16, 213–16, 225–26. The plan also urged the state legislature to authorize municipalities to control the design of structures.

21. Ibid., pp. 171, 190–91, 212.

22. Ibid., pp. 50–51.

23. Ibid., pp. 52–53, chaps. 2, 4, 7.

24. Ibid., pp. 50–53. In this section the plan noted that the Model Homes Company, a philanthropic enterprise, was remodeling and converting abandoned buildings such as the old Good Samaritan Hospital into housing, and recommended other undertakings of this sort. Ibid., pp. 51–55.

25. This and what follows, unless indicated otherwise, draws from Fairbanks, *Making Better Citizens,* chaps. 5–9; and from Robert B. Fairbanks and Zane L. Miller, "The Martial Metropolis: Housing, Planning, and Race in Cincinnati, 1940–1955," in Robert W. Lotchin, ed., *The Martial Metropolis: U.S. Cities in War and Peace* (New York: Praeger, 1984), pp. 200–204.

26. Kenneth T. Jackson, *The Crabgrass Frontier: The Suburbanization of the United States* (New York: Oxford University Press, 1985), pp. 195–215; Fairbanks, *Making Better Citizens,* pp. 143–44; Charles Casey-Leininger, "Making the Second Ghetto in Cincinnati, Avondale, 1925–1970" (M.A. thesis, University of Cincinnati, 1989), p. 81.

27. Urban Land Institute, *Proposals for Downtown Cincinnati: A Digest of the Report . . . by Walter S. Schmidt . . .* (Chicago: Urban Land Institute, January 1941), esp. pp. 3, 8, 10–13.

28. Fairbanks, *Making Better Citizens,* p. 157.

29. For an account of Bettman's role in the movement for a new master plan, see Robert A. Burnham, " 'Pulling Together' for Pluralism: Politics, Planning and Government in Cincinnati, 1924–1959" (Ph.D. diss., University of Cincinnati, 1990), pp. 191–200. Bettman knew about growing opposition in the 1940s to master planning by expert consultants among critics who advocated the elimination of independent planning commissions and more intense involvement of private citizens and organizations in the day-to-day operations of a planning bureaucracy directly responsible to the executive branch of city government. But he felt that popular participation in each stage of the planning process would impinge upon the quality of the plan and undermine confidence in the planning profession. And he continued to defend the independent planning commission

as an indispensable guardian of the master plan's vision of the welfare of the city as a whole in what he still viewed as a pluralistic polity of socially determined cultural groups. See Robert A. Walker, *The Planning Function in Urban Government* (Chicago: University of Chicago Press, 1941); Philip J. Funigiello, *The Challenge to Urban Liberalism: Federal-City Relations during World War II* (Knoxville: University of Tennessee Press, 1978), pp. 165–67.

30. Fairbanks and Miller, "The Martial Metropolis," p. 202. Leaders of Cincinnati's business elite agreed to take care of returning veterans by promoting private economic development efforts and public works projects after the war, which they felt had mitigated the depression by artificially stimulating the economy. They took this stance under the prodding of the Committee for Economic Development, a national coalition of businesspeople established in 1942 under the leadership of Paul G. Hoffman to encourage planning to forestall a postwar depression by providing "plenty of work for the soldiers when they come home." See Karl Schriftgiesser, *Business Comes of Age: The Story of the Committee for Economic Development and Its Impact on the Economic Policies of the United States, 1942–1960* (New York: Harper & Brothers, 1960), esp. pp. 37–38; Fairbanks and Miller, "The Martial Metropolis," pp. 201–2. The standard accounts of planning and housing activities during and after World War II, including those about sunbelt cities, overlook the role of the Committee for Economic Development, which organized 2,497 local CEDs in every state before 1945.

31. Fairbanks, *Making Better Citizens*, p. 159.

Chapter 2

1. Cincinnati City Planning Commission [hereafter cited as CPC], *Cincinnati Metropolitan Master Plan and the Official City Plan* (1948), pp. 4, 26, 74, 85–86. The Planning Commission noted that the plan had been prepared with the participation of officials of every governmental unit in the area, and with the advice of civic-minded individuals, who often expressed themselves through organized groups, especially the Cincinnati Citizens Development Committee, "which was organized expressly to represent the public, to inform it regarding the Commission's proposals and to co-operate with the Commission in the formulation of the Plan" (p. 4).

2. CPC, *The Population of the Cincinnati Metropolitan Area* (1945), esp. pp. 1–6, 19, 46, 55–57, 72–78, 85–93. The planning commissioners thought their plans would yield more people over thirty years in the metropolitan area (787,044 in 1940 to 872,497 in 1970), in Hamilton County (from 621,987 to 682,945), and the city of Cincinnati (from 455,610 to 474,319), but they noted and worried about not only the continuing decline of the basin population (7 percent between

1930 and 1940, from 127,089 to 118,069), but also another startling phenomenon, a decline in the population of the census tracts immediately surrounding the basin. The planners argued that the black population, unlike the white, had not decentralized significantly, and they observed but did not treat as problematic the continued concentration of blacks in the basin's West End. The planners also noted the area's insignificant foreign-born population (5.7 percent in the city and 4.4 percent in the metropolitan area) and questioned the conventional idea that Cincinnati had received in the 1930s a large number of rural migrants from the southern Appalachian region. The planners pointed to the low rate of white migration from the South and stressed that a large percentage of in-migrants from Kentucky, the source of most of the white migration to Cincinnati in the 1930s, had moved from towns and cities, especially those just across the Ohio River within the Cincinnati metropolitan area.

3. CPC, *Plan of 1948*, pp. 11, 27–34, fig. 17; CPC, *Residential Areas: An Analysis of Land Requirements for Residential Development, 1945 to 1970* (1946), fig. 2.

4. CPC, *Communities: A Study of Community and Neighborhood Development* (1947), pp. 2–6.

5. Ibid., pp. 6, 21–22.

6. Ibid., pp. 21–22.

7. Ibid., p. 9.

8. CPC, *Residential Areas*, pp. 17–18.

9. Ibid., p. 18.

10. Ibid., pp. 42–50.

11. Ibid., pp. 76–78.

12. Ibid., pp. 13–14, 54; CPC, *Plan of 1948*, fig. 10.

13. CPC, *Residential Areas*, p. 48.

14. Ibid.

15. Ibid., p. 49.

16. See Robert B. Fairbanks, *Making Better Citizens: Housing Reform and the Community Development Strategy in Cincinnati, 1890–1960* (Urbana: University of Illinois Press, 1988), p. 172. The standard study of the federal interregional highway act is Mark H. Rose, *Interstate: Express Highway Politics, 1939–1989* (Knoxville: University of Tennessee Press, 1979; rev. 1990).

17. CPC, Minutes, vol. 17, February 19, 1951, pp. 16–17, 169.

18. Mayor's Friendly Relations Committee, Board Minutes, September 3, 1951, pp. 2–4, Urban Studies Collection, University of Cincinnati Libraries.

19. Fairbanks, *Making Better Citizens*, pp. 169–70, 171.

20. Ibid., pp. 171–74, 275 n. 98; Mayor's Friendly Relations Committee, Board Minutes, June 10, 1954, pp. 1–3.

21. Zane L. Miller, *Suburb: Neighborhood and Community in Forest Park, Ohio,*

1935–1976 (Knoxville: University of Tennessee Press, 1981), pp. 19–22, 39–42; Mayor's Friendly Relations Committee, Board Minutes, April 15, 1954, p. 2.

22. CPC Staff, "Review of Urban Renewal Project Selection," 1960, typescript, pp. 4–5, Department of City Planning; Charles F. Casey-Leininger, "Making the Second Ghetto in Cincinnati: Avondale, 1925–1970," in Henry Louis Taylor, Jr., ed., *Race and the City: Work, Community, and Protest in Cincinnati, 1820–1970* (Urbana: University of Illinois Press, 1993), pp. 232–57.

23. *Cincinnati Enquirer*, August 24, 1956, 1; Office of the City Manager, *Workable Program for Urban Renewal: Recertification Request No. 2* (May 1957), p. 13.

24. Office of the City Manager, *Workable Program for Urban Renewal: Recertification Request No. 3* (1958), p. 12; Herbert S. Stevens, Memorandum to the City Planning Commission, September 11, 1958, CPC Papers, box 9, Local Government Records Collection, University of Cincinnati Libraries; CPC, Minutes, vol. 24, July 27, 1959, p. 91.

25. CPC, Minutes, vol. 23, November 10, 1958, pp. 118–19, November 24, p. 125; vol. 24, January 5, 1959, pp. 2–3.

26. Charles F. Casey-Leininger, "Park Town Cooperative Homes, Urban Redevelopment, and the Search for Residential Integration in Cincinnati, 1955–1965," *Queen City Heritage* 52 (Fall 1994): 36–52.

Part Two: Introduction

1. Dorothy Ross, "Grand Narrative in American Historical Writing: From Romance to Uncertainty," *American Historical Review* 100 (June 1995): 659–60; Alan I Marcus, *Cancer from Beef: DES, Federal Food Regulation, and Consumer Confidence* (Baltimore: Johns Hopkins University Press, 1994); Joanne Meyerowitz, ed., *Not June Cleaver: Women and Gender in Postwar America, 1945–1960* (Philadelphia: Temple University Press, 1994); Douglas Tallack, *Twentieth-Century America: The Intellectual and Cultural Context* (New York: Longman, 1991), esp. p. xv and chap. 6; Alan Brinkley, *The End of Reform: New Deal Liberalism in Recession and War* (New York: Vintage Books, 1996), esp. pp. 266–67, particularly the references to problems insoluble by governmental action. The fear of a "soft" totalitarianism was not a peculiarly American phenomenon. See, e.g., Arjun Appadurai and Carol A. Breckenridge, "Public Modernity in India," in Carol A. Breckenridge, ed., *Consuming Modernity: Public Culture in a South Asian World* (Minneapolis: University of Minnesota Press, 1995), pp. 1–5.

2. Arthur M. Schlesinger, Jr., *The Vital Center: The Politics of Freedom* (Boston: Houghton Mifflin, 1949), p. ix. See also Friedrich A. Hayek, *The Road to Serfdom* (Chicago: University of Chicago Press, 1949), esp. pp. 210–12; the list of books in Zane L. Miller, *Suburb: Neighborhood and Community in Forest Park, Ohio, 1935–*

1976 (Knoxville: University of Tennessee Press, 1981), pp. 250–52; David Riesman, *The Lonely Crowd: A Study of the Changing American Character* (New Haven: Yale University Press, 1950); Theodore W. Adorno et al., *The Authoritarian Personality* (New York: Harper and Row, 1950); Ralph Ellison, *Invisible Man* (New York: Random House, 1952); Sloan Wilson, *The Man in the Gray Flannel Suit* (New York: Simon and Schuster, 1955); and Daniel Bell, ed., *The Radical Right* (1955; New York: Doubleday, 1963); and, more recently, Anthony Giddens, *The Transformation of Intimacy: Sexuality, Love and Eroticism in Modern Societies* (Stanford: Stanford University Press, 1992), esp. p. 30.

3. On the rise of interest in self-fulfillment as self-actualization, see Muzafer Sherif, "Self-Concept," in David L. Stills, ed., *International Encyclopedia of Social Sciences* (New York: Macmillan, 1968), vol. 14, p. 150; R. H. Stensrud, "Self-Actualization," and R. C. Wylie, "Self-Concept," in Raymond J. Corsini, ed., *Encyclopedia of Psychology* (New York: John Wiley and Sons, 1994), vol. 3, pp. 359–60. For a description and commentary on the pervasiveness since 1950 of this "mutable sense of identity" (Robert Jay Lifton called it "the protean self") in American life, see Michiko Kakutani, "An Era When Fluidity Has Replaced Maturity," *New York Times*, March 20, 1995, B1. For analyses of some other consequences of the revolt against determinism that date its inception later than we do, see Terrence J. McDonald, ed., *The Historic Turn in the Human Sciences* (Ann Arbor: University of Michigan Press, 1996). For a view closer to ours, see David A. Hollinger, *Science, Jews, and Secular Culture: Studies in Mid-Twentieth Century American Intellectual History* (Princeton: Princeton University Press, 1996), esp. chaps. 5 and 8.

4. To our knowledge no one else has attempted a history of treatments of slums and the inner city (or anything else) since 1920 in the context of the rise in the 1920s of socially determined cultural group determinism and its rejection after 1950 in favor of cultural individualism. But see Stanley Buder, *Visionaries and Planners: The Garden City Movement and the Modern City* (New York: Oxford University Press, 1990), pp. 205–9, 210–16; and Hamilton Cravens, *The Triumph of Evolution: Scientists and the Hereditary-Environment Controversy, 1900–1941* (Philadelphia: University of Pennsylvania Press, 1978), pp. 191–92. The same shift took place in American popular music, as, e.g., the "cooperation, teamwork, and enforced civility" of the big bands of the 1930s and early 1940s that gave way after 1945 to "an explosion of individual voices." Stephen Holden, "Wartime Dreams Revisited," *New York Times*, July 23, 1995, Arts and Leisure, p. 30. The most influential city planning advice based on the new mode of thought remains Jane Jacobs, *The Death and Life of Great American Cities* (New York: Random House, 1961), which consists of ideas hatched in the 1950s. See also the "theoretical" planning literature listed in Thomas H. Jenkins, "The 1960s—A Watershed in

Urban Planning and Renewal," in Zane L. Miller and Thomas H. Jenkins, eds., *The Planning Partnership: Participants' Views of Urban Renewal* (Beverly Hills: Sage, 1982), pp. 47–50.

5. Robert Fisher, *Let the People Decide: Neighborhood Organizing in America* (Boston: Twayne, 1984); John Clayton Thomas, *Between Citizen and City: Neighborhood Organization and Urban Politics in Cincinnati* (Lawrence: University Press of Kansas, 1986).

Chapter 3

1. City hall analysts estimated that about one-fourth of the city's population (133,000 people) would be affected by the clearing and redevelopment of all the inner-city slums, that it would cost the city as much as $1 million, and that small projects in the central business district and central riverfront might be undertaken with "very little or no relocation." See Cincinnati City Planning Commission [hereafter cited as CPC] Staff, "Review of Urban Renewal Project Selection," 1960, typescript, pp. 9–12, 21–22, Department of City Planning.

2. Charles F. Casey-Leininger, "Creating Democracy in Housing: Civil Rights and Housing Policy in Cincinnati, 1945–1980," (Ph.D. diss., University of Cincinnati, 1993), chaps. 2 and 3, and, for a longer account of the Avondale-Corryville project, chap. 4.

3. CPC, *Residential Areas: An Analysis of Land Requirements for Residential Development, 1945 to 1970* (1946), pp. 46–48.

4. U.S. Code, Congressional and Administrative News, 83rd Congress, 2nd sess., 1954, vol. 1, Laws, Messages, Committees, Housing Act of 1954, esp. pp. 715–18, 725–26.

5. Cincinnati Urban Renewal Division, *A Workable Program for Urban Renewal* (Office of the City Manager, May 1955), pp. 3–4, 24.

6. Ibid., pp. 32–36.

7. Cincinnati Department of Urban Renewal, "A Preliminary Report to City Council on the Undertaking of Surveys and Plans for Renewal Area #3," June 13, 1956, revised September 7, typescript, pp. 1, 4–5, Municipal Reverence Library; Casey-Leininger, "Creating Democracy," pp. 141–47, 151–55, 167. The Avondale-Corryville urban renewal plan began with the acknowledgment that it deviated from the plan of 1948, which indicated that rehabilitation could shore up a neighborhood for fifteen years, "after which time slum clearance and redevelopment would be necessary." But "current thinking does not share this view," the Avondale-Corryville plan asserted, for the cost of the rehabilitation treatment could not be justified if, "in such a short period of time, redevelopment were inevitable." As a consequence, the Avondale-Corryville plan prescribed

techniques for "lasting restoration and stability far beyond the scope of the treatment and expected results envisioned by the Master Plan" of 1948. CPC (and Department of Urban Renewal), *Avondale-Corryville General Neighborhood Renewal
Plan* (December 1960), pp. 1–2.

    8. Ibid., pp. 4–7.

    9. Ibid., pp. 7–8.

    10. Ibid., p. 8 .

    11. Ibid., pp. 9–10.

    12. Ibid., pp. 11–12, 13–14. The Planning Commission institutionalized co-
ordinative planning in the late 1970s as a system for keeping track of goals, objectives, policies, and physical plans drawn from plans and programs developed by
all agencies of city government and neighborhood plans and programs. See CPC,
Coordinated City Plan and Process: Policy Paper (February 1977); CPC, *Coordinated
City Plan, Vol. 1: Strategies for Physical Development* (1980); CPC, *Coordinated City
Plan, Vol. 2: Strategies for Comprehensive Land Use* (1980).

    13. Martha S. Reynolds, "The City, Suburbs, and the Establishment of Clif-
ton Town Meeting, 1961–1964," *Cincinnati Historical Society Bulletin* 38 (Spring
1980): 9–12; John Clayton Thomas, *Between Citizen and City: Neighborhood Organizations and Urban Politics in Cincinnati* (Lawrence: University Press of Kansas,
1986), p. 28. City officials while working out the Avondale-Corryville urban renewal plan encouraged the residents of Clifton and North Avondale, neighborhoods with very different histories and not scheduled for urban renewal, to
create civic associations to work with the Planning Commission in devising conservation plans and programs to foster their development as stable neighborhoods with a character peculiar to each.

    14. CPC, Minutes, vol. 29, November 15, 1963, p. 154.

    15. CPC Staff, *Cincinnati Central Business District Space Use Study: A Summary*
(August 1956; rev. June 1957), front matter, n.p.

    16. Ibid., unpaginated map labeled "The Central Business District and Its
Sub-Areas," dated 1956.

    17. Ibid., pp. 5, 8, 9.

    18. CPC, *Central Business District Plan: Part Two, Land Use and Building
Groups* (1957).

    19. For more on the new vision of downtown and the two-shift concept, see
Geoffrey Giglierano and Zane L. Miller, "Downtown Housing: Changing Plans
and Perspectives, 1948–1980," *Cincinnati Historical Society Bulletin* 40 (Fall 1982):
167–90.

    20. CPC, *Business District Plan,* pp. 9, 43.

    21. Jana C. Morford, "Preserving a 'Special Place': The Lytle Park Neighbor-
hood, 1948–1976," *Queen City Heritage* 44 (Fall 1986): 3–22.

22. Ibid., pp. 7, 21 n. 32; *Charter of the City of Cincinnati* (Cincinnati: Webster W. Posey, Clerk of Council, 1983), pp. 18–20, esp. p. 19; CPC, *Inventory and Appraisal of Historic Sites, Buildings and Areas* (November 1960), p. 1.

23. CPC, *Inventory and Appraisal*, pp. 1, 5, 6, 15, 73, 95, figs. 1–3.

24. Jonathan Barnett, "A New Planning Process with Built-In Political Support," *Architectural Record* 139 (May 1966): 142–45; Archibald Rogers et al., *The Plan for Downtown Cincinnati: Report on the Plan for the Central Business District, Cincinnati, Ohio* (City of Cincinnati, December 1964), pp. 8–9, 45.

25. CPC, *Central Business District Urban Design Plan* (1964), p. 7.

26. Ibid., pp. 6, 7, 29.

27. Ibid., pp. 43, 110. Uptown already had one institution of higher education, the Ohio Mechanics Institute, but its programs catered to younger people seeking advanced training in various vocational areas, not adults in the managerial class or retirees.

28. A survey of opinion on proposals in 1941 for Cincinnati's downtown noted an agreement on "the good planning principle to so zone central business districts to provide for a segregation of office buildings, amusements, women's shopping areas, etc." Walter S. Schmidt, *Proposals for Downtown Cincinnati: A Digest of the Report Submitted by Walter S. Schmidt to the Urban Land Institute* (Chicago: Urban Land Institute, January 1, 1941), p. 8. The designation of Over-the-Rhine as part of the Downtown Fringe did not prevent the city, in the mid-1960s, from widening Liberty Street to improve traffic flow between I-75 and I-71, an improvement that destroyed 194 buildings. S.v. "Liberty Street," index to the Planning Commission minutes; and *Cincinnati Enquirer*, July 17, 1997, B16.

Chapter 4

1. See, e.g., Cincinnati Better Housing League, *Tenement Housing Survey* (1921), which delineated four different housing sections in the basin according to the Housing League's view of the given characteristics of each section's inhabitants. The new assumptions had significant implications for all post-1950 efforts to reconstruct metropolitan areas, including central business district and suburban planning. See Geoffrey Giglierano and Zane L. Miller, "Downtown Housing: Changing Plans and Perspectives, 1948–1980," *Cincinnati Historical Society Bulletin* 40 (Fall 1982): 167–90; and Zane L. Miller, *Suburb: Neighborhood and Community in Forest Park, Ohio, 1935–1976* (Knoxville: University of Tennessee Press, 1981), pp. xxiv–xxvi. On the historical study of neighborhoods and community organization, see Patricia Mooney Melvin, "Changing Contexts: Neighborhood Definition and Neighborhood Organization," *American Quarterly* 37 (1985): 357–67.

2. Council on Social Agencies, *Cincinnati Report* (1952). The literature on

the origins of community action neglects the diversity of those origins by focusing on such programs as Mobilization for Youth, the experimental delinquency program in New York City, and Columbia University social work professors Richard Cloward and Lloyd Ohlin's *Delinquency and Opportunity: A Theory of Delinquent Gangs* (New York: Free Press, 1960) as the antecedents of the war on poverty.

3. Community Health and Welfare Council and Group Work and Recreation Federation, *The Basin Area: An Appraisal of Its Leisure Time Services* (May 1959).

4. Ibid., pp. 6–15, 16. See also Zane L. Miller and Bruce Tucker, "The Revolt Against Cultural Determinism and the Meaning of Community Action: A View from Cincinnati," in Jack Salzman, ed., *Prospects: An Annual of American Cultural Studies*, vol. 15 (New York: Cambridge University Press, 1990), pp. 418–22.

5. Community Health and Welfare Council, *Community Indexes* (1962), p. 7A.

6. Community Health and Welfare Council, *Neighborhood Center Study* (1962), p. 36.

7. Henry D. Shapiro, *Appalachia on Our Mind: The Southern Mountains and Mountaineers in the American Consciousness, 1870–1920* (Chapel Hill: University of North Carolina Press, 1978), chap. 10. See also Zane L. Miller, "Pluralizing America: Walter Prescott Webb, Chicago School Sociology, and Cultural Regionalism," in Robert B. Fairbanks and Kathleen Underwood, *Essays on Sunbelt Cities and Recent America* (Arlington: Texas A&M University Press, 1990), pp. 151–76.

8. See Oscar Handlin, *The Uprooted: The Epic Story of the Great Migrations That Made the American People* (Boston: Little Brown, 1952). On the significance of individual choice in ethnic identification in Handlin's work, see Andrea Tuttle Kornbluh, "From Culture to Cuisine: Twentieth-Century Views of Race and Ethnicity in the City," in Howard Gillette and Zane L. Miller, eds., *American Urbanism: An Historiographical Review* (Westport, Conn.: Greenwood Press, 1987), pp. 55–58.

9. Handlin, *The Uprooted*, pp. 305–6.

10. *A Decade of Service, 1930–1940* (Public Library of Cincinnati and Hamilton County, 1941), p. 42; Arnold B. Walker, "Will There Be a Race Riot in Cincinnati?" *Bulletin of the Division of Negro Welfare*, August 1943, pp. 2, 5, Urban League of Greater Cincinnati Papers, box 24, folder 6; *Cincinnati Times-Star*, February 21, 1944, 5:1.

11. The conference was organized by the Social Service Association of Greater Cincinnati and the Mayor's Friendly Relations Committee, a volunteer organization established in 1943 to promote harmonious race relations. *Cincinnati Enquirer*, April 30, 1954, A:16:4.

12. Roscoe Giffin, *Report of a Workshop on the Southern Mountaineer in Cincinnati, April 24, 1954* (Mayor's Friendly Relations Committee, 1954), pp. 32–33.

13. Ibid., pp. 6, 8, 12.

14. Ibid., pp. 33, 35. For a similar view of mountaineers as an urban problem, see Albert N. Votaw, "The Hillbillies Invade Chicago," *Harper's* 216 (February 1958): 64–67.

15. See *Cincinnati Enquirer,* July 14–20, 1957, for a series of articles on mountaineers in Cincinnati that defined the problems of urban migrants. See esp. "It's Not So Easy: Ways of the City Become Cruel Barriers to Hill Folk Trying to Get Ahead," July 15, A:1:1.

16. Giffin, *Report,* p. 12.

17. Russell Porter, "When Cultures Meet" (Mayor's Friendly Relations Committee, 1962), pp. 7–9; Father Aloys Schweitzer, "Who Is SAM? A Friendly Study of the Southern Appalachian Migrant," 1963, typescript, p. 2, Foster Library, Cincinnati; WCKY Radio, "The Southern Mountaineer: An Audio Study of a People, a Place, and a Condition," September 1963, transcript, pp. 45, 65, Foster Library.

18. Porter, "When Cultures Meet," p. 3; WCKY Radio, "Southern Mountaineer," p. 7; and Schweitzer, "Who Is SAM?," p. 8.

19. *Cincinnati Enquirer,* September 9, 1957, A:6:1; Stuart Faber interview, April 1, 1986; and Mary Jo Herr, "Ernie Mynatt, Prophet of the Inner City," *St. Anthony Messenger,* December 1966, p. 20.

20. "Proposal for Establishment of Committee on Migration," November 7, 1966, Cincinnati Human Relations Commission Papers, box 12, folder 5, Department of Archives and Rare Books, University of Cincinnati. Although the Council on Appalachian Migration appears to have been active between 1963 and 1965, records of its activities in these years have not survived.

21. Chancellor of the Archdiocese to Reverend John E. Sherman, January 30, 1954, Alter Papers, general files, St. Mary's folder B, Archives of the Archdiocese of Cincinnati; *Catholic Telegraph,* March 9, 1962, 1:1.

The Main Street Bible Center was one of three such centers established by the students of Mount St. Mary's Seminary. See Report on the Main Street Bible Center, September 21, 1964, Alter Papers, Saint Mary's Bible Center Folder, Archives of the Archdiocese of Cincinnati. See also Edmund M. Hussey, *A History of the Seminaries of the Archdiocese of Cincinnati* (Norwood, Ohio: Mount St. Mary's Seminary of the West, 1979), p. 56; "An Interview with Michael Maloney," *Appalachian Journal* 17 (Fall 1989): 38–41; Reverend John Porter interview, April 21, 1986; Philip Obermiller interview, December 12, 1986. Underlying these programs were some assumptions about both the past role of the Catholic Church in Over-the-Rhine and its potential contribution to the community in the present. First, the archdiocese saw the neighborhood's past, symbolized by St. Mary's start as an immigrant church, as a basis for the revival of Catholicism among recent newcomers in the inner city. Second, church workers assumed that poor people needed opportunities and choices in employment, health care, education, and housing as well as food and clothing, and that the church should act as a liaison between the poor and outside individuals, agencies, and institutions, especially Catholic ones, that wished to provide such opportunities in poor neighborhoods. Third, the initiation of community organizing activities by church workers indicated that they had abandoned the policy of helping poor people move out of the neighborhood in favor of assisting them in their struggle to rehabilitate both their own lives and the neighborhood itself. *Catholic Telegraph,* March 19, 1965, A:3:3; Most Reverend Edward A. McCarthy to Right Reverend Monsignor Ralph A. Asplan, September 6, 1968, Alter Papers, Catholic Commission on Poverty folder, Archives of the Archdiocese of Cincinnati; and *Catholic Telegraph,* September 18, 1965, A:6:3, and December 11, 1964, A:3:2. For a theological articulation of this point of view in the mid-1960s, see Harvey Cox, *The Secular City: Secularization and Urbanization in Theological Perspective* (New York: Macmillan, 1965). Urban historians have come late to the study of religion and the inner city, a recurring theme in part 2 of this book. But see also John T. McGreevy, *Parish Boundaries: The Catholic Encounter with Race in the Twentieth-Century Urban North* (Chicago: University of Chicago Press, 1996).

22. *Cincinnati Enquirer,* September 8, 1966, Star Page 16.

23. Cincinnati City Planning Commission [hereafter cited as CPC], Minutes, vol. 29, January 24, 1964, p. 15.

24. CPC Staff, "The Dayton-Findlay Neighborhood: Report and Recommendations to the City Planning Commission, March 1964," typescript, pp. 1–4, Planning and Management Support System.

25. Ibid., pp. 5–6.

26. CPC, Minutes, vol. 29, April 10, 1964; Board of Trustees, Cincinnati Historical Society, Minutes, March 16, 1964.

27. CPC, Minutes, vol. 29, March 6, 1964, p. 35, March 13, p. 39, April 3, p. 44.

28. CPC, *Dayton Street Preservation Area Study* (February 1965).

29. CPC, Minutes, vol. 30, April 23, 1965, pp. 60–61, April 30, p. 66. Council enacted the Dayton Street Protection Area Ordinance, as amended by the Planning Commission, on June 16, 1965, after a public hearing on June 9. See Ordinance Nos. 159-1964 and 243-1965, Dayton Street Protection Area File, Urban Conservator's Office. Sec. 1 of the ordinance limited its duration to a period of fifty years.

30. For an account of the variety of perspectives on the urban renewal project that emerged from this situation, see Zane L. Miller and Thomas H. Jenkins, eds., *The Planning Partnership: Participants' Views of Urban Renewal* (Beverly Hills: Sage, 1982). See also Cincinnati Department of Urban Development, "History of

Progress," Annual Report, 1965–66, pp. 14–15; R. Jerome Jenkins, "Images of
the Future: A Case Study of the University of Cincinnati's Interdisciplinary Planning Team's Interface with the Queensgate II Urban Renewal Project" (Ph.D.
diss., University of Cincinnati, 1974), pp. 54–66, 76–88, 248–56.

31. Cincinnati Department of Urban Development, "History of Progress,"
pp. 14–16, 21. Six community councils, including Over-the-Rhine's, joined the
West End Community Council in protesting the building of a new stadium in the
neighborhood. See R. J. Jenkins, "Images of the Future," p. 59.

32. The Task Force was chaired by Edgar "Buddy" Mack, treasurer of the
Cincinnati Symphony Orchestra (the major tenant of Music Hall) and an officer
of Seasongood and Mayer, investment counselors. Other members of the Task
Force included representatives of the Planning Commission, the city's Department of Urban Development, the Cincinnati Public School District, the Metropolitan Housing Authority, the Greater Cincinnati Chamber of Commerce, and
the St. Peter in Chains Roman Catholic Cathedral across from the city hall building on the eastern boundary of the West End. See Thomas H. Jenkins, "The West
End Task Force: Community Participation and Policy Planning," in Miller and
Jenkins, *Planning Partnership,* pp. 84–85.

33. See Zane L. Miller, "Queensgate II: A History of a Neighborhood," in
Miller and Jenkins, *Planning Partnership,* pp. 51–81; and T. H. Jenkins and Jay-
anta Chatterjee, "Managing a University Team in Partnership Planning," in ibid.,
p. 182.

34. The Task Force adopted the alternative housing policy that some members of the university consulting team thought would produce little if any integration. See Zane L. Miller and Hayden B. May, "Housing: The Critical Nexus,"
in Miller and Jenkins, *Planning Partnership,* pp. 141–56. Two of the black participants in the Queensgate II policy planning process later contended that they
aimed from the outset to "provide for the continuous development of black communities over time," a goal that implied an immediate strategy of racial residential segregation. See Jerome R. Jenkins and Richard W. Lewis, "Queensgate II
and 'the Movement': A View from the Community," in ibid., pp. 106–7.

35. Institute for Metropolitan Studies, University of Cincinnati, *Queensgate
II Development Program,* vols. 1 and 2, submitted to Peter Kory, director, Department of Urban Development, City of Cincinnati, August 28 and 31, 1970, copies
in the Project Files.

36. *Cincinnati Enquirer,* August 1 and August 21, 1970; *Cincinnati Post and
Times-Star,* September 10, 1970.

37. Cincinnati Department of Urban Development, "Report on the Implementation of the Queensgate II Development Program," August 28, 1970, typescript, pp. 1–11. For a discussion of what happened to this plan and in

Queensgate II after the adoption of the plan, see Miller and Jenkins, "Postscript," in Miller and Jenkins, *Planning Partnership,* pp. 191–97.

38. See Jenkins and Lewis, "Queensgate II and 'the Movement,' " p. 107.

39. For one version of that history, see Miller, "Queensgate II," pp. 51–80. For the use of elements of that history for the purposes of building ethnic pride and cohesion, see Jenkins and Lewis, "Queensgate II and 'the Movement,' " pp. 112–13.

Chapter 5

1. Kevin A. Shepard, *Cincinnati Housing Policy: An Analysis of Cincinnati's Housing Problem and Governmental Response* (Institute of Governmental Research, University of Cincinnati, 1982), pp. 43–44.

2. Cincinnati City Planning Commission, *Annual Report: Achievements of 1965* (May 6, 1966), p. 7.

3. William A. McClain to the Urban Development, Housing, and Zoning Committee of Council, December 19, 1967, Better Housing League Papers, box 8, folder 22; Better Housing League, "Report on a Relocation Plan: The Washington Park Housing Sponsor," August 1970, typescript, esp. pp. 1–3, and an attachment to the document dated June 25, 1970, Planning and Management Support System 04-0322-0012. The League then worked with the housing committee of the Emmanuel Community Center to establish a short-lived not-for-profit corporation that rehabilitated two large buildings in the area, gave current tenants first priority in renting the remodeled units, and established a relocation program to take care of displaced residents.

4. Ernie Mynatt interview, January 10, 1986; John Porter interview, April 21, 1968; Minutes of the Uptown Basin Council, February to May 1986, Urban Appalachian Council Archives; *Catholic Telegraph,* August 19, 1965, A:8:3.

5. *Catholic Telegraph,* June 24, 1966, B:1:2.

6. *Cincinnati in Action* 2 (November 1966): 2. Virginia Coffey interview, April 10, 1986; "The Hub: A Monthly Report of HUB Activities for July 1967," typescript, Urban Appalachian Council Archives; Bruce Tucker, "An Interview with Michael Maloney," *Appalachian Journal* 17 (Fall 1989): 42–43; Robert Routt interview, May 13, 1986.

7. *Cincinnati in Action,* p. 2.

8. Madelaine Hertzman interview, April 8, 1986; Maureen Sullivan interview, June 11, 1986.

9. Robert Routt interview; "Interview with Michael Maloney," p. 42; "The Hub."

10. City of Cincinnati, *Application to the Department of Housing and Urban Devel-*

opment for a Grant to Plan a Comprehensive City Demonstration Project (Office of the City Manager, April 26, 1967), Part IV, p. 1.

11. Ibid., Part I, p. 1, and Part II, sec. A, p. 2.

12. On the application's view of the problem of community council leadership, see Ibid., Part V, sec. B, pp. 5–6.

13. Ibid., Part II, sec. B, p. 6.

14. Ibid., Part II, sec. F, 1, pp. 3–4; Part III, sec. A, pp. 6–10, and sec. G, pp. 4, 13–17.

15. See E. Bruce Tucker, "Toward a New Ethnicity: Appalachian Ethnic Consciousness in Cincinnati, 1950–87," in Henry D. Shapiro and Jonathan D. Sarna, eds., *Ethnic Diversity and Civic Identity: Patterns of Conflict and Cohesion in Cincinnati since 1820* (Urbana: University of Illinois Press, 1992), pp. 225–47. See also Roscoe Giffin, "Appalachian Newcomers in Cincinnati," in Thomas R. Ford, ed., *The Appalachian Region: A Survey* (Lexington: University Press of Kentucky, 1962), pp. 79–84; and James S. Brown and George A. Hillery, "The Great Migration, 1940–1960," pp. 54–78.

16. On the discovery of poverty in the United States in the 1960s, see Michael Harrington, *The Other America* (New York: Macmillan, 1962). National interest in Appalachia had waned in the decade and a half after World War II. See Henry D. Shapiro, "John F. Day and the Disappearance of Appalachia from the American Consciousness," *Appalachian Journal* 10 (1983): 157–64. Two contemporary statements of the "rediscovery" of Appalachia in the 1960s are Ford, *The Appalachian Region;* and David S. Walls and John B. Stephenson, *Appalachia in the Sixties: A Decade of Reawakening* (Lexington: University Press of Kentucky, 1972). See also Harry M. Caudill, *Night Comes to the Cumberlands: A Biography of a Depressed Area* (Boston: Little Brown, 1962); and Jack Weller, *Yesterday's People: Life in Contemporary Appalachia* (Lexington: University Press of Kentucky, 1965). For an assessment of the consequences of this new definition of the relationship between Appalachia and America, see Allen Batteau and Phillip Obermiller, "Introduction: The Transformation of Dependency," in Allen Batteau, ed., *Appalachia and America: Autonomy and Regional Dependence* (Lexington: University Press of Kentucky, 1983), pp. 1–13.

17. See "Interview with Michael Maloney," pp. 44, 48.

18. See in particular WCKY Radio, "The Southern Mountaineer: An Audio Study of a People, a Place, and a Condition," September 1963, transcript in the Foster Library, in which several public officials and social workers are interviewed about the presence of Appalachians in the inner city. The series was billed as Cincinnati's response to the publication of *Night Comes to the Cumberlands.*

19. See the minutes of United Appalachia Cincinnati, 1968–70, Urban Ap-

palachian Council Archives, Foster Library; United Appalachia Cincinnati, by-laws, Urban Appalachian Council Archives. Michael Maloney interview, December 20, 1985; Ernie Mynatt interview. See also Kenneth Fox, *Metropolitan America: Urban Life and Urban Policy in the United States, 1940–1980* (Jackson: University Press of Mississippi, 1986), pp. 122–26.

20. Draft proposal, Appalachian Identity Center, Urban Appalachian Council Archives, n.d., folder 2; Ernie Mynatt to Virginia Coffey, n.d. (probably 1970), Appalachian Identity Center folder, Urban Appalachian Council Archives.

21. Michael Maloney, "The Appalachian Committee Proposal," p. 4, Urban Appalachian Council Archives; Minutes of the Appalachian Regional Commission Meeting with Mayor Eugene P. Ruehlmann, pp. 1–5, Urban Appalachian Council Papers, folder 2, Department of Archives and Rare Books, University of Cincinnati Libraries; "Interview with Michael Maloney," pp. 44–45.

22. *Cincinnati Enquirer,* April 13, 1971, A:40:1; *Cincinnati Enquirer Magazine,* April 29, 1973, pp. 9–17; Minutes of the Appalachian Community Development Association, December 12, 1973, ACDA Papers, folder 10, Department of Archives and Rare Books, University of Cincinnati.

23. "The Appalachian Festival: A Plan for Community Participation and Control," and Articles of Incorporation of the Appalachian Community Development Association, ACDA Papers, folder 10.

24. "Appalachian Heritage Project Proposal: Washington Park School and Community," Urban Appalachian Council Papers, Department of Archives and Rare Books, University of Cincinnati. See also Michael Henson interview, March 4, 1986; and Mike Henson, "Over-the-Rhine: Community Context of the Education Crisis," 1974, typescript, Urban Appalachian Council Archives; *Appalachian Advocate,* May–June, 1975, p. 1.

25. Michael Henson interview; Mike Henson, "Over-the-Rhine"; *Appalachian Advocate,* May–June 1975, p. 1.

26. Michael Maloney, "The Implications of Appalachian Culture for Social Welfare Practice," *Working Paper No. 2* (Urban Appalachian Council, September 1974). The Urban Appalachian Council took similar positions in working papers on education and health care, arguing that current practice required Appalachians to surrender their cultural identification as the cost of receiving effective service. The council contended that Appalachians would be more effectively served by agencies that developed empathic personalistic relationships with clients and that accepted Appalachian cultural values as a basis for communication. See Phillip Obermiller, "Ethnicity and Education: The Intercultural Dimension," *Working Paper No. 5* (Urban Appalachian Council, 1974); Thomas E.

Wagner, "Urban Appalachian School Children: The Least Understood of All," *Working Paper No. 6* (Urban Appalachian Council, 1974); Virginia McCoy-Watkins, "Urban Appalachian Health Behavior," paper delivered at the annual forum of the National Conference on Social Welfare, Cincinnati, 1974, reprinted in Steven Weiland and Philip Obermiller, eds., *Perspectives on Urban Appalachians* (Cincinnati: Ohio Urban Appalachian Awareness Project, 1978), pp. 288–92.

27. Michael Maloney, *The Social Areas of Cincinnati: Towards an Analysis of Social Needs* (Cincinnati: Human Relations Commission, January 1974), esp. p. 2.

28. Ibid., pp. 42–43.

29. *Cincinnati Post,* July 21, 1971, 1:2.

30. On bluegrass music, see *Cincinnati Magazine* 11 (October 1977): 90.

31. "Interview with Michael Maloney," p. 47.

32. Ibid., p. 47; Larry Redden interview, February 18, 1986.

33. The Urban Appalachian Council moved its offices from Over-the-Rhine to Lower Price Hill in 1982. See *Cincinnati Enquirer,* February 1, 1982, D:2:1.

34. Kevin A. Shepard, *Cincinnati Housing Policy: An Analysis of Cincinnati's Housing Problem and Governmental Response* (Cincinnati: Institute of Governmental Research, University of Cincinnati, 1972), pp. 43–44.

35. Pat Crum, Public Information Subcommittee, Working Review Committee on Housing, "A Comprehensive Strategy for the City of Cincinnati," August 1973, typescript, pp. 1–3, in Clifton Town Meeting Papers, box 5, folder 56, Department of Archives and Rare Books, University of Cincinnati Libraries; Clifton Town Meeting, *Bulletin,* December 1971, p. 4, Clifton Town Meeting Papers, box 4, folder 25.

36. For the presentation of the Working Review Committee on Housing's resolution to city council, see Arnold J. Rosenmeyer to Robert E. Turner, memo, October 29, 1974, Clifton Town Meeting Papers, box 5, folder 8; Charles Stocker to Zane L. Miller, telephone interview, July 7, 1987.

37. Resolution No. 228-1974, Clerk of Council's Office.

Chapter 6

1. *Cincinnati Post and Times-Star,* January 9, 1968, 6:1–4, and June 7, 17:5–8.

2. Harris Forusz interview, November 30, 1984, transcript, p. 38; Cincinnati Department of Urban Development, *Over-the-Rhine/Findlay Market Area Designs and Objectives* (n.d. [1971?]), p. 1.

3. Ibid., front matter, n.p., and p. 16.

4. Ibid., pp. 51–52, 63.

5. Ibid., p. 32.

6. Ibid., pp. 4–5.

7. Ibid., p. 35.

8. Ibid., p. 44.

9. Ibid., pp. 35–36, 51, 52ff.

10. Miami Purchase Association, *Guidelines for the Rehabilitation of the Findlay Market District* (Cincinnati: Department of Urban Development, n.d. [1971?]), pp. 2–3.

11. Ibid., p. 12.

12. Office of the City Manager, Cincinnati, "Updated Mid-Planning Statement," in *Cincinnati Model Cities Program, First Year Action Plan* (March 1971), pp. 1–2.

13. Ibid., pp. 2, 11–14.

14. Harris Forusz interview, January 29, 1985, transcript, pp. 1, 3–5, 8–9, 11–12, 14, 18–20, 22–24, 26–28, 31–35, 37–41, 44–48.

15. Cincinnati Model Cities Physical Planning Program, *Over-the-Rhine/Clifton Heights/Fairview Neighborhood Development Plan* (1975), esp. p. 307.

16. Zane L. Miller, "Planning and the Politics of Ethnic Identity: Making Choices for Over-the-Rhine, 1971–85," in Henry D. Shapiro and Jonathan D. Sarna, eds., *Ethnic Diversity and Civic Identity: Patterns of Conflict and Cohesion in Cincinnati since 1820* (Urbana: University of Illinois Press, 1992), pp. 253–55.

17. Model Cities Planning Program, *Neighborhood Development Plan*, pp. 98–114, 117, 134–35.

18. Ibid., pp. 307, 318.

19. Ibid., pp. 319–21.

20. Ibid., pp. 317, 320–21. The plan offered no additional guidelines for this procedure, except to note that the Commission should have "the ear of [city] council" and that city council would decide which grievances to refer to the Commission.

21. Ibid., pp. 321–22.

22. Ibid., pp. 322–23.

23. Not everyone would agree with the plan, Forusz conceded in an afterword, but taken as intended, "as a *process* [authors' emphasis] for overall individual, community, neighborhood and city betterment," it would "promote changes that would respond to the needs of many users."

24. Hubert Guest to Zane L. Miller, interview 3, February 5, 1986, transcript, pp. 12–26; interview 2, December 16, 1985, transcript, pp. 8–9, Project Files.

25. Guest to Miller, interview 1, December 10, 1985, transcript, pp. 14–16, Project Files.

Chapter 7

1. Charles B. Hosmer, Jr., *Preservation Comes of Age: From Williamsburg to the National Trust, 1926–1949* (Charlottesville: University Press of Virginia, 1981). The Cincinnati metropolitan master planners of 1948 justified the preservation of Lytle Park because of its association with nation-building activities (the site of Fort Washington) during the late eighteenth and early nineteenth centuries. See Cincinnati City Planning Commission [hereafter cited as CPC], *Riverfront Redevelopment* (1946), pp. 46–47. Between 1920 and 1950 historic preservation centered not only on tourism but also on national patriotism and connoisseurship. The movement rallied around the preservation of sites, buildings, or localities associated with prominent persons and events in the nation's political and cultural history, particularly those of the preindustrial era. Connoisseurship led to an emphasis on authentic restoration, as in colonial Williamsburg, where preservationists tore down nineteenth-century buildings to authenticize the setting for older structures, and in historic Charleston and the Vieux Carré of New Orleans, which to some connoisseurs seemed natural museums of authentic colonial and early national architecture and ways of life.

2. Organization of American Historians, *Historic Preservation: A Guide for Departments of History* (Bloomington, Ind.: Organization of American Historians, 1982), p. 4; U.S. Code, Congressional and Administrative News, 89th Congress, 2nd Sess., 1966, vol. 1, Laws, Historic Properties—Preservation, pp. 1082–87.

3. U.S. Code, vol. 1, pp. 1082–87.

4. Iola O. Silberstein, *Cincinnati Hillsides: The Evolution of Environmental Quality Zoning* (Cincinnati: Institute of Governmental Research, University of Cincinnati, 1980), pp. 1–7; Citizens Task Force on Environmental Quality, *Report* (Cincinnati: n.p., May 1973), foreword.

5. Silberstein, *Cincinnati Hillsides*, p. 7; CPC, Minutes, vol. 36, July 7, 1971, pp. 88, November 5, p. 136; vol. 37, January 7, 1972, p. 6, January 21, p. 12, June 16, p. 85, June 23, pp. 87–89, June 30, p. 90, July 28, p. 96, August 25, pp. 103–4; Citizens Environmental Task Force, *Report*, p. iii.

6. CPC, Minutes, vol. 38, January 19, 1973, p. 16, February 2, p. 19, February 9, p. 22, February 16, pp. 25, 30, March 30, pp. 45–46; Cincinnati Ordinance No. 169-1973 (Clerk of Council's Office), pp. 1–5.

7. Citizens Environmental Task Force, *Report*, pp. 51–57, 67–72.

8. CPC Staff, "Review of the Report by the Citizens Task Force on Environmental Quality, July 1973," typescript, pp. 5–6, PAMSS Office, doc. no. 99-0915-0288. Ibid., pp. 1–3, 7–9.

9. Clerk of City Council, *Zoning Code, Cincinnati, Ohio*, January 1983, typescript, pp. 387–90.

10. In 1954 the Planning Commission staff suggested the demolition of Findlay Market and its replacement with "a modern shopping center with an adequate parking area in line with modern planning concepts." This proposal lay dormant until 1964, when the Planning Commission reversed its stance. Director of planning Stevens offered at that time to eliminate the Court Street Market but at the same time proposed to save and enlarge Findlay Market. John B. Sheblessy to CPC, "Use of Findlay Playground as an Off-Street Parking Facility," November 18, 1954, Findlay Market File, Historic Conservation Office, Department of City Planning; CPC, Minutes, vol. 19, November 22, 1954, p. 104; Herbert W. Stevens to CPC, May 12, 1964, Findlay Market File, p. 3.

11. H. W. Stevens to Peter Kory, July 29, 1971, Findlay Market File. Stevens apparently did not take this issue to the Planning Commission for its consideration.

12. CPC, Minutes, vol. 39, December 20, 1974, pp. 169–71; CPC Staff, "Report and Recommendation on a Proposed Change of Zoning to Establish Interim Development Control (IDC) District No. 3 in the Vicinity of Findlay Market," April 22, 1975, mimeograph, p. 3. The IDC district encompassed fifty-four properties and five acres of land that qualified for IDC and environmental quality district protection because of the adoption in 1972 of an urban design plan for the vicinity that had yielded expenditures of $1 million for the renovation of the market building and $2 million for the construction of the Pilot Center social services building. In addition, the staff report noted that the immediate environment around the market building constituted a "historic interest area" containing "excellent" examples of nineteenth-century architecture and set down historically sensitive guidelines for reviewing proposed work in the IDC district.

13. CPC Staff, "Application Review Guidelines for Interim Development Control District No. 3 (IDC No. 3), Findlay Market Vicinity," April 1975, stenciled, p. 1; CPC Staff, "Report and Recommendation," p. 2; CPC, Minutes, vol. 40, April 25, 1975, pp. 64–65; Cincinnati Ordinance No. 335-1975; Cincinnati Ordinance No. 357-1976, pp. 1–4. For the hearing examiner ordinance see Cincinnati Ordinance No. 358-1976. The Planning Commission approved a single permit in that IDC district, a permit for exterior repairs at 108 Elder Street. CPC, Minutes, vol. 41, March 5, 1976, p. 39, October 29, p. 150, November 19, p. 160, December 17, p. 171; vol. 42, January 7, 1977, p. 2; Cincinnati Ordinance No. 63-1977.

14. Documentation for these activities may be found in the Music Hall File, Department of City Planning, Historic Conservation Office. See also Zane L. Miller, "Music Hall: Its Neighborhood, the City and the Metropolis," in Zane L. Miller and George F. Roth, *Cincinnati's Music Hall* (Virginia Beach, Va.: Jordan, 1978), pp. 46–50.

15. Morton Rabkin to Winston E. Folkers, February 15, 1974, pp. 1–2, City Solicitor's File No. 1607-4.

16. CPC, Minutes, vol. 39, July 26, 1974, p. 101, November 15, p. 152.

17. CPC (for the Department of Urban Development), *North Frame CBD: General Planning Guidelines: Phase I* (June 1971; rev. January 1972).

18. Urban Design Associates, *Washington Park: The Plan, The Park, The Village* (3 documents) (Cincinnati: Department of Urban Development, September 1977).

19. Both the story on the Washington Park plan and Towe's column appeared in the *Cincinnati Post,* December 31, 1977, 17A.

20. Ibid.; Ohio Historic Preservation Office, National Register of Historic Places in Ohio as of 10/10/85, Hamilton County, Cincinnati, Apostolic Bethlehem Temple Church, 1205 Elm Street (4-11-73), and Hamilton County Memorial Building, Elm and Grant Streets (12-4-78).

21. Herbert W. Stevens to Zane L. Miller, telephone interview, November 11, 1987.

22. CPC, Minutes, vol. 42, December 9, 1977, p. 151, December 30, p. 161.

23. CPC, Minutes, vol. 43, February 24, 1978, p. 31. Stevens also reached beyond the Planning Commission to drum up support for a historic preservation planning program. In late March 1978 he authorized staff member Sanford Youkilis to participate in a discussion of the effectiveness of historic preservation with a field representative of the National Trust for Historic Preservation, Fred Mitchell of the MPA, professors Bruce Goetzman and Sam Noe of the College of Design, Art, Architecture, and Planning at the University of Cincinnati, and Pope Coleman, a leading actor in the drive for environmental quality zoning in Cincinnati. Miriam Tremontozzi, to Sanford Youkilis, March 29, 1978; and Sanford Youkilis and H. W. Stevens to C. C. "Bud" Haupt, April 7, 1978, Historic Planning Program-1978 File, Historic Conservation Office.

24. Fred Mitchell to Zane L. Miller, telephone interview, January 13, 1978; U.S. Department of the Interior, *Preservation Planning Series: Manual for State Historic Preservation Review Boards* (Washington, D.C.: National Park Service, 1984), p. 87.

25. H. W. Stevens to CPC, April 17, 1978, Historic Planning Program-1978 File.

26. Sanford Youkilis to H. W. Stevens, "Historic Preservation Proposal (Inventory Status)," June 5, 1978, typescript, Historic Planning Program-1978 File; William V. Donaldson to CPC, "Cincinnati Historic Inventory," June 12, 1978, Historic Planning Program-1978 File.

27. Donaldson, "Historic Inventory," pp. 1–2; H. W. Stevens to CPC, "A Pro-

posal for an Urban Conservation Strategy and Memorandum from the City Manager on Development Programs and Historic Preservation," typescript, June 13, 1978, pp. 1, 5–6.

28. Henry G. Alexander to Internal Revenue Service, June 27, 1980, Re: Queen City Housing Corporation-Application for Tax Exempt Status, Corporate Records, Queen City Housing Corporation, in possession of W. Joseph Dehner.

29. Fred Lazarus III, Report of the Queen City Club Breakfast Meeting of the Board of the Queen City Housing Corporation [hereafter cited as QCH], June 25, 1980, p. 1, Corporate Records; W. Joseph Dehner to Zane L. Miller, telephone interview, November 4, 1987.

30. Fred Lazarus III to Cincinnati Business Committee, "Downtown Development Task Force Report," updated typescript, p. 1, in possession of Carl Westmoreland.

31. Articles of Incorporation of QCH, E0543-1513, January 17, 1979, p. 1, Corporate Records; Alexander to IRS, p. 3; Initial Meeting of the Board of Trustees, QCH, Minutes, February 5, 1979, p. 1, Corporate Records.

32. QCH, Minutes, April 5, 1979, p. 1, Corporate Records; Henry G. Alexander to Rachel DeMarcus, August 20, 1980, Re: QCH Application for Tax Exempt Status, pp. 1–2, Corporate Records.

33. Minutes of the Meeting of the Incorporators of the Heritage Development Corporation, June 1, 1979, p. 1, Corporate Records, Heritage Preservation Development Corporation.

34. Neighborhood Housing Services of Cincinnati, Inc., Over-the-Rhine Proposal (to the Ford Foundation), May 1, 1979, typescript, Westmoreland Papers, Project Files; W. Joseph Dehner to Jim Wimberg, Carl Westmoreland, Fred Lazarus III, Nelson Schwab, Jr., Memorandum Re: Denhart Proposal to QCH, Corporate Records.

35. R. A. Anderegg to Lyle Everingham, July 6, 1979, attached to QCH, Minutes, July 12, 1979, Corporate Records.

36. Keith James Goodwin, "You Can Beat City Hall: Redefining the Mission and Relocating the Alcoholic Drop-In Center, 1967–1978," esp. pp. 3–34, Department of Archives and Rare Books, University of Cincinnati Libraries.

37. Fred Lazarus III, "Over-the-Rhine Meeting, May 21, 1979, City Hall," typescript, pp. 1–3, attached to QCH, Minutes, May 25, 1979, Corporate Records.

38. CPC, Minutes, vol. 44, December 7, 1979, p. 229. In October 1979 planning director Stevens persuaded the U.S. Department of the Interior to hold up the consideration of the nomination by the American Association for State and

Local History of Over-the-Rhine as a National Historic Landmark because dealing with it and the National Register nomination simultaneously would be "extremely disruptive." See Horace J. Sheely to H. W. Stevens, October 22, 1979, Over-the-Rhine Nomination 1980 File, Goetzman Papers, Project Files.

39. [No author, probably Lazarus], "Over-the-Rhine, Status Report, October 10, 1979, Revised 11.14.179," typescript, p. 1, attached to QCH, Minutes, November 26, 1979, Corporate Records.

40. W. Joseph Dehner to H. W. Stevens, December 10, 1979, IDC No. 12, Washington Park Area File, Zoning Division, Department of City Planning.

41. Sanford A. Youkilis to CPC, Report identifying the Washington Park area (Over-the-Rhine Community) as a potential historic conservation zone; and a recommendation to establish an Interim Development (IDC) District No. 12 in the vicinity of the Washington Park area, December 12, 1979, pp. 2–3, IDC No. 12, Washington Park Area File.

42. CPC, Minutes, vol. 44, December 14, 1979, pp. 235–36. The Planning Commission initiated and ran the community assistance program but voted to transfer the community assistance teams to the Office of Community Assistance in July 1977. See CPC, Minutes, vol. 42, July 2, 1977, p. 99.

43. CPC, Minutes, vol. 44, December 14, 1979, p. 236; Cincinnati Ordinance No. 579-1979, pp. 1–3, Clerk of Council's Office.

44. Sanford A. Youkilis to CPC, "Authorization to Prepare and Submit a Grant Application to the U.S. Department of the Interior for a Washington Park Historic Conservation Plan," January 23, 1980, typescript, p. 1, Over-the-Rhine Grant including Washington Park File, Schuckman Papers, Project Files; CPC, *Washington Park,* Project Aspects of Minority and Community Significance, December 1979, in Washington Park Study File, Schuckman Papers; Steven L. Schuckman to Buddy Gray, February 27, 1980, Over-the-Rhine Grant including Washington Park File; CPC, Minutes, vol. 45, January 25, 1980, p. 22.

45. CPC, Minutes, vol. 44, June 29, 1979, p. 140, August 24, p. 162, September 7, p. 165.

46. Jack Towe, "A Proposal: Rebuilding Older Communities in Cincinnati; Submitted to the Urban Conservation Task Force, Preliminary Draft," October 1978, typescript, pp. 1–5, in Anti-Displacement Ordinance File, Schuckman Papers. Towe did not mention historic conservation districts.

47. Michael A. Miller et al., "The Displacement Issue in Cincinnati," February 8, 1979, typescript, pp. 1–28, Anti-Displacement Ordinance File.

48. Gregory A. Shumate to Jack Towe, April 3, 1979, Anti-Displacement Ordinance File; Jack Towe, "Displacement Realities: Report to the Anti-Displacement Committee," n.d., typescript, pp. 1–2.

49. John Schrider to Zane L. Miller, telephone interview, December 11, 1987; John Schrider (untitled draft of an anti-displacement ordinance marked in print as "Public Sector"), April 24, 1979, typescript, rev., pp. 1–5, Anti-Displacement Ordinance File.

50. John Schrider to Zane L. Miller, telephone interview, December 24, 1987.

51. Thomas A. Luebbers to Tecumseh X. Graham, "Displacement/Relocation Assistance Resolution," July 26, 1979, typescript, pp. 1–7, Interdepartment Correspondence Sheet, Anti-Displacement Ordinance File.

52. Sylvester Murray to Urban Development, Planning, Zoning and Housing Committee, Interdepartment Correspondence Sheet, 1/8/90, Anti-Displacement Ordinance File; Manager's Recommended Displacement Ordinance, January 1, 1980, typescript, Anti-Displacement Ordinance File.

53. We use the term *separatists* rather than segregationists after 1950 because separatist connotes residential choice by individuals in neighborhoods, while residential segregation connotes a government policy (separate but equal) recommended by experts and adopted by elected and appointed authorities (before the 1950s), a practice that may be traced in southern and northern cities back to the 1870s.

Chapter 8

1. Cincinnati City Planning Commission [hereafter cited as CPC], Minutes, vol. 45, January 25, 1980, p. 22; vol. 45, April 25, 1980, p. 87; Cincinnati Ordinance Nos. 189-1980, 190-1980, 191-1980, 238-1980, Clerk of Council's Office.

2. *Cincinnati Enquirer,* December 17, 1981, A1, December 22, 1983, A1, A4.

3. *Cincinnati Enquirer,* December 22, 1983, A1, A4; Joel Hempel interview with Bruce Tucker, September 5, 1986, transcript, pp. 1–17.

4. Sanford A. Youkilis to CPC, "Summary of Public Hearing on Proposed Nomination of the Over-the-Rhine Community to the National Register of Historic Places," March 1980, typescript, pp. 1–2, Over-the-Rhine File, Historic Conservation Office, Department of City Planning.

5. Ibid., pp. 2–3.

6. Ibid., p. 3. On McCrackin's other protest activities, see Judith A. Bechtel and Robert M. Coughlin, *Building the Beloved Community: Maurice McCrackin's Life for Peace and Civil Rights* (Philadelphia: Temple University Press, 1991).

7. Youkilis, "Summary," p. 3. Klimoski's speech did not impress the next speaker, Sister Beverly Stark (residence and affiliation unidentified), who said, "Damn the buildings, save the people."

8. The letters may be found in Over-the-Rhine Nomination 1980 File, Goetzman Papers, Project Files, and in the Ohio Historic Preservation Office, Columbus.

9. Brunn did not note that the city justified the anti-displacement ordinance as an effort to promote the integration of neighborhoods.

10. See, e.g., Steven L. Schuckman to Buddy Gray, February 27, 1980, Over-the-Rhine Grant including Washington Park File, Schuckman Papers, Project Files; Steven L. Schuckman to Zane L. Miller, telephone interview, December 17, 1987; CPC, Minutes, vol. 45, March 28, 1980, pp. 70–71; H. W. Stevens to Sylvester Murray, copies to Nell Surber and Hubert Guest, "Joint Planning Program for Over-the-Rhine," March 31, 1980, Over-the-Rhine Grant including Washington Park File.

11. Fred Lazarus III, "June 25, 1980 Meeting [of the Queen City Housing Board] at Queen City Club Breakfast," typescript, p. 1, Corporate Records, Queen City Housing Corporation, Project Files.

12. Ibid., pp. 1–2.

13. Ibid., p. 2.

14. Ibid., p. 3.

15. Ibid.

16. Sylvester Murray to Laura Goodell, August 8, 1980, in Over-the-Rhine Planning Task Force File, December 2, 1980, Department of City Planning.

17. Heritage Preservation Development Corporation, Minutes, July 8, 1980, pp. 1–2, August 13, p. 3, September 10, pp. 1–2; Queen City Housing Corporation, Minutes, November 13, 1980, p. 1; CPC, Minutes, vol. 46, July 9, 1980, pp. 135–37; Cincinnati Post, October 17, 1980, B1; Cincinnati Enquirer, October 18, 1980, D2.

18. Cincinnati Ordinance Nos. 337-1980 (Over-the-Rhine) and 338-1980 (Findlay Market).

19. Sanford A. Youkilis, "Findings Report and Recommendation to Extend IDC District #12 (Washington Park Area) for an Additional Twelve Months," November 20, 1980, typescript, p. 1, Over-the-Rhine including Washington Park File; Steven L. Schuckman to CPC, "Preliminary Objectives and Findings Report for the Washington Park Area of Over-the-Rhine," Nov. 20, 1980, typescript, pp. 1–3, Over-the-Rhine including Washington Park File; CPC, Minutes, vol. 46, November 21, 1980, pp. 209–10; Cincinnati Ordinance Nos. 553-1980 and 534-1980.

20. Over-the-Rhine Planning Task Force [hereafter cited as PTF], Minutes, October 21, 1980, Schuckman Papers; Cincinnati Post, October 21, 1980, B1.

21. PTF, Minutes, December 2, 1980, December 9, January 6, 1981, February 17, March 3; PTF, Housing Committee, Minutes, February 12, 1981, Schuck-

man Papers. The city manager sent his message to the Task Force through James Bower. See James Bower to PTF, December 15, 1980, typescript, pp. 1–2, Over-the-Rhine including Washington Park File.

22. Sylvester Murray to PTF members, "Guidelines for a More Effective Task Force Planning Process," April 7, 1981, PTF File, Department of City Planning.

23. Tommie Birdsall to Over-the-Rhine Plan Policy Team, Policy Team Meeting, April 4, 1981, pp. 1–13, Over-the-Rhine Plan File, Schuckman Papers. The statements of Birdsall, Nell Surber, Stevens, and Barbara Lichtenstein may be found in this same file.

24. *Cincinnati Enquirer,* April 19, 1981, B1.

25. PTF, Housing Committee, Minutes, April 19, 1981, pp. 1–3, Schuckman Papers.

26. Richard A. Castellini to H. W. Stevens, Housing Preservation Ordinance, May 19, 1981, pp. 1–2, Over-the-Rhine including Washington Park File. No one then or later tried to change the law on fees or to test it in court.

27. Sylvester Murray to James Bower and PTF members, Initial City Goal Statement for Over-the-Rhine Planning, May 27, 1981, pp. 1–5, Over-the-Rhine including Washington Park File.

28. PTF, Minutes, June 2, 1981, pp. 1–2, Schuckman Papers.

29. PTF, Housing Committee, Minutes, June 23, 1981, pp. 1–2, Schuckman Papers.

30. Genevieve H. Ray interview with Nancy K. Shapiro, January 29, 1984, transcript, pp. 7–8, Project Files.

31. PTF, Housing Committee, Minutes, July 7, 1981, p. 1, Schuckman Papers; Ken Robinson to H. W. Stevens, July 13, 1981, Schuckman Papers.

32. Father William Schiesl to invited participants, August 19, 1981, pp. 1–2, Schuckman Papers. CPC staff followed up the invitations by mailing a packet containing information about federal and local housing subsidies and community development regulations and programs, including historic conservation measures. It also described legislation from other places that sought without historic preservation to control demolition of buildings and to protect low-income housing, including the Seattle ordinance and legislation from Portland, Oregon; Arlington County, Virginia; Ramapo, New York; and Petaluma, California. A final section of the packet analyzed the federal Tax Act of 1981, recently signed by President Ronald Reagan, and the use of its incentives for low-income housing production and the rehabilitation of old buildings for the benefit of low-income persons. CPC, The OTR Charette: More Than Just a Meeting, information package, September 8, 1981, sections A, B, C, Schuckman Papers.

33. Steven Bloomfield interview with Nancy K. Shapiro, May 17, 1984, tran-

script, pp. 17–18; Genevieve H. Ray interview with Nancy K. Shapiro, p. 20, Project Files; [CPC Staff], Conservation District Issues, draft, September 15, 1981, pp. 1–2, Schuckman Papers; *Cincinnati Enquirer,* September 17, 1981, B3.

34. CPC Staff, Neighborhood Conservation District (NCD), rev. draft, September 18, 1981; Amended Historic Legislation Proposal and Conservation District Proposal, September 21, 1981; A. Historic District(s) in Over-the-Rhine, B. Neighborhood Preservation Ordinance, and C. Low Income Housing Preservation Ordinance, September 26, 1981, Schuckman Papers.

35. CPC Staff, Neighborhood Preservation Ordinance; PTF Housing Subcommittee, Minutes, October 6, 1981, Schuckman Papers.

36. Cincinnati Historic Conservation Board, Minutes, October 12, 1981, pp. 1–3, Historic Conservation Files, Department of City Planning.

37. PTF, Minutes, October 20, 1981, p. 2; H. W. Stevens, Notice of Public Hearing, October 28, 1981, Schuckman Papers.

38. Comments by Sylvester Murray on Over-the-Rhine Housing Retention Draft Ordinance, n.d., pp. 1–2, handscript, Schuckman Papers.

39. Charlotte T. Birdsall to CPC, November 12, 1981, Proposed Amendments to the Housing Allocation Policy, Schuckman Papers.

40. CPC, Minutes, vol. 47, November 13, 1981, pp. 191–94, November 20, p. 197, December 4, pp. 202–6. The minutes for the December 4 meeting did not record the motion to approve the ordinance or the vote, but they appear in the minutes of the next meeting, December 11, p. 207.

41. City Council, Urban Development, Planning, Housing, and Zoning Committee, Public Hearing, December 8, 1981, tape recording, tape B, side 1, and December 15, side 2, Clerk of Council's Office.

42. Cincinnati Ordinance Nos. 521-1981 and 522-1981.

Chapter 9

1. Charlotte T. Birdsall interview with Nancy K. Shapiro, December 8, 1983, transcript, p. 19.

2. Business members of the Over-the-Rhine Planning Task Force [hereafter cited as PTF] to Sylvester Murray, January 18, 1982, PTF File, Meeting of January 19, 1982, Office of Charlotte Birdsall, Department of City Planning [hereafter cited as Birdsall Records].

3. Charlotte T. Birdsall, Notes from Sylvester Murray's Meeting, January 28, 1982, p. 1, PTF File, Birdsall Records.

4. Herbert W. Stevens to Zane L. Miller, telephone interview, August 29, 1991. The appointment of a replacement went to the city manager rather than the Planning Commission because a court ruled in the late 1970s in a personnel

dismissal case that the city charter did not specifically authorize the Commission to hire or fire its staff, although it had been doing so since 1926.

5. Birdsall interview, pp. 6, 18–20; Hubert E. Guest interview with Zane L. Miller, December 16, 1985, interview 2, transcript, pp. 3–5.

6. W. Ray Luce to David Mann, February 10, 1982, pp. 1–2, Schuckman Papers, Project Files; W. Ray Luce interview with Nancy K. Shapiro, June 11, 1984, tape recording, tape 1, side B.

7. PTF, February 16, 1982, pp. 2–3, Birdsall Records; Tommie Birdsall to Sylvester Murray and James Selonick, February 25, 1982, Schuckman Papers.

8. Cincinnati City Planning Commission [hereafter cited as CPC], Minutes, vol. 48, February 27, 1982, p. 33.

9. Genevieve Ray to Historic Conservation Board, Nomination of Over-the-Rhine to the National Register, March 2, 1982, pp. 1–2, 3–4, Historic Conservation Office, Department of City Planning.

10. Historic Conservation Board, Minutes, March 8, 1982, pp. 1–4, Historic Conservation Office, Department of City Planning.

11. CPC, Minutes, vol. 48, March 12, 1982, pp. 40–41.

12. The ayes consisted of Luken (D), Kenneth Blackwell (R), and Guy Guckenberger (R), while Mann (D), Thomas Brush (C), and Bobbie Sterne (C) voted nay. City Council, Proceedings, March 17, 1982, p. 94, Clerk of Council's Office. That same afternoon the *Cincinnati Post* ran a long op-ed article by Jack Towe against the nomination (15A).

13. William L. Mallory to Robert Ebinger, March 18, 1982; Helen Rankin to W. Ray Luce, March 18, 1982; William F. Bowen to Robert Ebinger, March 18, 1982, Goetzman Papers, Project Files.

14. Reverend James Willig to W. Ray Luce, March 17, 1982; Andrew Fox, O.F.M., to W. Ray Luce, March 16, 1982; Buddy Gray to W. Ray Luce, March 12, 1982; Grace Raines to W. Ray Luce, March 19, 1982, Goetzman Papers.

15. Genevieve Ray to Dana Baker, March 18, 1982; Shein Mei Li and Thomas Z. Li to W. Ray Luce, March 3, 1982; William F. Meyer to W. Ray Luce, March 9, 1982; Robert C. McIntosh to W. Ray Luce, March 17, 1982; Paul William Smart and Diane W. Smart to W. Ray Luce, March 9, 1982; Andrew L. Wolf to W. Ray Luce, March 18, 1982, Goetzman Papers.

16. *Cincinnati Post*, March 20, 1982, 12A.

17. W. Ray Luce to Buddy Gray, April 20, 1982, Goetzman Papers. Luce sent a blind copy of this letter to Genevieve Ray.

18. Diane Williams Smart to W. Ray Luce, May 4, 1982, pp. 1–2; *Cincinnati Post*, May 7, 1982, 8C.

19. W. Ray Luce to Diane Williams Smart, May 13, 1982, Schuckman Papers.

20. Appeal from the Ohio Historic Sites Preservation Advisory Board and

the Ohio Historic Preservation Office's Refusal to Approve the Cincinnati, Ohio, Over-the-Rhine District to the National Register of Historic Places by the Over-the-Rhine Property Owners Association, pp. 1–4, Goetzman Papers.

21. Charlotte T. Birdsall to CPC, Request to Establish a Neighborhood Housing Retention District (NHR) in the Over-the-Rhine Community, June 2, 1982, p. 1, Schuckman Papers.

22. CPC, Minutes, vol. 47, June 4, 1982, pp. 108–10.

23. Charlotte T. Birdsall, "Presentation to Urban Development Committee," June 29, 1982, typescript, PTF File-August 12, 1982, Birdsall Records.

24. Ken Blackwell voted against both the successful amendment and the amended ordinance. Cincinnati City Council, Proceedings, June 30, 1982, p. 255, Clerk of Council's Office; Cincinnati Ordinance No. 270-1982, Clerk of Council's Office. At the next meeting of the PTF Buddy Gray commended Birdsall for her statement to the Urban Development Committee and moved that the Task Force express its appreciation to Birdsall and planning director Guest for their support of the ordinance, a motion that passed by a vote of eight to zero with no abstentions. PTF, Minutes, July 13, 1982, p. 2, PTF File-August 12, 1982, Birdsall Records.

25. CPC Staff, An amendment to Chapter 15, the R-6 Multi-Family Districts to permit mixed use buildings containing business uses, March 18, 1982, pp. 1–3, Schuckman Papers. City council adopted the so-called R-B district zoning regulations on October 6, 1982. See Clerk of Council, *Zoning Code of the City of Cincinnati* (1985), pp. 431–35, 463. The Queen City Housing Corporation in May 1982 renewed its pledge of support for the Heritage Preservation Development Corporation's low-income rehabilitation housing projects in the Pleasant Street and Race Street sub-areas of Washington Park. Board of Directors, Minutes, May 14, 1982, Corporate Records, Queen City Housing Corporation.

26. Hubert E. Guest to Fred Zeidman, May 18, 1982, PTF File-May 25, 1982, Birdsall Records.

27. William H. Brabham for Carol D. Shull, to W. Ray Luce, July 27, 1982, Goetzman Papers.

28. Diane Smart to W. Ray Luce, August 12, 1982, telegram, Dehner Folder, Project Files; Diane Smart to W. Ray Luce, August 27, 1982, Heritage Preservation Records, Dehner Folder.

29. W. Ray Luce to Sylvester Murray, August 30, 1982; to Diane Smart, August 31, 1982; to James Bower, August 31, 1982, Goetzman Papers.

30. Hubert E. Guest to Paul Young, September 16, 1982, Goetzman Papers.

31. Charlotte T. Birdsall to W. Ray Luce, September 9, 1982, pp. 1–2, Goetzman Papers. Birdsall also sent copies of minutes of the Task Force meetings from

March 2 to September 21, 1982, a draft of the proposed land use plan for Over-the-Rhine (not yet approved by the Task Force), and a copy of the neighborhood housing retention district ordinance and the residence-business mixed use zoning ordinance.

32. Catherine Howard to Ohio Historic Preservation Advisory Board, September 16, 1982, Goetzman Papers.

33. Jack Towe to W. Ray Luce, September 11, 1982, pp. 1–2, Goetzman Papers.

34. Over-the-Rhine Property Owners Association to Members of the State Historic Preservation Advisory Board and W. Ray Luce, September 12, 1982, Goetzman Papers.

35. PTF, Minutes, October 2, 1982, pp. 1–2, PTF File-October 5, 1982, Birdsall Records.

36. Bonita Neumeier to Ohio Historic Conservation Board c/o W. Ray Luce, November 23, 1982; Jack Towe to Ohio Historic Sites Preservation Advisory Board, November 26, 1982; William F. Bowen to Ohio Historic Sites Preservation Advisory Board c/o W. Ray Luce, November 29, 1982, Goetzman Papers.

37. Steven F. Bloomfield to W. Ray Luce, November 30, 1982, p. 1; Philip A. Hawkey to Paul Young, December 2, 1982, pp. 1–2, Goetzman Papers.

38. Tommie Birdsall to Philip Hawkey, Over-the-Rhine Status, December 2, 1982, Goetzman Papers. Birdsall listed the components of the plan reviewed and commented on by the Task Force before the state preservation board meeting of September 17, 1982. She also listed the items requiring a review and comment by the Task Force: neighborhood improvement plans/preliminary development strategies (reviewed October 5 and November 16, 1982), the rezoning plan (reviewed November 30, 1982), and the printed version of the plan (review expected in late January 1983).

39. Genevieve Ray interview with Nancy K. Shapiro, January 24, 1984, transcript, pp. 23–25. This paragraph also draws on the recollections of Zane L. Miller, who attended the meeting as a member of the state advisory board.

40. Genevieve Ray interview, pp. 23–25, 26. For other accounts of this meeting, see Bruce Goetzman interview with Nancy K. Shapiro, January 30, 1984, side A; W. Ray Luce interview with Nancy K. Shapiro, May 1, 1984, side A; Zane L. Miller interview with Nancy K. Shapiro, December 12, 1983, side A; *Cincinnati Enquirer,* December 4, 1982, C1.

41. *Cincinnati Enquirer,* December 4, 1982, C1.

42. *Voices: Over-the-Rhine Community Newspaper,* December 1982–January 1983, pp. 6, 7, copy in Dehner File.

43. Ibid., pp. 7–8. Readers of the minutes of the Over-the-Rhine Task Force

meetings will notice that the residents on that body did indeed question the consultant and city staff every step of the way and prepared themselves for the minute scrutiny of each issue through assiduous homework. On the contentiousness of the Task Force meetings, see also Charlotte Birdsall interview with Nancy K. Shapiro, January 24, 1984, transcript, pp. 3, 8–9, 11–13.

44. *Voices*, p. 8.

45. W. Joseph Dehner to Ray W. Luce, Proposed Over-the-Rhine District, December 6, 1982, pp. 1–2, Dehner File; Mary A. Heller to W. Ray Luce, December 6, 1982, pp. 1–2, Goetzman Papers. The *Cincinnati Post* also urged the forwarding of the nomination to the keeper (December 14, 1982, 6A).

46. W. Ray Luce to Ohio Historic Sites Preservation Advisory Board, Over-the-Rhine Historic District Nomination, December 1982, Goetzman Papers.

47. W. Ray Luce to Carol Shull, December 22, 1982, pp. 1–3, Goetzman Papers.

48. *Cincinnati Enquirer*, December 23, 1982, C1.

49. W. Ray Luce to Carol Shull, January 19, 1983, Schuckman Papers.

50. Jerry L. Rogers to John Glenn, January 25, 1983, Dehner Papers; *Cincinnati Post*, February 15, 1983, clipping, Dehner Papers; *Cincinnati Post*, April 1, 1983, clipping, Dehner Papers; Catherine Howard to [City] Council Member, April 26, 1983, pp. 1–2, Schuckman Papers. This last letter revealed that the Community Council possessed a tape recording of the state advisory board meeting of December 2, 1982.

51. *Cincinnati Enquirer*, April 12, 1983, B1.

52. *Cincinnati Enquirer*, April 14, 1983, D1, April 23, C1; Mary A. Heller to Richard F. Celeste, April 15, 1983, pp. 1–2, Goetzman Papers. Celeste also sent an assistant, Paul Ryder, to Cincinnati to confer with various parties supporting the nomination. The Over-the-Rhine Property Owners Association and some city council members told Ryder that opponents of the nomination had since December 1979 used "deliberate delaying tactics to prevent the listing." Ryder also talked with deputy city manager Hawkey and Steven Bloomfield, head of the Department of Neighborhood Housing and Conservation, who assured him that the city worked only with low-income housing developers in Over-the-Rhine and that failure to list the district would force the city to find elsewhere $1 million to rehabilitate 100 units of low- and moderate-income housing. In addition, a representative of the Cincinnati Metropolitan Housing Authority (CMHA) supported the nomination. He explained the tax credit subsidy for low-income housing in National Register districts and noted that developers of such housing signed fifteen-year leases with the CMHA, which then rented the rehabilitated units to senior citizens and the poor through the Section 8 rehabilitation pro-

gram, which made up the difference between what renters could afford to pay and what developers had to charge to cover their investment. *Cincinnati Post,* April 22, 1983, clipping, Dehner Papers; *Cincinnati Enquirer,* April 23, 1983, C1.

53. *Cincinnati Post,* April 26, 1983, 13A. The article carried an insert identifying the authors of this statement as Reverend Randall LaFond, O.F.M., chair of the Catholic Coalition for Fair Housing; Rebecca Johnson, chair of the board, Contact Center, 164 Vine Street; Ira Crouch, Wishing Well Laundry & Cleaners, 1320 Vine Street; Michael Henson, tenant, author, 212 Orchard Street; Reverend Allen Mitchell, Wesley Chapel United Methodist Church, 80 E. McMicken Street; Jack Towe, homeowner, director of Sign of the Cross [development corporation], 1630 Republic Street; and the Over-the-Rhine Community Council, 1713 Vine Street, Catherine Howard, president, Nannie Hinkston, treasurer, and Buddy Gray, chair of the Housing Task Force. A week after the appearance of this piece Joe Dehner and Fred Lazarus sought to influence the decision on the nomination. Dehner sent Celeste a message urging the governor to return the nomination to Washington, and Lazarus tried to persuade U.S. senator Howard Metzenbaum (D) to support the nomination. Lazarus specifically addressed Buddy Gray's opposition to the nomination, which Lazarus dated to the late 1970s when his wife, Irma, tried to persuade city council not to provide $25,000 for the rehabilitation of a building near Music Hall for use by the Drop-Inn Shelter. Lazarus did not criticize Gray for helping alcoholics but thought that in protecting the Center Gray sought to "keep any kind of improvement from taking place in this area," including better housing for the poor. Lazarus charged Gray with stalling the completion of the Over-the-Rhine plan for more than two years, and complained that Gray picketed some of Heritage Preservation's rehabilitated low-income housing units "because they were created by businessmen." W. J. Dehner to Richard Celeste, mailgram, May 2, 1983, Dehner Papers; Fred Lazarus III to Howard M. Metzenbaum, May 9, 1983, pp. 1–2, Dehner Papers.

54. Kathryn Tefft-Keller to Joe Dehner, May 12, 1983, Dehner Papers.

55. *Cincinnati Enquirer,* July 22, 1983, C6.

56. Jerry L. Rogers to Buddy Gray, September 7, 1983, Over-the-Rhine File, Ohio Historic Preservation Office, Columbus.

Chapter 10

1. The biographical sketch derives chiefly from James Tarbell interview with Nancy K. Shapiro, March 1, 1984, audiotape, side A.

2. *Cleveland Plain Dealer,* August 28, 1983, 26A, August 29, 8A.

3. *Cincinnati Enquirer,* December 19, 1983, A4, December 22, A1, A4. Tar-

bell seems to have thought that the non-caring poor might be tolerated and in some cases assisted to change their behavior if they did not dominate the neighborhood numerically.

4. *Cleveland Plain Dealer,* August 29, 1983, 8A.

5. For an account of urban politics in Cincinnati from 1950 through 1985, see Zane L. Miller and Bruce Tucker, "The New Urban Politics, Planning and Development in Cincinnati, 1954–1988," in Richard M. Bernard, ed., *Snowbelt Cities: Metropolitan Politics in the Northeast and Midwest since World War II* (Bloomington: Indiana University Press, 1990), pp. 91–108. Council's dominant coalition after 1971 tried hard to keep its pledge of respect for and power to the neighborhoods. It expanded neighborhood health and recreation facilities, supported the Planning Commission's neighborhood planning program, brought Community Council representatives into the budgeting process and onto the citizens advisory committee on the spending of federal Community Development Block Grant dollars, and created in 1981 the Department of Neighborhood Housing and Conservation to spearhead the rehabilitation of old neighborhoods and their business districts. But this same council also worked vigorously to foster downtown redevelopment and rehabilitation.

6. Hubert E. Guest interview with Zane L. Miller, Dec. 16, 1985, interview 2, transcript, pp. 11–13; Hubert E. Guest to Fred Zeidman, March 3, 1983, Office of Charlotte Birdsall, Department of City Planning [hereafter cited as Birdsall Records]. Pressure from Guest to accommodate his views on the details of the plan, as well as the demand by the Task Force to control the content of the plan, prompted the consultant to seek an extension of the contract and put Birdsall, as she phrased it, in the position of "negotiating between the Arabs and Israelis." See Charlotte T. Birdsall interview with Nancy K. Shapiro, December 8, 1983, transcript, pp. 2–3, 20–21, Project Files.

7. Woolpert Consultants, *Over-the-Rhine Comprehensive Plan,* draft n.d., Appendix A, pp. 200–206. The Redevelopment Management Strategy and low-income housing emphasis attracted the fire of both Nell Surber, director of economic development, and Fred Lazarus, to whom Surber sent a copy of the draft. Lazarus thought the draft looked "pretty good from a land use perspective" but expressed serious reservations about the 5,520 units of low-income housing in the area, which by his estimate included 2,000 existing substandard units that required upgrading to meet building codes. He also attacked the Redevelopment Management Strategy because it proposed that developers of new and rehabilitated housing reserve half of the units for subsidized low-income rental, a goal he regarded as "impossible in the foreseeable future" because of the paucity of federal Section 8 rent subsidy funds. Nell Surber to Hugh [sic] Guest, December

2, 1983, Draft Over-the-Rhine-Plan, pp. 1–2, Over-the-Rhine 1983 File, Schuck-
man Papers, Project Files; Fred Lazarus III to Queen City Housing Board of
Trustees, December 2, 1983, Summary Report—Over-the-Rhine Community
Plan, Heritage Preservation Corporation Records, Heritage Preservation 1983
File, Dehner Papers, Project Files.

8. Over-the-Rhine Planning Task Force [hereafter cited as PTF], Minutes,
December 6, 1983, typescript, pp. 1–2, Schuckman Papers. By December 31,
1982, five business representatives had officially resigned from the Task Force.
See "Over the Rhine Planning Task Force Members, Alternatives, and Affiliations," typescript, pp. 1–2, Birdsall Files, copy in Project Files. Thomas A. Dutton,
assistant professor of architecture at Miami University in Oxford, Ohio, on the
northern edge of the Cincinnati metropolitan area, and a volunteer consultant to
the Task Force, raised additional objections. He denounced the draft plan for saying too little about how to protect and produce more low- and moderate-income
housing and belittled both the neighborhood strategies, which he described as a
mere list of vague objectives marginally related to low-income housing, and the
Redevelopment Management Strategy, which struck him as "hypothetical" because it lacked specific proposals geared precisely for Over-the-Rhine.

9. Thomas A. Dutton, "The Over-the-Rhine Community Plan—A Response," December 6, 1983, typescript, pp. 1–2, Project Files. In the interim,
however, Jack Towe presented an argument against the idea of fighting poverty
in Over-the-Rhine by providing jobs for residents through commercial development, suggesting instead that poverty in Over-the-Rhine could not be eliminated, at least not in the foreseeable future. It could not be done by outside
entrepreneurs, Towe contended, because they hired their friends and relatives
for all but the most menial jobs. Towe argued that Over-the-Rhine could "grow
as a prospering community" only if it possessed many "inside" resident entrepreneurs, which it lacked and would not likely develop. He closed by conceding that
neither he nor the city government knew how "to aid a low income community to
bootstrap itself," a hint that he too regarded neighborhoods like Over-the-Rhine
as inevitable products of American capitalism. Jack Towe, Response to the Urban
Development Critique of the Over-the-Rhine Plan, January 30, 1984, p. 1, Birdsall Records.

10. PTF Members, Community Representatives, "Over-the-Rhine Comprehensive Plan Critique," February 2, 1984, typescript, pp. 1–28, Birdsall Records.

11. Ibid., pp. 3–4.

12. Ibid., p. 5.

13. Ibid., pp. 6–8.

14. Ibid., pp. 14–21.

15. PTF, Minutes, February 7, 1982, pp. 1–6, February 14, 1984, pp. 1–3, Birdsall Records. Fred Zeidman of Woolpert Consultants recalled that he showed the draft plan first to Hubert Guest, who wanted some changes, which Zeidman made. Zeidman then submitted it to the Task Force, which wanted to make a lot of changes. He tried to accommodate the Task Force until it came to inserting material on the acquisition by the Community Council of the Peaslee School for use as a community center and the history of Over-the-Rhine prepared by the residential representatives on the Task Force, items that Zeidman did not regard as appropriate for inclusion in the plan. Woolpert then "declined to maintain authorship" of the plan and requested listing merely as a consultant to the city on the project. Fred Zeidman to Zane L. Miller, telephone interview, August 2, 1989, notes in Project Files.

16. Over-the-Rhine Plan Review Committee, Minutes, March 6, 1984, pp. 1–3, March 13, pp. 1–3, Birdsall Records; Hubert E. Guest interview 2, pp. 12, 15.

17. Cincinnati City Planning Commission [hereafter cited as CPC], Minutes, vol. 49, July 6, 1984, pp. 203, 208–9; PTF, Minutes, September 19, 1984, p. 1, Birdsall Records.

18. PTF, Minutes, September 19, 1984, pp. 2–4.

19. *Cincinnati Post,* January 10, 1985, 1B, January 12, 1B.

20. Buddy Gray to Sylvester Murray, March 6, 1985, pp. 1–3, in Cincinnati City Planning Department, Advance Planning, Over-the-Rhine File, copy in Project Files.

21. Hubert E. Guest interview 2, pp. 13–15; Charlotte T. Birdsall interview with Nancy K. Shapiro, interview 2, July 11, 1985, side A; Roland T. Docter to Zane L. Miller, phone interview, April 7, 1992, notes in Project Files.

22. Roland T. Docter to CPC, May 3, 1985, Subject: Over-the-Rhine Comprehensive Plan . . . , pp. 1, 9, attachments B, E.

23. CPC, Minutes, vol. 50, May 3, 1985, pp. 78–83; *Cincinnati Post,* May 3, 1985, 1B.

24. Roland T. Docter to CPC, May 17, 1985, Supplementary Report on the Over-the-Rhine Comprehensive Plan, December 1984, typescript, pp. 1–3; CPC, Minutes, vol. 50, May 17, 1985, pp. 89–96.

25. CPC, Minutes, vol. 50, May 17, 1985, p. 97; Statement by Sy Murray on the Over-the-Rhine Comprehensive Plan, May 17, 1985, typescript, p. 1, Docter Over-the-Rhine File, Cincinnati City Planning Department.

26. Statement by Sy Murray, pp. 1–2.

27. CPC, Minutes, vol. 50, May 17, 1985, pp. 98–99.

28. Sylvester Murray to Zane L. Miller, telephone interview, April 17, 1992; Donald Mooney to Zane L. Miller, telephone interview, April 20, 1992, notes in Project Files.

29. Estelle Berman to Zane L. Miller, telephone interview, April 15, 1992; Donald Mooney interview; CPC, Minutes, vol. 50, June 7, 1985, p. 109.

30. CPC, Minutes, vol. 50, June 7, 1985, pp. 109–14, 115–19. Under the rubric of general goals, e.g., one alteration said that the plan intended to improve the quality of life of all neighborhood residents, "including" (instead of "particularly") low-income people, an amendment that simultaneously softened the emphasis on low-income housing and made the goal more compatible with the city's assisted housing allocation policy. The Planning Commission also added "historic character" to a goal endorsing the reinforcement of the mixed use character of Over-the-Rhine and added two goals involving historic preservation, one indicating that Findlay Market should be developed as a regional trade center, tourist attraction, and historic resource while respecting its tradition of serving local residents, and another calling for the retention of the historic urban qualities of scale, density, and architecture that contributed to the character and image of Over-the-Rhine. The Commission in addition added a general goal encouraging the development of housing "for all income levels," repeated that phrase in the new item making home ownership an objective, and eliminated an objective calling for a cap of 15,000 persons in the population of Over-the-Rhine, a gesture toward those who wanted to enlarge the housing stock by making it appealing to diverse income levels.

31. *Cincinnati Enquirer*, June 8, 1985, C2; *Cincinnati Post*, June 8, 1985, 1B.

32. CPC, Minutes, vol. 50, June 14, 1985, pp. 124–26. The land use section of this revised urban renewal plan designated the area around the Drop-Inn Shelter as neither a residential nor an office district but as a public/quasi-public district. See CPC, *Over-the-Rhine Urban Renewal Plan* (June 14, 1985), plate 6. The document contained a statement of the legal basis and authority for making the plan, a description of the location of Over-the-Rhine and the boundaries of its sub-neighborhoods (Mohawk, Findlay Market, Washington Park, Over-the-Rhine Central, and Pendleton), just over two pages of terse statements of existing conditions (assets as well as problems) in Over-the-Rhine, and a seventeen-page section of proposals for dividing the sub-neighborhoods into land use categories (but nothing on zoning). It also contained sixteen pages of goals and objectives, including sixteen general goals and goals and objectives for six "functional" areas of activity (housing, commercial/industrial, character/cultural diversity, traffic circulation/transit/parking, social services/facilities/recreation, and environment/public services), after which came five pages of development policies, including a recommendation to study districts and landmarks for possible historic designation (local), based on the large array of goals and objectives.

33. Cincinnati City Council, Urban Development Committee Public Hearing, July 2, 1985, tape recording, side 3, Clerk of Council's Office. In these

comments Gray noted that zoning did not specify income levels within residential zones. Before mixed land uses came into vogue, however, zoning sought to segregate the population into economic classes by designating several types of residential districts with regulations making housing more expensive in some districts (single-family home districts, e.g., as opposed to high-density residential districts).

34. Cincinnati City Council, Meeting of August 7, 1985, audiotape, sides 1–3, Clerk of Council's Office. Tarbell's remarks occur on side 2 of the tape and Gray's on side 3. An outline of the proceedings, including the title and number of the ordinance and the roll call votes, is recorded in Cincinnati City Council, Minutes, August 7, 1985, pp. 288–89. For the final version of the plan see CPC, *Over-the-Rhine Urban Renewal Plan* (adopted August 1985).

35. Charlotte T. Birdsall interviews with Nancy K. Shapiro, December 3, 1983, transcript, pp. 8, 13–14, 31, and July 11, 1985, audiotape, sides A and B; W. Joseph Dehner interview with Nancy K. Shapiro, March 8, 1984, transcript, pp. 14–17; Mary Heller interview with Nancy K. Shapiro, April 24, 1984, transcript, pp. 18, 20–21, 26–30, 32; Sister Ann Renee McCann interview with Nancy K. Shapiro, January 26, 1984, transcript, p. 11; Genevieve Ray interview with Nancy K. Shapiro, January 29, 1984, transcript, pp. 10, 16, 21, Project Files.

36. This stance seems evident in the behavior of the Gray faction from 1979 onward. But according to Sister Ann Renee McCann, who worked in the city's community assistance division during the late 1970s and early 1980s, Gray once said that the life styles of the poor, drifters, and "scum" should be left alone and that the city government should permit them to live in "a neighborhood which resembled their life style." See Sister Ann Renee McCann interview, pp. 19–23 (the quotation, a paraphrase of Gray by McCann, is on p. 20). See also Genevieve Ray interview, p. 18, and the biographical sketch of Gray and analysis of his views and activities in Over-the-Rhine by reporter Tom Shroder, *Cincinnati Enquirer,* December 22, 1983, A1, A4, Dec. 23, A1, A4. Syndicated newspaper columnist William Pfaff noted a few years later the tendency on "the left" in the United States to treat the "destitute . . . as a class phenomenon . . . apart from race—or as if their condition was a career decision or lifestyle choice." *Cincinnati Enquirer,* May 23, 1992, A7.

37. Complete and coherent statements of Tarbell's views may be found on the audiotape of the city council meeting of August 7, 1985, side 2, and on another audiotape, James Tarbell interview with Nancy K. Shapiro, March 13, 1984, sides A and B, Project Files. See also the biographical sketch and analysis of Tarbell's views and activities in Over-the-Rhine by Tom Shroder in *Cincinnati Enquirer,* December 22, 1983, A1, A4.

38. For one attempt to link historic preservation, residential racial integration, and the welfare of both particular neighborhoods and the city as a whole, see Zane L. Miller, "History and the Politics of Community Change in Cincinnati," *Public Historian* 5 (Fall 1983): esp. 30–35.

Epilogue

1. Charlotte T. Birdsall to Honorable City Planning Commission, "A Report . . . on Extending the Time Period of the Over-the-Rhine Housing Retention Districts [*sic*] . . . ," March 8, 1991, Office of Charlotte Birdsall, Department of City Planning, copy in Project Files; *Cincinnati Enquirer*, May 6, 1992, B2.

2. Housing Opportunities Made Equal, Inc., "Over-the-Rhine: A Permanent Ghetto?" typescript, July 1, 1991, pp. 1, 4; *Cincinnati Enquirer*, August 16, 1991, D1.

3. Housing Opportunities, "Over-the-Rhine," pp. 6–8.

4. Irvine explicated the citywide intent of her views on Over-the-Rhine in a guest column called "Housing beyond the Inner City" for the *Cincinnati Enquirer*, February 22, 1992, A8. Irvine argued that experience had demonstrated that residents of predominantly white neighborhoods would not object to a few low-income persons, including black ones from ghettos, moving into a few houses within their neighborhoods. The same experience indicated that black low-income families making such a move felt more secure in their new neighborhoods, earned higher incomes, felt happy about the move, and reported little isolation and few incidents of racial harassment. See also Paul B. Fisher, *Is Housing Mobility an Effective Anti-Poverty Strategy? An Examination of the Cincinnati Experience* (Cincinnati: Stephen H. Wilder Foundation, 1991), p. vi. While conceding the inevitability of some ghettos, Irvine again in 1992, in the wake of the Los Angeles ghetto riot of that spring involving random physical assaults by blacks on whites, called for a limitation on the size of such places. "Public policy that continues to expand the ghetto is suicide for urban (and suburban) America," she wrote. See Housing Opportunities Made Equal, *Annual Report, 1991–1992* (May 14, 1992), p. 7.

5. For an attempt to forge a strategy for housing the Cincinnati area's poor from this broader perspective, see Merrill Goozner, *Housing Cincinnati's Poor* (Cincinnati: Stephen H. Wilder Foundation, January 1982 [actually 1983]). Goozner's strategy, never adopted, would have involved a coalition requiring cooperation among all the actors in the Over-the-Rhine story. His vision of what Cincinnati as a physical and social environment might and ought to become resembled Irvine's.

6. The continuing conflict over the future of Over-the-Rhine produced in 1993 a lawsuit against the city that challenged the policy of making low-income housing the top priority in revitalizing the area. A proposed out-of-court settlement of the case produced another loser, Buddy Gray and his allies, who responded with hostility to what they called the plaintiff's "quota" program for integrating Over-the-Rhine by class and race as a violation of their civil rights. See *Cincinnati Enquirer,* June 30, 1993, F1, July 2, C5; *Cincinnati Post,* June 29, 1993, 5A, June 30, 14A. The city won the suit in a local court, and the plaintiffs considered appealing but backed off when the city eliminated low-income housing as the top priority for Over-the-Rhine and altered some other policies in the direction favored by the plaintiffs. Robert E. Manley to Zane L. Miller, phone conversation, July 25, 1995. Before the conclusion of that case, however, HOME and the Legal Aid Society filed an administrative complaint in April 1994 (still pending) with the U.S. Department of Housing and Urban Development alleging that the city of Cincinnati had denied housing opportunities to low-income African Americans by using federal subsidies to provide low-income rental housing primarily in low-income minority neighborhoods, including Over-the-Rhine. See Geraldine Taylor et al. vs. City of Cincinnati, "Housing Discrimination Complaint," n.d., typescript, Project Files; Karla Irvine to Zane L. Miller, letter of June 27, 1996, Project Files.

Squabbling continued within the neighborhood as well. A newspaper investigation of Over-the-Rhine in the summer of 1995—prompted by the appearance of a business revival (mostly restaurants, bars, and nightclubs) along Main Street—turned up essentially the same cast of characters from the 1970s and 1980s making the same arguments about the neighborhood's destiny and what to do about it. See *Cincinnati Enquirer,* July 16, 1995, A1, C1, July 17, A1, C1, July 18, A1, C2. A year later an Urban Land Institute panel ticketed the continued factionalization of Over-the-Rhine as still the chief obstacle to its revitalization as a place with room for everyone. See *Cincinnati Enquirer,* June 29, 1996, B1.

7. For an early warning by a political scientist about the eclipse of the public interest after the 1940s, see Theodore J. Lowi, *The End of Liberalism: Ideology, Policy, and the Crisis of Public Authority* (New York: W. W. Norton, 1969). Lowi misleads us, however, by associating with only the left the eclipse of the public interest, a phenomenon that spanned and spans the political spectrum.

8. Vaclav Havel, "The New Measure of Man," *New York Times,* July 8, 1994, A15. For another reminder that all of "civil society" is not civic-minded and a call for "*civitas;* that is, public-spiritedness, sacrifice for the community, citizenship, even nobility," see Fareed Zakaria, "Bigger Than the Family, Smaller Than the State," *New York Times Book Review,* August 13, 1995, pp. 1, 25. See also John Gray,

NOTES TO EPILOGUE ■ 215

"Does Democracy Have a Future?" *New York Times Book Review,* January 22, 1995, pp. 1, 24–25.

9. *Cincinnati Enquirer,* November 16, 1996, S1, S4, A6.

10. *Cincinnati Enquirer,* November 20, 1996, B1.

11. See, e.g., *Cincinnati Post,* November 18, 1996, 8A, November 20, 12A; Randy Katz, "Buddy Gray: A Warrior Falls," *Everybody's News* (Cincinnati), p. 2.

12. See, e.g., *New York Times* (national), November 30, 1996, Y9.

13. *Cincinnati Post,* November 25, 1996, A10.

14. *Cincinnati Enquirer,* November 19, 1996, A4. In the late 1990s some Over-the-Rhine improvement advocates finally started systematically to place the problems of the neighborhood in the context of citywide and metropolitan poverty and racial residential segregation. See Marge Hammelrath, "Over-the-Rhine Can Be Much More than Warehouse for Poor," *Cincinnati Post,* March 18, 1997, A12.

INDEX

adaptive reuse, versus authentic restoration, 97
African Americans, 65
  Appalachians compared to, 75–76
  in Avondale area, 47–48, 50–51
  enclaves: brought about by displacement, 157–58; confinement to, 26; inner city seen as home for, 45–46; during 1920s in the basin, 21, 160–62; viewed as ghetto areas, xx–xxi, 156, 163, 172 n. 7
  in Over-the-Rhine, xix, 6, 81, 158, 160–61
  Queensgate I I land use proposal, 69–70
  relocation attempts, 38, 40, 178 n. 2
  role as community activists, 70–71, 72, 81
  See also population; separatist movement
age, neighborhoods classified by, 34–35
alcoholics, street, 96, 105–6, 112, 207 n. 53
anti-displacement ordinance: proposed, 108–9. *See also* displacement
apartheid, residential, Over-the-Rhine viewed as, xx
apartments, as residential units, xix, 33, 50, 93
Apostolic Bethlehem Temple Church (formerly St. John's German Evangelical and Reform Church), 102
Appalachian Committee, CHRC, 78
Appalachian Community Development Association, 78
Appalachian Fund, 64
Appalachian Identity Center, 77–78

Appalachians: attempts to constitute Over-the-Rhine as community for, 73–83; compared to African Americans, 75–76; as migrants, 6, 178 n. 2; migration to Over-the-Rhine, 61–62; Queensgate I I land use proposal, 69–70; workshop on working with migrants, 62–63, 185 n. 11
application form, for Model Cities Act grant, 74–76
"Architectural Resources Clusters," of Redevelopment Management Strategy draft plan, 145
artifacts, Appalachian, 79
Asbury, Mary, 120, 129
assimilation, Handlin's view of fluid society, 61–62
Augur, Tracy, 28
Aunt Maudie's Kitchen, 81
Avondale-Corryville neighborhoods, 159; city projects for, 48–53, 66, 89, 182 n. 7; as proposed areas for displaced blacks, 39–40
Avondale neighborhood, 17, 22, 35, 48, 50–51, 58
Avondale Neighborhood Association, 82

basin, the, 5, 53, 60; 1920s TAC report, 17; 1925 proposals for major changes, 17–21; 1930s north and west central plan, 23–26; seen as deteriorated area in 1948 plan, 34, 35. *See also* West End
Berman, Estelle, 150
Better Housing League, 189 n. 3
Bettman, Alfred, 16, 27, 37, 177 n. 29

217

URBAN LIFE AND URBAN LANDSCAPE SERIES

Zane L. Miller *and* Henry D. Shapiro, *General Editors*

The series examines the history of urban life and the development of the urban landscape through works that place social, economic, and political issues in the intellectual and cultural context of their times.